"THIS—IS LONDON . . ."

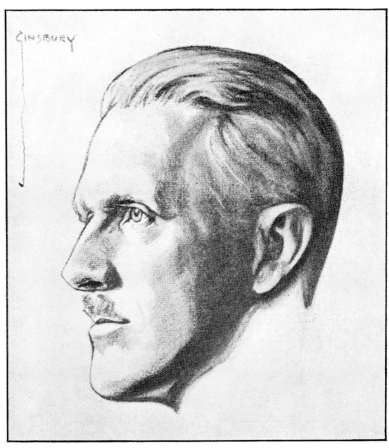

THE AUTHOR
(From an original drawing by Ginsbury)

" THIS—IS LONDON . . ."

BY

STUART HIBBERD

LONDON

MACDONALD AND EVANS

8 JOHN STREET, BEDFORD ROW, W.C.1

1950

First published 1950
Second impression

PRINTED IN GREAT BRITAIN BY RICHARD CLAY AND COMPANY, LTD.,
BUNGAY, SUFFOLK

" While thou livest keep a good tongue in thy head "
The Tempest

LIST OF PLATES

CARTOONS IN THE TEXT

PREFACE

FOR many years I have kept a Diary. Originally it was a very sketchy affair—a few notes scribbled down as a check on dates and events in my life, which came in useful as an aid to memory. But when I joined the B.B.C. I realised the importance of keeping a record of events which could be read in conjunction with the published programmes, and I began to take my diary more seriously. This was particularly so during the General Strike of 1926, when events of the utmost national importance began to move swiftly, and I found myself ideally placed as an observer.

From that time onwards I made a rule of keeping a day-to-day diary, written up each twenty-four hours, and the book which follows consists of extracts from this diary, together with a number of short sketches of famous men and women as I have known them as broadcasters.

In covering this period of twenty-five years I have made no attempt to link events so as to form a continuous narrative, except where they form a natural sequence—for example, those leading up to the Declaration of War—but I have arranged them chronologically.

Knowing the many pitfalls in the use of the spoken word, I have ventured to include some remarks on this most important subject at the end of the book, and also some references to the work of the B.B.C. Pronunciation Committee, which I trust may be of use to Producers and News Editors, as well as to announcers.

My object throughout has been to try to take my readers behind the broadcasting scenes, and to give them an eye-witness account as I, myself, have seen them. I have tried to make it a human picture, and have not attempted to include events or programmes in which I have not been concerned. Therefore what follows cannot be regarded as a history of broadcasting : it should, however, provide some useful data for the historian, particularly as many of the B.BC. records and News Bulletins were destroyed in the Blitz.

My thanks are due to my former colleague Mr. R. T. Clark, and my fellow-announcer Mr. Denys Drower, and to Major E. J. B. Raymond, M.C., for their invaluable help and advice and for kindly reading the proofs. I must also thank Miss Ruth Cockerton, for her help in selecting the photographs, and Miss M. J. Shearman for compiling the Index.

STUART HIBBERD.

October, 1950.

ACKNOWLEDGEMENTS

The Author and Publishers wish to make acknowledgement and offer their thanks to all those who have kindly given permission for the use of copyright material.

A. F. Buck, Esq., for allowing the inclusion of part of " Into This World of Sorrow ", by Sir Percy Buck.

Messrs. Chappell & Co., Ltd., for the inclusion of part of Noel Coward's lyric, " Auntie Jessie ".

H. B. Carter, Esq., and the British News Association for the original tape message reporting the death of King George V.

The Editor of the *Daily Express* for the Lancaster Cartoon on page 229.

The Greyhound Racing Association, Ltd., and Harringay Arena, Ltd., for the two photographs facing pages 296 and 297.

Messrs. William Heinemann, Ltd., for an extract from " The Island," by Francis Brett Young.

Messrs. Thomas Nelson & Sons, Ltd., for an extract from " My Own Country ", which appears in " The Four Men " by Hilaire Belloc.

The Norfolk News Co., Ltd., for the photograph facing page 281.

The Proprietors of *Punch* for the two poems appearing on pages 21 and 247.

The Editor of the *Radio Times* for the drawings on pages 15, 24, 25, 59, facing page 88, and the Frontispiece.

The Editor of *The Star* for the cartoon by Low appearing on page 19.

The Editor of *The Tatler and Bystander* for the cartoon facing page 233 and the photograph facing page 201.

The Musicians' Benevolent Society and their Secretary Mr. Frank Thistleton for the poem by John Masefield on page 249.

Messrs. A. P. Watt & Son for an extract from " Daventry Calling ", from the Collected Poems of Alfred Noyes.

Miss Ruth Cockerton, Head of Display Section, for the remainder of the photographs which are B.B.C. copyright.

1924–1925

IT was quite by chance that I came to London. I had answered an advertisement in the *Morning Post* for a vacancy on the staff of the B.B.C., which turned out to be for the post of Director of the Cardiff Station, and this led to an interview with the Controller in London.

I have the clearest possible recollection of that interview, and I remember how my heart thumped as I walked up the steps of 2 Savoy Hill and saw on my left the large polished brass plate informing me that this was the Registered Office of the British Broadcasting Company, Ltd.

I was received most politely by Arbuckle, the commissionaire, who asked me what my business was, and I recall how impressed I was by his reply to a telephone inquiry for John Dodgson, the announcer. . . . "Oh no, sir; I'm sorry I cannot get hold of him now; he's in the studio, broadcasting." Then I noticed that a red light was burning over one of the doors just to the right of the lift-shaft. Soon afterwards I was being conducted up the stairs and into "the presence". Admiral Carpendale, a slim, lithe, blue-eyed, good-looking man, about 5 feet 9 inches in height, shook hands with me and waved me to a chair in front of his desk, having a good look at me as he did so. He got out my papers and proceeded to ask me about my education and war service, my hobbies, my likes and dislikes, any special qualifications I had, what games I played, and so on, and soon came to the conclusion that I was not the man they were then looking for, because I had had no journalistic experience and knew nothing about Wales, to which, incidentally, there had been no reference in the advertisement. At his suggestion, however, I agreed that my name should remain on the Company's books, and this in the early autumn led to a second interview, which resulted in my appointment as an assistant announcer in London.

I remember that at this second interview the "Admiral" gave me a reading test, and afterwards asked me various questions. To these I replied quietly, being rather nervous, and he turned on me and said, " Speak up, man, and don't mumble."

Although famous for his quarter-deck manner, behind a severe expression there was a heart of gold. He could not suffer fools gladly, and I do not blame him for that. He had a grand sense of humour, with a twinkle in his eye, and loved a joke and a good story, and his smile was one of the most charming I have ever seen.

Rex Palmer was then the London Station Director, and I was attached to his staff. Rex was very well known for his News reading and presentation of concerts and talks, and also as " Uncle Rex " of the Children's Hour, where his pleasant baritone voice, with its clear diction—so important for radio—was in great demand. His London Station staff and the Headquarters staff were housed in the same building—No. 2 Savoy Hill, next to the Savoy Hotel on the Embankment. The office windows either overlooked the Savoy Hotel or the graveyard of the Savoy Chapel, between Savoy Hill and the Strand.

I was introduced to Miss Lilian Taylor, Palmer's friendly and business-like secretary, who at once took me in hand, showing me round, and introducing me to the rest of the staff, which included Kenneth Wright, Lindsay Wellington, Stanford Robinson and Dan Godfrey.

.   .   .   .   .

There were then only two studios in use at Savoy Hill: No. 1, a large orchestral one on the ground floor, pleasantly decorated in blue and gold, and another general-purpose studio—No. 3—on the second floor. Both these studios were heavily draped with curtains, hanging in folds from ceiling to floor, the idea being to eliminate echo, because without such damping down speech would have been unintelligible, with the microphone and amplifiers then at our disposal. Those curtains certainly damped down the echo most successfully, the studios being as dead as mutton—often compelling artists to force their tone because they could not hear themselves normally. They also collected an incredible amount of dust. For ventilation, exhaust fans were fitted in the roof, but as they made a " hum " when switched on, it was seldom possible to use them during transmission; consequently when there was a choir and a full orchestra in the studio for hours at a stretch the atmosphere and heat were appalling.

Savoy Hill is quite near the river, and the noise of hooters of tugs or river-steamers could often be heard coming through the ventilation shafts in the roof, and these sounds must sometimes have been broadcast during talks or News Bulletins.

   •   •   •   •   •

The three things that impressed me most, as a newcomer, were the general atmosphere of friendliness, the way I was at once made to feel at home—one of the family, as it were—and the all-pervading pioneering spirit, which seemed to proclaim from the house-tops, "Here's a wonderfully worth-while job. Nothing matters but broadcasting, unless it is still better and more extensive broadcasting."

   •   •   •   •

For two days I followed John Dodgson around in the studios and watched him announce, listened to his voice, and saw how he acted as host, studio manager and cashier, as well as announcer. I learnt, too, the first principle of radio announcing—to make friends with your engineers and consult them on every possible occasion; then they will never let you down. But almost before I had time to realise it—or, mercifully, to think about it—I found myself taking over and reading the News. Broadbent, the night-duty announcer, did not turn up on the Saturday of my first week there. I did not worry about this until the time for the News approached; but when the Editor brought up the bulletin five minutes before it was due to go out, something had to be done. The senior engineer on duty came down to the studio, and while we were talking, the red light began to flicker—the signal for the broadcast to begin. I remember Rex Haworth's exact words : " Well, it's like this : if you don't do it I shall have to, as the News has got to go out." " All right," I said, " I'll do it," and, taking up the News bulletin—typed on thick pieces of foolscap—I gave the return light to Control Room and, with my heart in my mouth, began, " This is London calling, 2L.O. calling. Here is the First General News Bulletin, copyright by Reuter, Press Association, Exchange Telegraph and Central News." How many scores of times was I to use that opening, until, later on, it was mercifully contracted to " copyright reserved ".

Apparently Broadbent, who was a fine cross-country runner, had been out with some harriers in Surrey that afternoon, and had been held up in a homeward-bound traffic jam, and was unable to telephone to us to let us know.

. . . . .

In 1924 we only broadcast a little in the afternoon, mainly schools and tea-time music, and the evening programmes ended at 10.30 p.m. in the studio, with dance music following from the Savoy Hotel until midnight. On Sundays, in order not to keep people from church or chapel, broadcasting did not begin until 3 p.m. Do you remember the Bach Cantatas which were broadcast each Sunday at this time ? On Sunday nights the station closed down at 10.35, after the Epilogue at 10.30. The Epilogues started in a very simple way—just a few verses from the Old or New Testament, chosen by Mr. Stobart—who was then in charge of religious broadcasting— or myself, the idea being to remind listeners that though they may have been enjoying a superb concert from the studio or elsewhere, it was not an ordinary night of the week, but a Sunday night.

Soon to verses from the Bible was added a hymn or psalm or a sacred song. Rex Palmer's singing of " Abide with me " and " Nearer, my God, to Thee " created a deep impression. Later, the Wireless Singers were brought in, and the Epilogue began to take on its present well-known form, the choir consisting of eight unaccompanied voices.

. . . . .

In the mid-nineteen-twenties dance-band leaders were not allowed to announce their own numbers, there being no Outside-Broadcast-speech microphones available—only those suspended from the roof for broadcasting the dance music. Dancing couples, seeing the microphones and knowing a broadcast to be in progress, were often tempted to " put across " a message or greeting to their friends, and the " O.B." Engineers controlling off-stage had to be constantly on the alert. Generally these messages were of the " Hello-George-can-you-hear-me " type, but there was always a chance of a possible advertisement, and the rule about no advertising was strictly enforced. We were even supplied with a cut-out

4

switch on the studio microphone-stand, which could be operated at once without any signal to Control Room.

We announcers used to enjoy going over to the Savoy. We could dance if we wanted to, but most of us were content to change after closing down in the studio at 10.30, and get to the Savoy just before 11, in time to announce, back-stage, the numbers which had been played. An excellent supper was provided by M. de Mornys, the Savoy Entertainments Manager, in a private room upstairs—my mouth waters as I think of the food of those days, especially the omelettes and sweets—and we came down again to make two further announcements, one at 11.30, and one just before Big Ben at midnight. Generally the two bands—the Savoy Orpheans and the Savoy Havana Band—changed over at those times.

.   .   .   .   .

I find it difficult to realise in these days, when no fewer than ten News bulletins are broadcast each day, that in 1924 no News bulletin was permitted to be broadcast before 7 p.m.

We were not in a position to collect data for our News, but obtained it all by an agreement with the Agencies. The newspapers, especially the evening papers, feared that an earlier bulletin would seriously affect their sales, and not until the national emergency of the General Strike of 1926 were we allowed to broadcast news *before* 7 p.m. It was not until World War II that we were able to institute regular early morning and mid-day News bulletins.

This attitude of the Press of regarding broadcasting as a serious competitor was quite intelligible, and, as wireless was so new to the world, probably a wise precaution. But it was soon realised that broadcast news was something which was complementary to, not a substitute for, the written word. I can vouch for the truth of this from my own experience. Many hundreds of times have I read two or three bulletins a night, but I have always bought an evening paper to read in the train going home.

This fear of wireless competition was by no means restricted to the Press; as soon as it was obvious that wireless had come to stay, all sorts of obstacles were placed in our path in our efforts to widen our sphere of action and give listeners a more varied and increasingly topical fare.

There were, for example, the theatre managers and concert agents, who said, in effect, " Here are we, doing our level best to attract people out of their homes to come to the theatres or concert-halls, while you are keeping them indoors by their firesides." This was a reasonable argument, but, as events turned out, a fallacious one, owing to the enormous publicity value of broadcasts of con-certs or excerpts from plays, which resulted in substantial increases in the box-office receipts.

Then there was the attitude of many members of the educated public, that nothing really worth while connected with the arts is ever properly achieved in this country. I remember hearing the following conversation about this time between two men coming out of the Queen's Hall after a symphony concert.

> 1st Patron : " Good performance of the Brahms to-night, I thought, didn't you ? "
> 2nd Patron (rather bored) : " Yes, I suppose so, but, then, I never really enjoy music unless I am on the Continent."

Thanks, however, to the patience, foresight and leadership of Mr. Reith, the Managing Director, who, though often severely criticised in the Press and by listeners, did not hesitate from the start to stress the public service attitude of British Broadcasting, in due course all these difficulties were overcome, and the number of licences increased steadily year by year.

.   .   .   .   .

Of my first B.B.C. Christmas I remember chiefly the carols sung on Christmas Eve by the Wireless Singers, under Stanford Robinson, in the ancient parish church of St. Mary's, Whitechapel—now, alas ! destroyed by the Blitz. This short carol service, with a five-minute address by the Rector, The Rev. John Mayo, was greatly appreciated, and became a feature of our Christmas programmes for many years. The " Padre ", as we called him, was a general favourite, and was the first person ever to broadcast a religious service. This, so he told me, was broadcast from the top-floor attics of Marconi House, Strand, on Christmas Eve, 1922. Dr. Fleming, the Presbyterian minister from Pont Street, spoke on the following Sunday. Then, to quote John Mayo, " I spoke again very soon. There was a request from the studio for hymns, and I supplied the books (music) and chose a couple for Sundays. Later a nonconformist minister ventured on a prayer and I on a short Scripture passage. I then suggested Anglicans and Nonconformists alternately, and this was done. This was the genesis of the Service."

. . . . .

In 1925 we broadcast some fine symphony concerts conducted by Sir Edward Elgar and Sir Landon Ronald, in addition to chamber concerts and song recitals—e.g. the Woodhouse String Quartet. In response to applications for programme time by some of the papers, a series of concerts was arranged—the *"Answers* Concert ", the *" News of the World* Concert ", the " *Evening Standard* Concert "—in which famous papers vied with one another in collecting constellations of stars. I remember in particular the " *Evening Standard* Concert ", because it included Ysaye, Dihn Gilly and Tetrazzini. I can see Rex Palmer now opening the studio door, as Madame Tetrazzini, a short and rather plump figure with her Titian hair catching the light, smilingly walks briskly into the studio for her first group of songs.

Several other great artists broadcast in our programmes for the first time that year—e.g. Lappas, the Greek tenor, and Paul Robeson, then playing in " The Emperor Jones ", who came to the studio after the theatre, and sang African songs with native drum accompaniment, as well as Negro Spirituals. Then there was Ben Davies, the Grand Old Man of Oratorio, and, most impressive of all, in November, a special studio recital by Chaliapin, who sang songs from " Boris Godounov " and other operas, in Russian, and of course the " Song of the Volga Boatman "—all with superb artistry. Then there were the broadcast plays, the Drama Department being under the direction of R. E. Jeffrey. Among these was Reginald Berkeley's grim war play, " The White Chateau ", and on 14th April we broadcast a play for radio called " The Dweller in the Darkness ", a creepy play by an author who was later to become famous as a commentator on international affairs, Vernon Bartlett. In addition to the plays broadcast on weekdays, we now began giving scenes from famous plays on Sunday afternoons, featuring well-known actors and actresses who were not available on week-days; on 28th June, Sybil Thorndike and Lewis Casson broadcast scenes from the " Medea ".

7

It was in this broadcast that I first met Howard Rose, who was playing the part of the messenger, and who later joined the staff as R. E. Jeffrey's assistant, eventually becoming Assistant Director of Drama, and being responsible for the production of many broadcast plays, which gave great pleasure to listeners, until his retirement in 1949.

It was in 1925, too, that Noel Coward was persuaded to come to the studio and entertain us for a few minutes at the piano, during which time he sang a song about a young married couple and their children, who were soon to be visited by a rich aunt, and, in view of the possibility of a legacy at some future date, must all make a point of being kind to Aunt Jessie.

This was one of the verses :—

> We must all be very kind to Auntie Jessie,
> For she's never been a mother or a wife.
> You mustn't throw your toys at her
> Or make a vulgar noise at her—
> She hadn't led a *very happy* life.
> You must never lock her playfully in the bath-room
> Or play tunes on her enamelled Spanish comb.
> Though her kiss is worse than death
> It's unkind to hold your breath;
> For Charity, you know, begins at home.

This was the first time any cabaret-type of programme was put on in the late evening in the studio, as distinct from the dance-music cabaret turns, like Norman Long's broadcasts from the Savoy.

At about this time we began interviewing famous personalities from America and the Continent as they came to this country, either on board ship or the boat-train at the ports, or, better still, if they would come to the studios in London.

Tom Mix came to Savoy Hill in April 1925 in an enormously wide Stetson hat and complete cowboy kit, including spurs. A swarm of small boys—autograph-hunters—gathered outside the building to greet him, many of them wanting to know if he had brought his famous horse " Tony " with him.

Then, later on, came Adolphe Menjou and Catherine Carver, and the great Will Rogers—a most charming, likeable, good-natured man, with a dry, stimulating wit. I remember announcing him and

8

telling him to go ahead and say what he thought of us. This is what he said :

" Well, I guess you'll be expecting me to say something about your weather over here, or your wonderful London policemen— but [with a pause and shake of the head] I'm not going to do anything like that. You know, we in the States are rather interested in a man you've got over here called George Bernard Shaw. We think him rather amusing; some folk think he's really funny [then after a long pause], but we haven't got to live with him like you have."

On 17th August I went to Luna Park with Gerald Cock, then attached to the Outside Broadcast Department, and afterwards " O.B." Director and the first Director of Television, to arrange for a broadcast from there that evening. We went round the shows and met a most entertaining person, named Bill Reeves, who introduced himself rather naïvely as " Fred Karno's original drunk ". " I am the man," he said, " who first took Charlie Chaplin over to the States and made him a millionaire."

.   .   .   .   .

Our transmitter for the 2L.O. programme had been situated at Marconi House in the Strand, but a new transmitter with a higher aerial system was now erected on the top of Selfridge's in Oxford Street, and on 6th April, 1925, all was ready, and we switched over to that transmitter permanently, holding the old Marconi House one in reserve for an emergency. Actually we had very few transmitter breakdowns. Occasionally there would be an S.O.S. asking for a three-minute interval to change a valve, but I can recall no serious delay because of transmitter trouble, with one exception. That was on 31st May, when 2L.O. was off the air for some nineteen minutes. A long and careful search for the cause of the trouble eventually revealed the charred remains of a mouse which had been incautious enough to venture in between the terminals of a high-capacity condenser. There were delays of three or four minutes caused by microphone trouble, usually only a matter of adjustment, but, all the same, a nuisance. We were then using the Round-Sykes Magnetophone, a microphone with a heavy magnet and a delicate frontal attachment, slung in a thick piece of sponge rubber mounted on a square wooden frame, the

B   9

legs of which were splayed out and fitted with casters, so that it could be easily pushed around the studio. To prevent nervous artists from being upset by its rather bizarre appearance, the apparatus was covered with a box-like cover overlaid with blue silk, making it look like a most artistic portable meat-safe, hence its nickname "the meat-safe".

Spare microphones were always kept in the studio, and when Control Room wished to change over, at an agreed point in the programme we said, "Three minutes interval, please", and then resumed as if nothing had happened, giving no explanation.

This microphone could not accommodate an unlimited volume of sound; it was a sensitive instrument and needed careful nursing, and I remember that so powerful was the voice of Lauritz Melchior, the Danish operatic tenor, that when he came to the studio the only way we could obtain even an approximate balance was to put the microphone in the passage at the far end of the studio and open the doors. He was not singing operatic arias with full orchestra, but songs with piano accompaniment, like Strauss' "Zueignung" and Grieg's "Ich liebe dich".

All this was years before "programme engineers" as we now know them came on the broadcasting scene. Nowadays, for all serious musical programmes they have to be both musicians and engineers. Their job is to find out, by trial and error, the best positions in the studio for the microphones at rehearsal, so that the finest balance may be obtained, and then at transmission to control the actual volume of current passing through the microphone and amplifier, so that all "peaks" are avoided and microphone blasting is eliminated. This necessitates a careful watch on the score, as well as actual control of the electrical instruments, and demands a great deal of skill. In my view, it is only after years of experience that really first-class programme engineers are made, and it is interesting to note how much conductors depend on their judgment and collaboration in rehearsing for a broadcast, as it is essential for the conductor to know if certain effects for which he is striving in the concert-hall or studio will reach the listener's ear.

Contrast this present-day elaborate process with the late nineteen-twenties when the announcer was frequently the only person available to attend to the balance. If he could not be present at the rehearsal—

which often happened, as he was engaged on other work—then, having started off a concert, he at once went into the "listening box"—a cubicle in the studio like a public telephone call-box—where he put on headphones and did his best to listen to the balance, going into the studio again to move the microphone perhaps two or three times before the right spot was found. This did not matter very much if an orchestra were playing and the microphone was carefully moved. But if one began to move the microphone when a singer was in the middle of a song, it was disconcerting, to say the least, and if he stopped altogether, he could hardly be blamed.

. . . . .

An announcer's job in these early days of broadcasting was very varied. He had to act as host, try to make nervous artists at home in the studio to ensure a good broadcast, deal with any programme troubles, make any last-minute decisions, frequently turn over for artists, and finally either pay them their fee or sign an authority card for the cashier as they went out.

Many are the experiences I have had in turning over—my worst, when I was asked to turn over for a two-piano recital in the large studio at Maida Vale, just as I was about to announce. I had to walk almost the length of the studio before I got to the piano. Meanwhile the pianists had begun to play. It was a modern Dutch work in manuscript, with frequent—much too frequent for me—changes of time signature, so that I never even found my place at all on the first page. Only by carefully watching the left hand and looking at the bass in the score did I pick it up in the middle of page 2—an awful feeling, because it is so easy to let an artist down if you lose, or do not find, your place.

On another occasion Professor Tovey was giving a talk on Beethoven in the studio, with illustrations at the piano. Not only did he ask me to turn over for him, but also to turn over the pages of his notes, written in a small hand on thin pieces of notepaper. I had an anxious half-hour, with the climax just at the end of the talk. He had been talking about Beethoven's use of the dominant, and proceeded to give some illustrations from full miniature scores, which I had some difficulty in seeing. The slow movement was easy enough to follow, but when it came to the scherzo I had to watch my step. All seemed to be going well, when suddenly he yelled, " Look out ! " I was scared, wondering what had gone wrong. However, we got through it all right, and after the broadcast he smilingly explained that what he had meant was " Look out for the dominant ". I felt rather limp for the rest of the evening.

Cecile Dixon (Sophie), who was for many years the staff accompanist at Savoy Hill and Broadcasting House, told me that on one occasion before I came she asked someone in the studio to turn over for her, when she was accompanying a violinist who was playing a very fast two-in-a-bar piece, and there was a difficult turn, because of a loose leaf. Apparently the person concerned could not read music, but did his best to turn over when Sophie nodded, but unfortunately let the page fall on to the floor. He dived for it and replaced it as quickly as he could—upside down.

On another occasion a singer, who brought his own accompanist, was singing, without music, some of Somervell's " Shropshire Lad " songs. When he came to the marching song, " The street sounds to the soldier's tread ", he forgot his words, turned away from the microphone, seized the piano copy, and left the wretched accompanist " pompomming " with his left hand as best he could, till the song ended.

.   .   .   .   .

In May 1925 the second year of the Wembley Exhibition was opened by His Majesty the King, and we broadcast the opening ceremony, including the music by the massed bands of the Brigade of Guards. On 27th July our new high-powered transmitter at Daventry was opened by the Postmaster-General, with a special programme from there to celebrate the occasion, which included a poem by Alfred Noyes, " Daventry Calling ".

The opening of this high-powered transmitter at Daventry was a most important step forward in the history of British broadcasting, because it meant that events of national importance could now be heard by virtually the whole of the country. Daventry broadcast its own programmes from the London studios. They were quite distinct from the London programmes, the transmitter being connected by land line to London. This, of course, meant a large increase in the output from London, and we had to bring into use several new studios at Savoy Hill to cope with this situation.

Twice, I remember, artists engaged for a 5XX Daventry broadcast actually went to Daventry in Northamptonshire, in spite of a note on the contract stating that they were to go to the London studios. There was a small emergency studio at Daventry, and they were able to broadcast from there, although this made the presentation of their programme a complex matter.

1925 was the year in which Lord Knutsford ("the Prince of Beggars") made his famous appeal from the studio for the London Hospitals and netted nearly £20,000 as a result of an appeal lasting a little under ten minutes. This stood as a record for several years, and immediately opened people's eyes to the immense possibilities of wireless as an aid to charitable bodies appealing for funds. So great was the demand for time on the air for this purpose that we had to set up an Appeals Advisory Committee to help us to allocate broadcast appeals on a fair basis.

On 30th November Queen Alexandra died, and, following the announcement of her death at 7 p.m. we closed down until 7.30 p.m., when a studio service was broadcast, after which we again closed down until 10 p.m., when I read both General News bulletins, which were compressed into one. Then we closed down for that night. The next night T. P. O'Connor broadcast a talk about her life. I think that this was the only time he ever broadcast, for soon afterwards he, too, died.

It was in 1925 that Bransby Williams, Vivian Foster (the Vicar of Mirth), Norah Blaney and Gwen Farrar, Sir Harry Lauder and, last but not least, the Nightingale, all made their first appearance in our programmes, and won countless admirers.

On August Bank Holiday we broadcast, also for the first time, the sound of the waves of the sea from Great Yarmouth; and attempted to broadcast the noise of the horses galloping past Tattenham Corner on Derby Day on 27th May : at that time we were not allowed to broadcast a running commentary. But luck was against us. It was a pouring wet day, our men were soaked and the going was so soft that one could hear next to nothing of the horses rounding the Corner. Added to which there was line trouble, and I made a note in my diary that, " The broadcast from Tattenham Corner was a fiasco; I spent most of the afternoon putting out apologies from the studio ".

In spite of this, somebody managed to shout out the name of the winner near enough to the microphone for it to be clearly heard.

. . . . .

In the late nineteen-twenties, when "the Wireless", as it was called, was becoming more and more popular and the number of licences issued each year was increasing rapidly, reputations were being swiftly made by little-known artists, and the importance of broadcasting as a publicity medium was becoming widely recognised.

There was Willie Rous ("Wireless Willie", as he was called), with his songs and jokes at the piano, Helena Millais, or "Our Lizzie", and John Henry, the henpecked Yorkshireman telling us of his exploits with his friend Joe Murgatroyd, and describing the tiffs he was having with "Blossom", his wife; a little later came Wish Wynne with her superb Cockney versions of nursery rhymes, and among the talkers were "A Bonnet Laird", who spoke about country life and customs, and Marion Cran, who gave weekly talks on gardening. These were mainly about the flower-garden, for she had a most wonderful eye for colour, and was an adept at suggesting pleasing effects for the small garden. Her approach was very feminine. She had a small, soft voice, often pitched in a minor key, which, though it won her many admirers and brought her a very heavy fan mail, was the despair of the engineers, who had great difficulty in getting her to produce a sufficient volume of sound to ensure a good broadcast. She was a well-known writer on gardening subjects, and while at the height of her fame brought out a book with the intriguing title *The Story of my Ruin*. This had nothing to do with any personal experience of hers, as one might be led to expect, but was an account of an old, almost derelict, house she had bought in South-East England. In the book she described how she had had it renovated, and the enchanting gardens she had designed for it, transforming it into an old-world dream house.

1926

ONE of the earliest entries in my diary for this year is "4th January, first day of evening dress for announcers". I know, of course, that caricaturists traditionally depict the announcer as an individual dressed in faultless tails and white tie,

"GOOD EVENING, EVERYBODY. XXX
CALLING! WE WILL NOW HAVE A FUGUE"

or a short coat and a neat black bow, usually wearing horn-rimmed spectacles and standing in front of a microphone suspended from the ceiling. Well, it all starts from this date. Personally, I have always thought it only right and proper that announcers should wear evening dress on duty. After all, announcing is a serious, if new, profession, and the wearing of evening dress is an act of courtesy to the artists, many of whom will almost certainly be similarly dressed if they are taking part in a programme from 8 p.m. onwards.

There are, of course, certain disadvantages. It is not ideal kit in which to read the News—I myself hate having anything tight round my neck when broadcasting—and I remember that more than once the engineers said that my shirt-front creaked during the reading of the bulletin.

.   .   .   .   .

This year will always be remembered in the history of British Broadcasting because it demonstrated the tremendous power of the spoken word. The first example of this was Father Ronald Knox's talk on 16th April, the second the General Strike, when most of the country had to depend on radio for their news. Father Knox was speaking from Edinburgh, letting his imagination run riot, in describing a fictitious revolution in this country called "Broadcasting the Barricades". Of course, there was the usual studio opening announcement explaining that what followed was fiction, but the difficulty was that so many listeners either did not hear or did not understand that announcement, or began to listen after the talk had started, and thought it was an actual description of scenes of mob violence in London at that very moment.

I was on duty at Savoy Hill, and, as Knox was speaking from Edinburgh, I did not listen at the beginning, but soon so many 'phone calls from apprehensive listeners were coming through that I had to listen. Obviously the whole thing was a "spoof"; you had only to hear sentences like "The mob are now swarming into Hyde Park and throwing ginger-beer bottles at the ducks on the Serpentine" to realise this; after all, it was night, and bitterly cold, with ice and snow everywhere in the London area. But still the telephone calls came in, and we had to put out a reassuring announcement at the end. Sometime later that evening a call was put through to me from a commercial traveller, who told me that he had only just got home after a very long day. He found the wireless switched on, both his wife and his sister-in-law, who was staying with them, drunk in the sitting-room, and his best bottle of brandy empty under the table.

" What are you going to do about it ? " he inquired.

. . . . .

At this time a man named A. J. Alan was being acclaimed as a story-teller at the microphone. He appeared only very occasionally, and his name carried an aura of mystery about it, as he had not been heard of before, and there was some doubt as to whether this was his real name. In fact A. J. Alan was the mystery man of radio. " Tell me, who is this fellow Alan ? What does he look like ? Is Alan his real name ? " (How many times had I been asked such questions !)

I always remember A. J.'s entrance to the studio : the slim, neat figure in the perfectly cut dinner-jacket, the eye-glass, the thin black brief-case, the cheerful smile, which seemed to say, " I'm feeling on top of the world; I hope you are, too ! "

Who discovered him, and how did he come to begin broad-casting ? One night Sir William Bull, a Director of the original B.B.C., Ltd., happened to tell a short story from 2L.O. which Alan heard while listening at his home. The next day he called on Rex Palmer, who was then the Director of the London Station, and told him about it, and went on to say that he had some ideas for several short stories, and asked for an audition. Rex was so struck by his personality and performance that he engaged him at once, and in his very first broadcast—a story called " My Adventure in Jermyn Street "—Alan made such a hit that whenever his name appeared in the *Radio Times* thousands of listeners noted the date and time in their diaries.

When broadcasting he used to sit on a high stool close to the microphone—originally the old meat-safe magnetophone type—with his manuscript, pasted on to sheets of cardboard, in a pile on his knees. He spoke very quietly at the microphone. (If you fidgeted or creaked your chair you got a black look !)

He took himself most seriously when broadcasting, and would never smoke or drink for at least a week beforehand. But he obviously enjoyed it, and knew that he was giving pleasure to countless people.

As he was a Government servant—his name was not Alan—he

did not have to broadcast for a living, and was careful to nurse the demand he created, by appearing in the programmes only twice or three times a year.

The idea of the sheets of cardboard was to eliminate any possibility of paper-rustle, which would have destroyed the illusion he was out to create—namely, that he was sitting by his own fireside, relating some incredible adventure that had just happened to him.

Once, in the late nineteen-twenties, he saw in the paper that the lights had gone out while I was reading the News, but that I managed to carry on with the aid of matches and a candle, until the bulletin ended. The next time he came to the studio he insisted on having the candle lit in the reading-lamp beforehand. The electric light did not go out, but the candle did—suddenly with a loud click, for there was only a stump of it—and the spring in the reading-lamp jerked it out, throwing grease all over him, but A. J., unperturbed, carried on as if nothing had happened. After that experience he decided never again to trust B.B.C. candles, but always brought his own candle in a candlestick, and solemnly lit it before he began.

" No," he said, " I'm taking *no* chances."

What was the secret of his art—for art it certainly was ? In the first place, I should say that he was a born raconteur, with ideas, imagination and a keen sense of humour, and, being a first-class radio technician, saw in a flash the great possibilities of radio as a medium for his own particular line.

He also thoroughly understood the intimate nature of the microphone, and made each listener think that he was telling the story to him, and to him alone; it was done in such a natural, detached and effortless way.

But you must not imagine that his stories were just reeled off without effort or thought beforehand. He took the very greatest care in the preparation and rehearsal of the manuscripts, and having written and timed a story—he was most meticulous about timing—he would record it, play it back to himself, noting where to put in the little asides which always seemed so spontaneous. Then he would ask one or two trusted friends to come to his house to listen and criticise, adding a pause here, altering a downward inflection of the voice there, until he himself was reasonably satisfied.

The result was certainly a work of originality; in fact he was one of the first to explore the uncharted continents of broadcasting. He was, indeed, the inimitable A. J. Alan.

THE GENERAL STRIKE

Towards the end of April a crisis arose in the coal industry over a dispute between the miners and coal-owners, threatening a General Strike, and on 30th April the News included a statement that a " deadlock in the negotiations existed, and a strike seemed inevitable ". On the following night—Saturday, 1st May—Mr. Reith came in and broadcast a message from the Prime Minister, Mr.

A LOW CARTOON DURING THE GENERAL STRIKE

Baldwin : " Keep steady; remember that peace on earth comes to men of goodwill."

The next evening a message about the coal crisis was broadcast by me from Daventry 5XX at 6.6. p.m.—the first time a News item had ever been broadcast before 7 p.m. The message came from Reuters, and I had Mr. Reith's permission to put it out. Broadcasting continued normally on the following day, but I have a note to say that I kept in constant touch with Mr. Reith, and on Tuesday, 4th May the strike started.

At once we began to broadcast special News bulletins. As no newspapers were being published, except the *British Gazette* and the

British Worker, these usually ended with a long list of trains due to leave London the following day, the announcer becoming a kind of vocal Bradshaw. Now and again accidental asides were broadcast—e.g. on 5th May "Hell! More trains again. Shut the door, Brennan"—but on the whole the News bulletins were broadcast without much difficulty. Owing to the volume of news, they went on for half or three-quarters of an hour, sometimes even longer. To help out, several senior members of the staff came and read one or more bulletins each day; on Saturday, 8th May Mr. Reith read the News—this was the day on which the Prime Minister broadcast to the nation, beginning, "I am a man of peace"; on Sunday, 9th May, the bulletins were shared by P. P. Eckersley—the Chief Engineer—and Admiral Carpendale, the Controller.

By this time it was realised how important a part the spoken word was playing in the drama of the strike, and we were given a heavy police guard at Savoy Hill; the building seemed to be full of police, and only certain people with specially endorsed passes were allowed in the Control Room—the nerve-centre of the broadcasting machine.

On 11th May a large box of kippers and haddock arrived for me from Pembroke. They came from a kind trawler owner who thought we might be running short of food at Savoy Hill. It was the same man who, earlier in the year, having just installed a wireless set, listened to our 5XX weather forecasts, and so saved his nets from destruction in a gale. He now thought he must try to do something for us in return.

On 12th May the strike ended. Mr. Reith read the one o'clock News, as we had heard that a meeting had been arranged between the Prime Minister and representatives of the T.U.C. for 12 noon at No. 10 Downing Street, and this was mentioned in the News.

I was acting as Liaison Officer between the News Editor, Mr. Strutt, and Mr. Reith, and while he was reading, a message came through on the tape to say that the strike had terminated. I ran down to the studio with it, exactly as it had come through, and, waiting until he had reached the end of a paragraph, put it in front of him. He paused, read it through, and reflected, then signed to me for a pencil and wrote on the back of the paper: "Get this confirmed by 10 Downing Street." Some ten minutes later I obtained the necessary confirmation, and he at once announced the end of the strike to the world, and cut out the rest of the bulletin.

The following day the Prime Minister made a statement in the House, which was broadcast by Mr. Reith to the nation at 9.30 p.m.; I followed him with the News at 9.40. Soon the necessary agreements were drawn up and signed, and things gradually returned to normal.

.   .   .   .

The terms of the Railway agreement were broadcast on Friday, 14th May, and Mr. J. H. Thomas, the N.U.R. leader, spoke about them that night.

I noted that the first L.C.C. tram to pass along the Embankment in charge of " regulars ", as distinct from volunteers, went by at 2 p.m. on Friday, 14th May; also, that the first News on 15th May, scheduled for ten minutes, actually took thirty-eight.

At about this time the following poem appeared in *Punch* :—

Gaunt pole that rises into upper air,
    High o'er my clumps of holly and genista,
How my whole soul revolts to see thee there,
    Bisecting what was once a high-class vista !
Not—oh, believe me—not from whim or choice
    Would I maintain an object so appalling,
But lo ! from thy slim apex comes the Voice
    That nightly tells me " This is London calling ".

And when industrial peace is wearing thin,
    Or Hobbs and Root are making cricket history,
I seize my crystal set and listen-in,
    Nor grudge thee ample credit for the mystery,
When, winged upon the ether overhead,
    That silken Voice whose sweetness never varies
Bids me look under Uncle George's bed,
    Or notes a cyclone crossing the Canaries.

Wherefore stand on, O eyesore unalloyed,
    Seeing thou bearest that so potent cable
That snares all news, all knowledge, from the void
    And drops it neatly on my study table;
Ay, and the Voice, that disembodied tongue,
    That I so oft have sought in playful fancy
To add a face to, shall not go unsung
    While I've a voice to praise thy necromancy.
                                        ALGOL.

.   .   .   .

Unlike other Prime Ministers I have met, Mr. Baldwin nearly always made a point of coming to the studio to broadcast, rather than speak from 10 Downing Street. I announced him on several occasions, and was always impressed by his humanity and friendliness, also his great concentration while speaking at the microphone. In fact his broadcasts were an object lesson. He had one or two little mannerisms, which probably resulted from this intense concentration on what he was saying, and I doubt if he was conscious of them. Apart from Hugh Walpole, Mr. Baldwin was, as far as I can remember, the only person who ever spoke into the microphone without a manuscript, and, watching him in action, I am sure a manuscript would have bothered, and not helped him. He spoke somewhat slowly and deliberately, without using very much voice—a good point this, for a House of Commons man—from a few headings written on a piece of folded paper, rather like a spill one uses to light a pipe; and this he kept twisting and turning nervously around his fingers as he spoke. Now and again, in searching his mind for the right word, he would momentarily open and close his lips without any sound emerging, but generally his thoughts flowed swiftly and his sentences were short, crisp and clear—in fact, ideal for broadcasting purposes. He kept his body quite still—unlike many other famous broadcasters—made no gestures with his hands, and remained all the time looking directly at the microphone, as though engaged in earnest conversation with a man immediately opposite him in the room.

As soon as he had finished and the red light had gone out he would take his cherry-wood pipe from his coat pocket and start filling it, ready to light up immediately he got outside the studio.

While waiting for the Engineer's report on his broadcast he would laugh and joke like a schoolboy, and talk in the most homely and natural way.

Here was the man, I thought, for whom "England was the country and the country was England".

.   .   .   .   .

On 26th May we broadcast from Parliament for the first time, not a Parliamentary Debate, but a speech by H.R.H. the Prince of Wales on the occasion of a banquet given by permission of H.M.

the King in the Royal Gallery of the House of Lords by the International Parliamentary Commercial Conference.

. . . . .

On 8th June we broadcast Melba's farewell concert from the Royal Opera House, Covent Garden. It was most memorable, but sad to think that it was the last time we would hear that wonderful voice, with its exquisite quality and diction. There was something so individual about her singing, especially the pathos expressed in the part of Mimi in " La Bohème ", that surely those who heard her will never forget. Then at the end the tumultuous applause, the pathetic little speech in broken sentences in front of the curtain, and we, who were listening, realised that she was passing from reality to the realms of memory.

. . . . .

One of my earliest memories of Savoy Hill is of being shown a list of place and proper names, many of them Scottish, posted up on the wall of the Announcers' Room, on the principle of " you have been warned ". It included names like Glamis, Dalziel, Milngavie, Kirkcudbright and Cholmondeley. Place and proper names were constantly cropping up in Talks and News bulletins, and were an ever-present problem. By 1926 the B.B.C. decided that something must be done about them. A committee of eminent persons was therefore assembled under the chairmanship of Robert Bridges, with Bernard Shaw as vice-chairman; and including such authorities as Logan Pearsall-Smith, Daniel Jones and Lloyd James. Its main task was to advise announcers as to the pronunciation of difficult names, and, in the case of words which could be pronounced in two or more ways, which one to use when broadcasting.

As the date of the first meeting (5th July, 1926) drew near there was a rush to collect words for the Committee from the various departments—chiefly Talks, Schools and News—and in due course its decisions were published, and created a great deal of interest in the Press.

Unfortunately, there were one or two misprints in this list, and I remember that *Punch* made the following selection :—

Upanishad to be pronounced Oo-pan-i-shad.

Ogive to be pronounced O-jive.
Cinema to be pronounced Sinne-mah.
Zoological Gardens to be pronounced Zoojolical Gardens.
Fauteuils to be pronounced Fotils. . . .

and then enquired :—

Will you come with me to the fotils of the Sinne-mah or

UNRECOGNISED HEROES
THE ANNOUNCER WHO SAID
" BROADCASTED "

are you going to the zoojolical gardens to see the ojives and the oopanishads ?

Later on the Committee produced a number of " Spoken English " booklets dealing with place and proper names both at home and abroad, which were, and still are, of the greatest possible service to broadcasters. Their compilation was a long and difficult business, and they were admirably edited and introduced by Mr. Lloyd James. In the case of British place-names the principle was to get at least two authentic rulings on the pronunciation of each place-name. With this object in view, the postmasters and vicars of all the smaller towns and villages were written to; and in a large number of cases the postmaster did not agree with the vicar. Nevertheless, this gave us the rulings of two authorities to enter up in our card index. Sometimes there were as many as five alternatives—

A TERRIBLE FEAR THAT HE IS ABOUT
TO SNEEZE HIS HEAD OFF

e.g. Uttoxeter, which can be pronounced either Uttoxeter, Yew-toxeter, Uxeter, Uxter, or Utcheter.

. . . . .

In the autumn of 1926 we broadcast a number of programmes from a studio which had been specially fitted up at the Radio Exhibition at Olympia. The walls were mostly made of glass, and all day queues of people walked slowly past or stood with their noses pressed to the windows, watching us at work. After a while we got used to it, but it was very disconcerting at first, and many of us had what was known as " that goldfish feeling ".

As it was a box within a box, with practically no ventilation, the heat and " fug " became almost unbearable after an hour or so, and how the players managed to keep their instruments in tune I shall never know. Incidentally one of the performers was Tommy Handley, who appeared in " The Awful Revue ", making everyone laugh with a tongue-twisting song, " What I want is a proper pot of coffee ".

In the field of light music, De Groot and his Piccadilly Hotel Orchestra and Sandler and his Grand Hotel Orchestra from East-bourne had both become very popular, the clarity of the broadcasts from Eastbourne being outstanding.

Another resounding success was the broadcast of the first of the new series of National Concerts from the Albert Hall on 30th September. To open this series there was a huge orchestra of 150 conducted by Sir Hamilton Harty, Olszewska, the Covent Garden Opera star, being the soloist.

Two famous men, both pre-eminent in their own particular sphere, had by this time become popular with listeners, Sir Oliver Lodge and Sir Walford Davies.

Sir Oliver resumed his scientific series in the autumn on the difficult and abstruse subject " Worlds and Atoms ", beginning on 6th October with " The Atom of Matter ".

He was a tall, venerable figure with a slight stoop. He had a short grey beard and a most wonderfully formed head : it was dome-shaped, and the area from the eyes to the apex of the skull in propor-tion to the area of the face was much greater than any other I had ever seen. He had, too, a pair of penetrating bright blue eyes and a humorous mouth, and his voice was a resounding basso which seemed to match the profundity of his utterances.

He had a little trick of clearing his throat immediately after he had been announced and before he began to speak. So regularly was this sound produced that we used to call it his " signature tune ".

SIR OLIVER LODGE

SIR WALFORD DAVIES

He could talk simply, directly, effortlessly, and with great humility, in non-technical terms, about complex scientific subjects, giving the impression that he was taking you into his confidence and that you and he were sharing secrets together—in fact, he was a real master of the microphone.

.   .   .   .   .

For Sir Walford Davies music was life, and life meant everything in the realm of music. Towards the close of his career he devoted all his energies to spreading the gospel of music, using broadcasting most effectively to that end. He was a fine musician and an able pianist with a most sensitive touch. He had a charming personality and a sympathetic, well-modulated voice. He loved all that was best in music, literature and the arts—especially Shakespeare—and together with these gifts went a vivid imagination. Small wonder, then, that he was one of the first to appreciate and seize with both hands—in more senses than one—the vast opportunities which wireless afforded.

He was the ideal broadcaster, friendly and confidential at the microphone. He used the piano with consummate skill, and had that sense of intimacy—of having a little chat with one listener or one family only—which, broadly speaking, is the pre-requisite of all successful broadcasting.

He took the greatest care in preparing his notes and rehearsing his illustrations—sometimes, when rehearsing with the B.B.C. Singers, going on too long, and giving them little time for food between rehearsal and transmission. But all this was because his standards of performance were so high, especially in music of a religious nature—nothing but the best would ever do.

Through his talks to schools many a grown-up has been converted to an appreciation of good music; I myself know of several who had never written a note in their lives, but were persuaded by him to try their hand at composing simple melodies. His vast unseen audience through his broadcasts to schools and his series "Music and the Ordinary Listener", "Music for Worship", and "Melodies of Christendom", made him by far the best known of all broadcasters.

He was most kind and encouraging to us, realising at first hand some of our problems. Of all the many facets of his personality, the one which most impressed me was his great humanity and consideration for others. Most of the engine-drivers on the Paddington trains to the West and Wales knew him, because he always talked to them, and thanked them at the end of a journey. Then there was his schoolboy-like keenness, his power of concentration, and the personal magnetism with which he persuaded others not only to be good listeners, but to try their hand at music-making, too.

Sometimes his keenness was a source of embarrassment to us, when he ran over his allotted time, but when the broadcast ended, I was always disarmed by his charming apology which immediately followed :

" Oh, I'm so sorry, Hibberd. I'm afraid I've been a naughty boy again."

" Yes," I would reply, " a very naughty boy; you over-ran by nearly two minutes. Next time I shall have to fade you out ! "

.   .   .   .   .

At the end of the year the old British Broadcasting Company, Ltd., itself faded away, like an old soldier who has served his time, and the new British Broadcasting Corporation was born.

1927

ONE of the most memorable concerts yet broadcast was given in the National series at the Royal Albert Hall on 20th January, just after we had received our charter as a corporation.

It was devoted to the works of Berlioz, and given by the National Orchestra of 150 players, the Hallé Chorus, brought down specially from Manchester, and four brass orchestras drawn from "The Besses o' the Barn" and Irwell Springs Band, conducted by Sir Hamilton Harty, who had a great reputation as a conductor of Berlioz.

The first part of the concert consisted of the "Grande Messe des Morts", a work scored for a very large combination of instruments. The volume of sound was tremendous, and the sensitive singing of the choir and the fine ensemble made a deep impression on all who heard it. Incidentally, we had to wait just twenty years before again hearing this huge work broadcast from London.

Ten days later, on 30th January, we broadcast a special Delius programme conducted by Geoffrey Toye, which included the violin concerto played by Albert Sammons on the occasion of the composer's sixty-fourth birthday, and I read a message of greeting to him, knowing that he was listening at his home at Grez-sur-Loing in France.

About this time a singer with a most unusual voice, who was very popular, frequently appeared in our programmes—Ruby Helder, the lady tenor.

Her voice was unlike any I had ever heard, and though in the studio or concert-hall it appeared to differ from an ordinary tenor in the quality of the tone—but not in range or pitch—yet when broadcast it was most effective and pleasing to the ear.

On Sunday, 13th February I sang two verses of the hymn "The

radiant morn hath passed away " with the choir in the Epilogue. I had been in the studio all the evening. When I went outside afterwards there was thick fog, the trains were held up, and I did not reach home until one o'clock in the morning !

· · · · ·

On Sunday, 20th March, Tallulah Bankhead was making the Week's Good Cause appeal for King's College Hospital. She was very nervous at rehearsal, and seemed most excited at the thought of speaking to unseen millions. I did my best to calm her, without much success. After the opening announcement she took a deep breath and dashed through her script, speaking so fast that she was difficult to follow. Then, as soon as the red light went out, she collapsed on the studio floor, much to my embarrassment. Luckily Derek McCulloch was near at hand to help me carry her out into the fresh air, and I left her in his capable hands while I hurried off to read the News.

· · · · ·

11th April was Budget Day, and the Chancellor of the Exchequer, Mr. Winston Churchill, sat down in the House of Commons after finishing his speech at 6.20 p.m. Ten minutes later we were broadcasting details of the Budget in the News, almost all of it taken straight off the tape-machines as it came in, with practically no editing at all. Sometimes the Editor, blue pencil in hand, would be checking through the last paragraph while I was broadcasting the first one. It meant solid concentration the whole of the time, as of course I had not seen the script before, and the broadcast lasted for half an hour.

· · · · ·

There was a standing instruction that all studio equipment must be tested by the engineers immediately before a broadcast. It was always interesting, after a rehearsal, to watch the Control Room engineer at work testing the plugs, leads, etc., with the help of Control Room, who replied to his questions with a series of signals on the red light.

" Hello, Control Room ! Can you hear me ? Here is the plug, the earth-pin, now the leads "—as he handled each in turn. " One if you can, two if you can't. Now the mike. I am speaking about a foot away from it. 'Mary had a little lamb, whose fleece was white as snow ' . . . Monday, Tuesday, Wednesday, Thursday. . . . Can you still hear me, Control Room ? Now the grams."

He would then go out of the studio and into the adjoining "listening room", which was separated from the studio by a wall in which was a large glass sound-proof window, and soon from the loud speaker in the studio you would hear the conversation continue, ending with the "Teddy Bear's Picnic", a record especially chosen for this purpose because of the wide variety of frequencies involved. This was the tune that eventually became generally known as the Engineers' Signature Tune.

On Friday, 20th May, I happened to read the first News Bulletin, and the next day I heard that it had been relayed by the new Dutch short-wave station P.C.J.J. of Eindhoven, Holland, to the East Indies and heard clearly in Sydney, Christchurch (New Zealand), Calcutta, Cape Town and Durban. It produced a sensation in the overseas Press, which reported that "London Calling" sounded like "uncle in the next room". Apparently it was picked up and relayed by the Sydney Station (2BL) between 3 and 6 a.m., Australian time. Listeners could not believe their ears; they telephoned the Sydney Station to find out if it were a hoax or not, and were surprised and delighted when they learnt that they had indeed been listening to London. An article about it in one of the papers ended : " It has proved that London's programme can be put into the air for Australia between 3.30 and 5 a.m., Sydney time. Certainly, nearly all Sydney will stay up the whole night next time there is a broadcast of 2LO's programme." The orchestral programme of light music from the Prince of Wales Playhouse, Lewisham, before the News was also clearly heard.

In New Zealand the Press began a campaign urging their Government to collaborate with the British Government in casting a wireless girdle round the Empire, and in South Africa the opinion was expressed that "the experiment was sufficiently successful to warrant the hope that a regular service of relayed London programmes may soon be available to South African wireless enthusiasts"—one Durban listener writing, " What a thrill we had here to-day when we heard that crisp, clear voice 'London Calling', followed by the

News and Cricket Scores ! " The home Press was swift to ask why this successful broadcast should have been carried out by a foreign short-wave station, and not a British one, and the cautious official reply was at once given by our Engineers that it was one thing to broadcast a programme to the Empire on one night, when conditions happened to be exceedingly good; it was quite another to be able to put out a regular service. We were experimenting with short waves and collecting data about long-distance reception.

The next chapter in this interesting story begins on Armistice Day, when our new short-wave transmitter at Chelmsford G.5SW was brought into use on an important occasion for the first time. We broadcast the British Legion Rally at the Royal Albert Hall, which was attended by H.R.H. the Prince of Wales, and for the first time I was able to say in the opening announcement :

" This is the British Broadcasting Corporation calling the British Isles, the British Empire, the United States of America and the Continent of Europe, from London, England, through Daventry 5XX, and through Chelmsford 5SW.

We are now going over to the Albert Hall, London, to take the Remembrance Festival which is organised under the joint auspices of the *Daily Express* and the British Legion, and includes an address by His Royal Highness the Prince of Wales.

Through our high-power long-wave station, Daventry 5XX, we are radiating this programme for the British Isles and the Continent of Europe; with our high-power short-wave transmitter, Chelmsford 5SW, in co-operation with broadcasting organisations overseas, we are undertaking an experiment in order that listeners in the British Dominions, Colonies, and Protectorates beyond the seas, as well as listeners in the United States of America, may have the opportunity of endeavouring to hear the address of the Prince of Wales and the Community Singing of war-time songs in the Remembrance Festival at the Royal Albert Hall to-night.

In the United States, New York City receiving stations

are standing by to pass on this programme for distribution by the networks of the National Broadcasting Company of America."

This led to the eventual formation of the Empire Service, which for various reasons, one of the chief being the problem of raising the necessary finance with which to start the service, did not materialise until 1932.

. . . . .

One of the earliest of the broadcasts from the Continent was the Memorial Service and ceremony at the opening of the new Menin Gate on 24th July, involving the use of long land lines. The results of the tests carried out beforehand for this important occasion were excellent, and the broadcast began well, but unfortunately, owing to line troubles, there was a four-minute break in the transmission during King Albert's speech. This gave us an anxious time at Savoy Hill. Apart from this break, the broadcast was very clear, and the ceremony most impressive.

To English listeners a strange feature of this memorable broadcast was the embarrassing applause that greeted Lord Plumer and others before making their addresses, in spite of the religious character of the ceremony.

. . . . .

When closing down the programme in the studio before the dance music, the announcer on duty always said good night to his unseen audience, each one doing so in his own particular way.

I used the double good night, counting a quick four beats to myself in between the two, thus : " Good night everybody . . . 1, 2, 3, 4 . . . good night "; the idea being to give listeners a chance to say good night back to me in between the two. This was greatly appreciated, especially by the old folks and invalids, and now and again there would be requests to say good night to a particular person on an agreed date, either to one over ninety, or a sick person, though not, of course, mentioning the individual by name.

One such request came on 22nd November, 1927, from Nottingham. The B.B.C. rang me up at my home about it just as I had got back from London, shortly after 7 p.m. Apparently a young girl named Edna Dent, who was known to be dying, had expressed the wish to hear me say good night to her. I returned to London in good time to close the programme down and say good night in my usual way. A few days later her aunt wrote to say that Edna had been listening, and heard me say good night, and said good night back to me. Early the next afternoon she died.

I realise that this was a pathetic case, which unfortunately was given a great deal of publicity in the Press, but it made me do some solid thinking about the vastness of the potential opportunities and responsibilities afforded by the microphone, and the immense power of the spoken word.

1928

LOOKING over some of our programmes broadcast in the late 1920's, I cannot help thinking that the Music Department sometimes included large-scale works—most expensive to perform—because they were exotic fruit, rather than the more tasty morsels usually served up to the public. I have already spoken of Berlioz' "Grande Messe des Morts", which was broadcast in the autumn of 1927, and pointed out that it was twenty years before we again heard this work.

Then there was Rimsky-Korsakoff's opera "Kitesh"—the invisible city—which, sung in Russian, was broadcast in a concert version from Covent Garden, with Russian singers brought from various parts of Europe for the occasion, apparently regardless of expense, and for one performance only; this was in March 1926.

But most memorable of all was the performance of Schönberg's "Gurrelieder", or Songs of Gurra, on 27th January, 1928. For this there was the same vast orchestra and chorus, plus four soloists and a speaker, with many rehearsals over and above the normal. Was the result a musical experience? Yes. Was it an outstanding work which forthwith took its place in the repertory? No. This is what one of the London critics said about it the following day :—

> "The 'Gurrelieder' have never been acclaimed as a popular attraction; essentially they remain caviare to the general."

He then goes on to discuss the work in detail, and ends :—

> ". . . a very remarkable work, that we shall, I suppose, never hear again."

(Up to now—1948—we have not heard another live performance, but records of the "Gurrelieder" were broadcast in the Third Programme in 1947, almost twenty years later.)

There is a story told about Schönberg and the first performance of the " Gurrelieder " here which has a very human background.

Schönberg spoke but little English, and in order to help him with his rehearsals, Edward Clarke of the Music Department was attached to him as liaison officer. There were many rehearsals, some with sections of the orchestra, some with the full orchestra and chorus. During a lengthy rehearsal with the wood-wind and brass, Clarke was called away to the telephone. It so happened that while he was out of the studio a long wood-wind passage was played, ending with a silent bar or two and then a few notes for the third horn—his only solo part. The conductor gave the cue to the horn-player, but instead of the solo, a voice was heard exclaiming, " What I told him was, he'll have to marry the girl " ! Schönberg, exasperated, looked round in vain for Edward Clarke, put down his baton and burst out with the only two English words he could muster, " Good morning " ! Of course the whole orchestra roared with laughter.

. . . . .

On Sunday, 25th March, Sir John Reith asked me to look after a friend of his, a Dr. Miller, who was giving the address in the studio service from London at 8 p.m. I met him when he arrived at 7.30 p.m., took him to the studio and explained the procedure, leaving him alone to meditate for a few moments at 7.45. As I came out I noticed that the choir was not in the waiting-room, as it should have been. When by 7.50 there was still no sign of a choir, I realised that something had to be done about it, and done quickly.

I consulted the engineers as to possible alternatives, and found that 5G.B.—Daventry Experimental—was broadcasting a service from Birmingham Cathedral, and that it was possible to broadcast this service from London also. The important and urgent thing to do was to get some kind of service on the air at 8 ; the next, to see if we could, somehow or other, fit in Dr. Miller's address. I therefore told the engineers to get into touch with Birmingham and find out from their Outside Broadcast engineers what the hymn before the sermon was, how many verses it had, and, most important of all, what was the last line of the last verse. I returned to the studio to explain to an anxious Dr. Miller what had happened, asked for his help, which he readily promised to give, and outlined my plan of action. This was to put out the 5G.B. service from Birmingham Cathedral at 8 p.m., and broadcast it up to the end of the hymn before the sermon, then to leave the cathedral and come over to the studio for his address. I told him that I myself would be with him and would give him an agreed sign when to begin. I then asked if he would kindly read two or three prayers after his address, explaining that it would be impossible to return to Birmingham, because the sermon there would probably not have finished, and we could not risk it. He agreed to do this, and while he was looking out the prayers, I rang Sir John Reith and explained the situation and what I had planned to do. Then I went in search of a suitable record as a voluntary after the prayers. The gramophone-record room was locked, but I found the commissionaire with the master key, and quickly chose some of Handel's organ music.

Everything eventually went well, and I was most grateful to Dr. Miller for helping me in an awkward situation. Apparently there had been a mistake in the date, and that was why the choir had not arrived. It was the first time I had ever purposely deceived listeners; I made no attempt to explain why such a hybrid service was broadcast.

As far as I can remember only two letters of protest were received about the change; my deception must therefore have been very nearly complete, and Sir John seemed quite happy about the result.

.   .   .   .   .

I had now been announcing just over three years, and had become fairly confident in dealing with Scottish place-names, and, though I had met and conquered some of the simpler Welsh names, such as Llandilo, Pontardawe, Bettws-y-Coed, on 1st March—St. David's Day—I met my Waterloo.

We broadcast a special programme from the Miner's Institute at Rhosllanerchrugog, near Wrexham, and this dreadful name came in three or four times during the evening! I decided to take some lessons in Welsh pronunciation, and have never regretted having done so: when you have a sound working knowledge of the structure of a language, nearly all pronunciation problems soon disappear.

.   .   .   .   .

In these days of modern scientific methods—1948—our Listener Research Department can tell us the percentage of listeners to any programme, and compile detailed reports explaining why some liked and others disliked it, and all this within a week or so after the broadcast. In 1928, however, our method of finding out what listeners thought of our programmes was a simple one. We asked them to write and tell us frankly what their opinions were and why they held them. This we did by broadcast announcements and by notices and articles published in the *Radio Times*, the B.B.C.'s official journal.

About this time the B.B.C.'s Music Critic, Dr. Percy Scholes, in the course of his weekly talks on broadcast music, was dealing with the music of Bartok, and in a talk entitled " Is Bartok Mad or Are We ? " he ventured to give his own personal opinion on some aspect of this music, and asked listeners to write and say what their opinions were on this subject. They acceded to his request beyond all expectations, and by the end of the week some eight and a half sacks full of letters had arrived at Broadcasting House, which meant that extra staff had to be engaged to deal with them. This taught us a lesson, and from that day onwards, while we continued to ask for criticism of our programmes in general terms, because it was valuable data for the Programme Board, specific broadcast questionnaires were *ultra vires*.

The main defect of this early method was the human one. The satisfied listener seldom bothered to write; it was the disgruntled one who at once put pen to paper.

.   .   .   .   .

On Saturday, 12th May, we broadcast, most successfully, the song of the nightingale from the Surrey woods. He had become a firm favourite with listeners, and at this time of the year was billed in the *Radio Times* to appear two or three times a week, during the late dance-music. At first the O.B. engineers invoked the aid of Miss Beatrice Harrison's 'cello to induce him to sing when required, she having discovered that certain passages on that instrument, especially trills, were irresistible; but later several satisfactory microphone positions were found, and the 'cello stimulus was no longer used.

When he was in good form we would broadcast snatches of his

glorious song three or four times in the course of an evening, fading out from the dance-music over to the microphone in the woods.

I was familiar with so many songs and poems about the love-song of the nightingale that I had accepted it as such without question. It therefore came as something of a shock when a well-known naturalist told me that the real object of the song was to distract attention from the female, sitting on the eggs in the nest some distance away. He went on to say, that when recently the song of the nightingale was being broadcast, he had placed his loud-speaker in the open window of his house facing some trees where a nightingale used to sing, and sure enough the local nightingale came nearer and nearer, doing his best to shout down the rival voice from the loud-speaker.

.   .   .   .   .

In addition to the General News bulletins broadcast at night, there were also periods following devoted to Local News, this time being used chiefly by provincial stations for broadcasting news and announcements of purely local interest—e.g. the cotton prices for Liverpool and district.

Frequently in London, after giving the other stations the agreed word-cue to cut out from London—" That is the end of the General News ; Local News will follow "—I found myself saying, " This is 2L.O. calling. There is no Local News to-night." On such occasions Cecile Dixon, the staff accompanist—" Sophie " of the Children's Hour, " the lady with the shy voice "—would step in and play a short piano piece, announcing the name of it herself. She was nearly always ready to come to our aid if programmes ran short or broke down, so much so that one of her many listener admirers said he was quite sure that she must sleep under the piano.

One night in June 1928, however, there was some Local News. It was to the effect that a dead whale had been washed ashore at Southend, and in spite of the fact that it was very dead, hundreds of people had been to the beach to see it. It was a large mammal, 52 feet long. By some mischance, probably because I was wondering if I should get an opportunity of speaking to the conductor before I started off the following orchestral programme, I said it was 512 feet long. I did not know I had done so until the next day, when I received a postcard : " Re. Local News last night. SOME WHALE " !

. . . . .

During the summer of 1928 a series of Bible-readings from the Old Testament, called " Songs of the Bible ", was broadcast at 5 p.m. each Sunday evening by well-known personalities, who, however, remained anonymous. One Sunday when I was on duty the reader failed to arrive, and I had to take over and read the passage myself at only about five minutes' notice. It was the Song of Deborah from Judges V—not an easy passage to read, even with adequate rehearsal, and I fear that my performance was not up to the requisite standard. However, I got through as well as I could in the circumstances, but was mercilessly ragged the next day by Stobart—who had chosen the reading—because, according to him, I had said, " Dan abode in his ships, but Asher remained on the seashore in his breeches "—instead of breaches, i.e. harbours!

. . . . .

In announcing musical programmes I have come across various amusing misprints or sequences. A simple change of one letter was responsible for turning Holst's Ballet " The Perfect Fool " into " The Perfect Foot " and a critic, when referring to Arthur Bliss's piano concerto, spoke of his " hormonic asperity "; similarly, an interchange of one word turned a famous soprano song from " Lo ! here the gentle lark—Bishop," into " Lo ! here the gentle Bishop—lark." Then there was the " Merry Pheasant " and the " Furry-breasted Pearl ". But in February 1928 the St. George's Singers began their programme with three Elizabethan madrigals which, read consecutively, made startling reading :—

" In going to my naked bed."
" Fair Phyllis I saw."
" To shorten winter's sadness."

. . . . .

On Monday, 15th October, I was on night duty, and we were half-way through a programme given in the studio by the Wireless Military Band—Robert Easton (bass) and Claude Pollard and Isobel Gray (two pianos)—when news came in via the control room from our experimental receiving station at Chelmsford that they were picking up an American broadcast of the landing of the

Graf Zeppelin at Lakehurst, New Jersey, and could I use it ?   I left
the studio and went to the control room, and with the senior
control-room engineer listened to the American transmission.   We
decided it was so good that it was an opportunity not to be missed.
I then rang up the Director-General (Sir John Reith), and he
agreed that I should go ahead and broadcast it.   I faded out the
Military Band, made a short explanatory announcement from
another studio, and over we went to Lakehurst at about 10.15 p.m.
Here is an account of what fol-
lowed :—

The loud, clear voice of an
announcer was heard describing the
preparations being made at the
landing-ground.   It was as clear
as if he were speaking from the
studio at Savoy Hill.   The noise
of the engines as the Zeppelin
passed overhead was clearly heard;
the landing of the airship was then
vividly described, the lowering of
the securing ropes, and the activities
of the ground crew, as she gradually
came to rest.   The announcer said,
" The ship has established a world's
record for continuous flight by
staying in the air for 111 hours 35
minutes."

"THE MARCH OF THE WOMEN"
DAME ETHEL SMYTH CONDUCT-
ING THE WIRELESS ORCHESTRA

It was a scoop for us, a fine
piece of work by our engineers at
Chelmsford, and the clearest relay from the United States heard in
this country up to that time.

.   .   .   .   .

On Sunday, 20th May, the concert after the Second General News
was devoted to the works of Dame Ethel Smyth; it consisted of
the overture " The Wreckers ", some part songs, and then her great
Mass in D, the Wireless Singers and Orchestra being conducted
by the composer.   Unfortunately we began the concert four
minutes late, and ran a minute over at 10.30, so that the Epilogue

did not begin until 10.32. Dame Ethel was very upset about the late start, as she had set her heart on putting in " The March of the Women " as an extra—a piece which she had written for the suffragettes when she herself was an active member of that movement. The Mass is undoubtedly a fine work, and I should like to hear it again; but to put in " The March of the Women ", however martial and stirring the music, after a Mass and before the Epilogue would have been an error of taste. So perhaps it was just as well that we did begin four minutes late.

.   .   .   .   .

The Roosters Concert Party, which had made a great name in France during the war, were at this time firm favourites with listeners, and used to broadcast at regular intervals from Savoy Hill. In 1928 they made a double-sided record of a battalion route march, giving a complete sound-picture from the " Shun " of the battalion commander to the command " Dismiss " at the end, including Cockney march-at-ease patter, such as " Hullo, Baby! how's Nurse ? " Christopher Stone broadcast this record in one of his weekly programmes, and, such was the publicity that broadcasting afforded, within a few days tens of thousands of this record were sold.

.   .   .   .   .

There had always been a strict rule in the B.B.C. that no advertising was allowed. At first even household words like Ford and Rolls-Royce were banned, and the announcer did not hesitate to use his cut-out switch on the microphone stand if an advertisement were slipped in. Later, however, things were slightly relaxed and certain agreements were made with the theatre managers, whereby the names of the theatre and the cast were broadcast when excerpts were included in our programmes. In the case of gramophone records, the make and number of the record were always announced, if time permitted.

It was seldom that any veiled advertisements were included in our programmes, but I recall one case in which the medium of radio was most cleverly employed for indirect advertisement, though we were all ignorant of the fact at the time.

There was an American broadcaster who came over to this country with a reputation as a story-teller. Several of his adventures were broadcast at the end of the studio programme, before the late-night dance music. In each case the setting was the same : a crusty old man, who had been a great traveller in his day, now spending his last years in a log hut in the American back-woods, and looked after by his grand-daughter. Supper over, the grand-daughter would settle him in his chair by the fireside, mix him a glass of grog, give him his pipe, and then ask him to tell her a story before they went to bed. At first he always refused, but eventually gave way to persuasion, and an excellent adventure story followed. He was a great success, and hundreds of listeners wrote to him, as requested in the closing announcement, which always gave the date and time of his next broadcast. It was not until some time after he had returned to America that we realised that each of his stories had been about a quest for some kind of precious stone, and that behind this there was a definite purpose. One was about the Klondyke Gold Rush, another about deep-sea pearl-fishing, a third about the search for diamonds in South Africa, and yet another about hunting for rubies in Burma, etc., etc. Each listener who had written to him received a courteous note of thanks in reply, with a card enclosed explaining that he was the European repre-sentative of a well-known New York firm of jewellers, and at their service. He was able to carry out this neat piece of indirect ad-vertising without in any way contravening the strict no-advertising rule of the B.B.C.

1929

IN the course of my work it has been my good fortune to meet many eminent men in almost all walks of life, and I had often reflected what a pity it was that no permanent record was being kept by the Corporation of their voices, and therefore of their personalities. It is true there were the scripts "as broadcast", retained in the files, but these were not generally available to the public, apart from a few extracts which were sometimes published in the topical columns of the *Radio Times*, and scripts are liable to be damaged or destroyed by fire or flooding, as indeed many of them were during the Blitz in 1940–41. I was thinking of men like Robert Bridges, the Poet Laureate, Sir J. J. Thomson, Sir Arthur Eddington, Sir Gowland Hopkins—how well I remember his fondness of the phrase " Now, this is very significant "—Lord Haldane, and J. C. Stobart; though we had recorded a fragment of Stobart's famous " Grand Good Night ", a New Year's Eve broadcast of outstanding originality and achievement. You may remember that on this occasion he referred to all professions and callings up and down the country, or almost all. He forgot dentists, and was reminded of his omission the next day. We also had an indifferent recording of Sir Oliver Lodge on " Worlds and Atoms ", and one of Sir Walford Davies on " Music and the Ordinary Listener ". But these were the few exceptions; the other early speakers have mostly passed and gone, and nothing remains that is audible, only a memory. Since 1932, however, the Corporation has gradually built up a Sound-Reference Library, which is now attaining enormous proportions.

In 1929 it was realised that if no recording of the spoken word were possible, there should at any rate be a written record available (apart from the original script), for use by listeners after the broadcast, which would be both complementary and supplementary to it. After protracted negotiations with the Press, and a good deal of opposition, the first number of the B.B.C.'s new paper *The Listener* was brought out on 16th January, 1929, its avowed object being " to carry home the more serious activities of the microphone in literature, drama and the many subjects covered by the talks ". Some original contributions were included, but by far the greater part of the material was based on matter that had been broadcast.

The opening number included contributions by such well-known broadcasters as Sir Walford Davies, Sir Oliver Lodge and Dr. Temple, Archbishop of York, and it undoubtedly supplied a frequently expressed demand by listeners.

This was particularly true in the case of the longer and more technical talks and special series, such as the National Lectures, an outstanding contribution to broadcasting and current thought, suggested by Sir John Reith, and begun on 28th February, 1929, by the Poet Laureate, Robert Bridges.

．　　　．　　　．　　　．　　　．

At the end of April and the beginning of May three party political broadcasts were given, with a few days' interval between each talk, in what was called the " Dissolution Series "—by Mr. Baldwin, the Prime Minister, for the Conservatives, Lord Samuel for the Liberals and Mr. Philip Snowden for the Labour Party.

It so happened that I announced each one, and it was interesting to watch and compare these three men in action as they made their appeals to the public. The microphone seemed to present no handicap to Lord Samuel, who spoke effortlessly and in conversational tones, and was obviously perfectly at ease from the moment he began. Not so Mr. Snowden, however, who, though clear and precise, seemed ill at ease and found it difficult to get away from the public-speaking approach, to which he was so accustomed. Both these men spoke from scripts, but Mr. Baldwin spoke only from a few notes scribbled on a piece of paper, and talked more slowly and deliberately than the others, looking hard at the microphone the whole of the time, as though deep in concentration on his subject-matter, though he, too, used conversational tones.

Here were these most experienced public speakers in unfamiliar surroundings, addressing probably the largest single audience they had ever had, and I could not help wondering how much consideration they had given to the psychology of the microphone before they began. In my view, sitting alone in a studio and speaking to thousands, there should be no mass psychology at all; rather the appeal must be made to the individual or the family, as the unit, the microphone forming the bridge between speaker and listener.

After the broadcast, we waited for a few moments to hear from the engineers whether it had gone over well or not, and if not, what were the criticisms.

While Mr. Baldwin was waiting after his broadcast, he threw himself on to the sofa in the studio and said, " Thank Heaven that is over. It's such a strain—solid concentration the whole of the time; and in the middle of it all I had the horrid feeling that nobody was listening."

.   .   .   .   .

On 9th November F. H. Grisewood was given his passing-out test as an announcer, and came through it with flying colours. It was a stiff test : a solid three-quarters of an hour at the microphone, with News-reading, poetry and prose readings, a situation test, i.e. an imaginary emergency with which he had to deal, orchestral programmes to announce, recitals, programmes in French, German and Italian, also an unseen short story as an intelligence test. All this was listened to in a special listening-room by a board of eight or nine seniors, with Mr. Lloyd James as technical adviser.

How many listeners, I wonder, realise the amount of training, experience and sound general knowledge that are required in order to pass such a test, everything having to be conveyed to the examiners through the medium of the voice—the most important factor of all. Fortunately, Grisewood was an experienced singer, with a fine and flexible voice. No wonder he cleared all the fences with ease.

.   .   .   .   .

For some years we had offered the public a free broadcasting S.O.S. service, which was greatly appreciated and widely used. At first there was some misunderstanding about the rules, and we used to get requests to put out S.O.S.s for lost cats, dogs, parrots and canaries, being regarded as a kind of inquiry agency for any lost individual or animal. We had therefore to make it quite clear that we could only accept an S.O.S. for a near relative of a sick person if he or she were dangerously ill, and this had to be confirmed by the doctor in charge of the case or the hospital authorities concerned. In the case of a missing person or a witness of a fatal accident being required, the request had to come to us from Scotland Yard or the Chief Constable of the county. In time, however, after many announcements and notices in the *Radio Times*, these rules became known, and we no longer received telephone inquiries asking how much it would cost to broadcast an S.O.S. for little Johnnie or cousin Tim.

There were one or two exceptions to these rules. One was when, on 25th November, 1929, I broadcast a most dramatic message about a wreck, at the end of the First General News. There had been wild weather all over the country, and most of the News was taken up with descriptions of the storms and the havoc that followed, and a gale was still blowing hard as the News began.

Suddenly the News Editor brought down this message, and I paused to glance at it, before putting it out :—

" Will any ship that may be in the vicinity of Wooltack Point, Cardiganshire, send, if possible, radio or visual signals to the steamer *Moseley*, which is ashore there, and breaking up, to the effect that the owners are sending them all possible assistance from Milford Haven—tugs, lifebelts and rocket apparatus ? "

We afterwards learned that three attempts were made by the Milford Haven lifeboat before it was possible to make fast life-lines to the stricken vessel. Eventually twenty-eight survivors were taken off safely, but unfortunately the Chief Officer's wife and seven of the crew were drowned.

1930

IN the early part of this year a new series of talks was begun, entitled " My Day's Work "; the idea being to outline a typical day's work in many trades and callings, so that people in one part of the country could get to know something about how those in the other part lived.   One of the contributors to this series was a Post Office night worker in a long-distance train—the night Irish Mail—and he described his duties throughout the journey.

He had written his script in the usual way, which, after some alterations at the suggestion of the Talks producer, was eventually rehearsed and timed in the morning.   He went home and tried it out on his family in the afternoon, and gained the impression that it was on the dull side.   He then sat down and tried to think out a plan to liven it up and make it more realistic.   After a while he had a bright idea, and, without saying anything to anybody, he slipped a whistle into his pocket, said good-bye to his family, who wished him good luck, and set out for Savoy Hill.

I was introduced to him by the Talks producer in the studio, and we had a little chat about procedure, which is normal practice. Then the red light came on, I announced him, and he was on the air.

After having described the Travelling Post Office and how he had to sort the mail en route, he paused and said, " Now will you come with me in imagination to Euston station, where the night Irish Mail for Holyhead is just about to leave ?   The engine-driver is looking out of his cabin along the platform, waiting for the signal from the guard to start, the doors are shut, the guard looks at his watch . . . now he's waving his flag . . . and we're off ! "   At this point he put his hand into his breast pocket, pulled out a whistle, and gave a long, shrill blast right into the microphone. He did this so quickly that I had no chance of stopping him, or even of signing to him or warning the engineers, who could then have taken " evasive action ".   Such high-pitched sound-frequencies

produced close to the microphone without warning meant a sudden
rush of current through the transmitter, causing serious damage to
the apparatus.   In this case the result was that Daventry was " off
the air " for three-quarters of an hour, and it cost the Corporation
about £350.

.   .   .   .   .

For some years the Corporation had included works by contemporary composers in their programmes, and, under the guidance of Edward Clarke of the Music Department, had strongly
supported the efforts of the International Society for Contemporary
Music, and had been instrumental in enabling listeners to hear
works by composers of such international eminence as Bartok,
Stravinsky, Schönberg, Webern, Honegger and Kodàly.   Most of
these had been large-scale works, such as the " Psalmus Hungaricus "
of Kodàly or the " Gurrelieder " of Schönberg, but concerts of
contemporary chamber music were also given.

One of these concerts was broadcast in February 1930, and consisted of works for wood-wind and strings.   Included in this
concert was a septet written in 1926–27 by a Russian named Gabriel
Popoff; it was scored for flute, clarinet, bassoon, trumpet, violin,
'cello and double bass—an unusual combination of instruments.
At the rehearsal, Haydn Draper, the clarinet, was most unhappy
about the ensemble, and said so to the conductor, asking if the
strange atonal effects produced were really what the composer
intended, as they sounded all wrong.   He was reassured, and told
that the work was going excellently.

The rehearsal was then resumed, and some most bizarre sound
effects were produced.   After a few moments the conductor
stopped the players on some small point of detail, and Draper
took this opportunity of again expressing his misgivings : " I seem
to be playing what is written in my part," he said, " but it sounds
like a succession of wrong notes."   Again the conductor had no
fault to find, and said that it was going splendidly, and in due
course the rehearsal ended without further comment.

It was only after the rehearsal was over that Draper discovered
that he had been playing with the clarinet in the wrong key; so
he *had* been playing wrong notes all the time.   But nobody seemed

to worry about it, and, what is more, nobody seemed to be aware of it, least of all the conductor !

.   .   .   .   .

In 1930 the Corporation formed the B.B.C. Symphony Orchestra from some of the finest players in the land, drawn from the old Wireless Symphony Orchestra and other famous orchestras, and including a fair sprinkling of younger players—recent graduates of the Colleges of Music. The leader was Arthur Catterall, the conductor Dr. (now Sir) Adrian Boult. Lauri Kennedy, the Australian 'cellist, was the principal 'cello, and among other principals were Frederick Thurston (clarinet), Archie Camden (bassoon), Aubrey Brain (horn), Jesse Stamp (trombone) and Harry Barlow (tuba). The orchestra was divisible into sections for small orchestral studio work, but for large-scale works, such as those by Berlioz or Strauss, it could muster, with extras, up to 120. It was a magnificent instrument, and soon made a deep impression on the public with its fine ensemble, superb wood-wind and brass, and the wonderful depth of tone of the strings.

It was not always possible to use either the Queen's Hall or the Royal Albert Hall, and the big studio at Savoy Hill was too small for the larger sections, though some of the smaller sections could play there. Another large studio had therefore to be found near Savoy Hill for rehearsals and studio transmissions. After a long search, an empty warehouse just across Waterloo Bridge, on the south bank of the river, was chosen. This was soon converted into a fine studio, and became known as No. 10. It was a most successful experiment, and this studio acted as the temporary home of the orchestra until a large skating rink was taken over in Maida Vale some three years later and converted into five fine studios, the largest being designed for the Symphony Orchestra.

Although No. 10 was an ideal studio for broadcasting, as the acoustics were excellent and there was enough but not too much resonance, it had several drawbacks. The situation on the water-front was not very pleasant, the studio being approached through narrow streets in a drab dockland district, where the smells varied in range from piano to fortissimo. The roof was not too good, and on one occasion after a heavy storm the water came pouring through, just above the conductor's head, and splashed the manuscript score he was using, so that " immediate action " had to be taken during the performance. As might be expected from the locality, there were many rats about, and several times during transmission they were seen running along the main iron girders of the roof, and on one occasion, on a Sunday night, a bat flew up and down over the heads of the players while a symphony was being broadcast. Luckily it did not swoop low enough to get caught in any of the ladies' hair, or a most awkward " technical hitch " might have arisen.

The main concerts of the week were then, as they are now in 1948, on Wednesdays and Sundays, the Sunday night Symphony Concert ending the programme, except for the Epilogue, which followed at 10.30 p.m.

For several Sunday nights in the late summer and early autumn programmes had run over their scheduled time and the Epilogue had begun late. So consistently bad had these timings been that many listeners waiting up especially for the Epilogue had complained about them, and a strict order was issued to the effect that in future the 10.30 timing of the Epilogue was to be regarded as a fixed point, just as nine o'clock is for Big Ben and the News.

I was announcing the Symphony Concert on a Sunday early in November in No. 10 Studio. The concert included a Mozart piano concerto played by Marcelle Meyer, the French artist, and ended with Delius's " Dance Rhapsody ". The programme was running late, and when the concerto had started it was obvious that there would not be enough time to play the "Dance Rhapsody", unless the Epilogue was again to begin at least three or four minutes late. The concerto ended at 10.20; the " Dance Rhapsody ", I knew, took thirteen or fourteen minutes. I had a hurried consultation with the conductor. Could he cut it in any way? He turned over the pages of the score, and then, shaking his head, said, " No, definitely not; it is a case of all or none ". Reluctantly I decided that we could not begin the work, as it would be impossible to finish it, and I went to the microphone and, adopting the principle I have always believed in, of telling listeners the truth, I told them the position, announced an interval of approximately nine minutes, until the Epilogue at 10.30, and said " Good night ". As soon as the red light went out, it was obvious that the conductor was very angry, having spent a great deal of time on the " Rhapsody " at the rehearsal. I went to him and explained why I had made my decision not to play it, and pointed out that the Epilogue had to start on time. Instead of dismissing the orchestra, he said to them in an angry tone of voice, " Now we will play the ' Dance Rhapsody ' " ! And play it they did—excellently, too, to the small studio audience who had been invited to come and listen. It ended at 10.34, vindicating my decision.

Naturally, there was an " inquest " the next day at Savoy Hill, and though I was blamed for an inept decision, the fact that I took it cleared the air. It was subsequently ruled that in future the announcer in charge of the programme should use his own discretion.

.   .   .   .   .

While on the subject of the Epilogue, it is interesting to note that it had always been something quite apart from the programme, and in the early days came at the end of the day's broadcasting. Originally it was a sort of addendum, and no mention was made of it in the *Radio Times*. Then, later, at the end of the Sunday programme items the single word " Epilogue " was printed. This led to requests from listeners for details, so that they could follow the Bible-readings at home, but these requests were refused, on the ground that the Epilogue would then become a programme item, and it was by definition something separate from the programme. Some months later a further request to publish the details was made by influential members of both Houses of Parliament and, after much discussion, a compromise was agreed on, whereby the details of the Epilogue (Bible-reading, hymns, psalm, etc.) were printed on another page of the *Radio Times*, so that the billing in that journal read as follows :—

10.30 p.m.   The Epilogue
(for details see page 673)

This principle seemed to work well and to satisfy those who had complained about the original billing, until it was decided to plan Epilogues weeks ahead in series under a general title, this and the sub-title being printed in the *Radio Times*.

I still have in my diary the cutting from the *Radio Times* which
reads as follows :—

> 10.30 p.m.   The Epilogue
> The Commandments
> " Thou shalt not commit adultery "
> (For details see page 140)

. . . . .

I do not think I am unduly superstitious—I should never worry
if I saw one magpie instead of two, or if I saw the new moon through
glass—but something did happen to me on Friday, 13th June.

I was taking Christopher Stone's weekly gramophone programme from 1.30 to 2.30 p.m., because he was unable to come to
the studio himself.   I was using No. 6 Studio in Savoy Hill—one
of the talks studios which were also used for gramophone programmes.   I sat at a desk fitted with two gramophone turn-tables,
on my right and left respectively, and in between was slung a Reiss
microphone, controlled by a three-way switch, the middle position
being for the microphone.   The leads were connected to a central
plug in the wall beneath the desk, and it was that plug which was
to prove my undoing.

I was thoroughly enjoying presenting this programme, and after
about fifteen minutes I came to a record of Berlioz' " Hungarian
March ".   It was a superb recording, conducted by Sir Thomas
Beecham, and as I listened to it on the headphones I began to beat
out the rhythm with my feet; then, more and more attracted by
this magnificent, irresistible tune, I began to sing it.

I must have been singing quite loudly—one usually does when
wearing head-phones—for half a minute or more, when two anxious
engineers rushed into the studio and silenced me by explaining that
it was all being broadcast.   Apparently there was a fault in one of
the connections, and though, from the position of the switch, the
microphone should have been dead, it was actually very much alive,
and every note I had sung had gone out.

After the programme the fault was traced to the plug in the
wall, which somehow or other must have become loose during
the programme, as it had been tested immediately before the broadcast began.   There could be only one possible explanation : I must

have knocked the plug with my foot without knowing that I had done so.

I still have a postcard in my diary to remind me that even announcers sometimes sing . . . at their work; it ran as follows :—

> " Congratulations on your vocal rendering of the Hungarian March in Christopher Stone's hour to-day. I wanted to hear more.   T.N.H."

.   .   .   .   .

At this time there was a school of experts at the Air Ministry who pinned their faith to the lighter-than-air machines and saw in airship development the solution of all Empire communications problems. With a view to testing this theory, an airship mast and shed were built at Cardington, Bedford, to house the newly constructed airship R 101, and a flight was planned to India and back early in October.

I well remember seeing the R 101 as she flew over Savoy Hill on one of her final trials on 1st October.   She was a wonderful sight, moving slowly and gracefully along, like a large silver floating cigar.

On Saturday, 4th October, she was due to start her flight to India, carrying a full crew and a number of senior officials and technicians from the Air Ministry, including Lord Thomson, the Minister for Air, and Sir Sefton Brancker.

I was on duty at Savoy Hill on the afternoon of the next day, Sunday, 5th October, and as I entered the building the commissionaire told me that he had an urgent message for me to ring up Gladstone Murray, our Director of Public Relations.   I did so at once, and he told me the sad news that the R 101 had crashed early that morning at Beauvais, in France, and we discussed when I should announce this to listeners, and together set about drafting the announcement.

The first programme of the day was the Bach Cantata, timed for 3 p.m., and, as no transmitters would have been working before then, we decided to put out the statement at 3 p.m., giving the news of the accident, and stating that no details were available, adding that a further announcement would be made at 4.15 p.m.,

before the concert by the Northern Orchestra, by which time it was
hoped that the official communiqué would be ready.

The official communiqué came in just before the end of the
Bach Cantata, and I read it out in full at 4.15, as arranged. It was
one of the most tragic announcements it has ever been my lot to
make.

1931

THE outstanding event at the beginning of the new year was the assembling of the Indian Round Table Conference at St. James' Palace, to tackle the thorny problem of the future of that continent.

It was attended by many famous Indian figures, including the Maharajah of Burdwan, and Mahatma Gandhi himself.

We broadcast the Prime Minister's speech on the conference following the 9 p.m. News on 20th January. I happen to remember it well, because I had had a long bulletin and was a little late with the News; the Prime Minister began nearly two minutes late in consequence, and I was admonished about this the next day.

Although it was then mid-winter, Mr. Gandhi came over to this country in his simple Indian dress of white cotton *dhoti* and sandals, but to keep his body warm, around and over the *dhoti* he was swathed in blankets. I could not help thinking how cold his legs must have been, because he wore no socks or stockings, and, apart from the sandals, nothing below the knees.

Simplicity had always been one of the principles of this great man's life. I remember meeting him in Delhi in 1921, at St. Stephen's College, where I was fortunate enough to have a long talk with him, and was much impressed by his pleasant personality, his quiet voice and flawless English, his strong opposition to Western ideas and the Western way of life—hence the *dhoti*, the *khaddar* or home-spun cloth, and the campaign in favour of the spinning-wheel. Gandhi, however, was not anti-British; he realised the great part Britain had played, and had yet to play, in helping India through the period of her adolescence. However much one may have disagreed with his views, one could have nothing but respect for his idealism.

.   .   .   .   .

On 5th February Sir Harry Lauder, supported by the B.B.C. Symphony Orchestra conducted by Stanford Robinson, gave a one-man performance lasting an hour—the only time I can ever remember the Symphony Orchestra being used to accompany a comedian.

I went to the rehearsal in the morning, and also announced the transmission in the evening, and was fascinated by his methods. What a showman he was, how well he knew his public and the value of cheerfulness, and a song with a good lilt and chorus, with plenty of sentiment thrown in, plus a few wisecracks about the excellent traditional Scottish characteristic of thrift.

The microphone did not hamper his music-hall style or make him nervous in the least. He had made many records with the gramophone companies, and his experience stood him in good stead; his concentration on the microphone to the exclusion of all else was an object lesson to all would-be successful broadcasters. He had a good voice, and sang songs about the lads and lassies of his native land, interspersed with sentimental songs like "Keep right on to the end of the road", linked by a monologue written out in a sixpenny note-book and spoken by himself, each section leading, on a cue, to another song.

His energy, for an old man, was astounding, and if he disliked anything he had no hesitation in saying so, in no uncertain way—I can hear him say, "Not so much of the old", as I write this sentence—and if the tempo of the orchestra was not exactly to his liking, he did not sign to the conductor, or go and tell him about it, but, ignoring him altogether, left his microphone at the earliest opportunity, and, facing the orchestra, and looking most pugnacious, proceeded to beat with both hands the tempo he wanted.

I felt most embarrassed when this happened, wondering what the conductor would do, but Stanford Robinson, with a wry smile and a wink at me, took his cue from the great little man, quickened the pace, and all was well.

. . . . .

Two famous artists of the Victorian and Edwardian eras broadcast in the early part of 1931—Fanny Davies in February and Sir George Henschel in March.

Fanny Davies, then an old lady of seventy, was playing a Mozart Concerto with the Symphony Orchestra conducted by Dr. Adrian

E   57

Boult. Here was a direct link with the Schumann tradition, for Fanny Davies studied under Madame Clara Schumann at Frankfurt in the 'eighties. She adopted the rather old-fashioned distant " stance ", compared with the more modern method of sitting close to the piano and almost caressing the keys. I remember that she had a pleasant speaking voice and that we discussed the presentation of the concerto. In addition to the material I had prepared, she brought me a most interesting note written in her own hand, explaining how Mozart used a theme taken from a short phrase of a bird's song. Here it is :—

" Mozart's concièrge had a delightful little piping finch of which he was very fond. The bird knew its master and whenever he saw him he piped :—

to him.

" Mozart wove this bird-tune into a theme for the last movement of the G Major Concerto (No. 17, K.453), and made variations most characteristic of his endless resources. Then for the Finale he put the ' bird-theme ' into its own proper time; much faster, of course, than the allegretto."

Fanny Davies played the Mozart effortlessly. It was crisp, clear playing, with no frills; but she was not quite at home in the atmosphere of a broadcasting studio, having had little experience of this type of work, being more used to playing before large audiences than to the soul-less void of an empty studio. It was the last time I ever announced her, for by then she had practically retired from the concert platform, and in 1934 she died.

Unlike Fanny Davies, Sir George Henschel, who also died in 1934, revelled in studio work. A great favourite with listeners, he was one of the few singers whom I announced who always accompanied themselves. The result was that his phrasing, tone-colour and diction were superb. He sang Brahms, Schubert and Schumann and his own " Morning Hymn ", but most memorable of all was his moving interpretation of Dvorak's lament " By the Waters of Babylon ".

BRISK BIOGRAPHIES—I
Drawn and written by Gavin Gordon

*T*HE *dreariest part of Schumann's life*
    Was being married to his wife.
    He of course was too un-hearty
    For Clara's kind of musical party ;
    And though her guests were terribly kind,
    The atmosphere unhinged his mind.
And that is why he lost his reason
At the height of the artistic season.

But in March 1931 he was not singing, but conducting the B.B.C. Symphony Orchestra in No. 10 Studio. He was then over eighty years old, and had recently returned from Boston, where he had conducted the same programme as at the opening concert there in 1881. For his broadcast with our orchestra he again chose that programme :—

    1. Overture, " The Consecration of the House." *Beethoven.*
    2. Aria " Che faro " (What can I do ?). *Gluck.*
    3. Symphony No. 102 in B Flat. *Haydn.*
    4. Ballet Music " Rosamunde ". *Schubert.*
    5. Overture, " The Mastersingers ". *Wagner.*

After the Gluck aria, Sir George, on again mounting the conductor's rostrum, turned to me, as I was about to announce the Haydn Symphony, and said, with a sly wink, " Now we're going to have some fun "—and we did.

If ever *joie de vivre* has been expressed in terms of music, then surely it is in the sparkling, breathless finale of this B Flat Symphony.

The players were all out to give this Grand Old Man of Music as good a performance as possible, and at the end of the concert, after " The Mastersingers " overture, they stood and cheered him to the echo, and it is not often that orchestral players let themselves go in this way.

    .   .   .   .   .

It was in August of this year that the Government crisis in economy came to a head, which eventually led to the resignation of Britain's first Labour Government and the formation of the National Government to succeed it. The Labour Government resigned on 24th August, and the following night the Prime Minister —Mr. Ramsay MacDonald—broadcast to the nation before the nine o'clock News. He was due to speak at 8.35, and I announced him at that time, but he was late in getting off the mark, and it was 8.41 before he actually began his broadcast. I learned afterwards from our Outside Broadcast director that he only began to dictate his speech just after 8 p.m., and was busily engaged in putting the finishing touches to it at 8.30; but in spite of the rather irritating delay it was a fine effort, and most effective.

    .   .   .   .   .

On Sunday, 30th August, the Week's Good Cause appeal was made by Dame Madge Kendal, on behalf of the Central London Throat, Nose and Ear Hospital. The appeal was scheduled for 8.45, the News following at 8.50, and this, in turn, was to be followed at 9.5 by the first of a new series of continental broadcasts from the Kursaal at Knocke, in Belgium.

Dame Madge had rehearsed her script, and had been asked by the producer to keep it well under the five minutes, so that the News could start on time. I went to see her in the studio, told her how I proposed to announce her, and explained that I could not remain until the end, because I had to read the News directly she had finished.

She began the appeal, and after about two minutes came to a passage in it which, she said, reminded her of her girlhood days. She was an old lady, and at this point pushed her script on one side, folded her hands, and went off at a tangent about what she did as a girl, and there was no stopping her.

Here was a quandary. I could not fade her out, as she was a person of such eminence that listeners would have regarded such action as an insult; I could not break in and interrupt her, as that would have sounded extremely rude, also she was quite capable of telling me to go away and not interrupt.

There was only one thing I could do, and that was to let her go on and hope for the best. So on she went, serenely, like a ship in full sail, eventually ending her " oration "—it was something much more than an ordinary appeal—after sixteen and a half minutes ! I do not think I have ever gabbled through a News bulletin so quickly. The editor helped by cutting it to ribbons, and I doubt if it can have lasted more than five minutes. We got over to the Kursaal at Knocke just as the second item in the programme was about to begin.

Naturally I protested to Stobart, then in charge of appeals, pointing out to him the anxious time I had had. He wrote me a charming note of apology, saying that I need not worry, as " she has now been placed on my list of unmanageable old ladies ".

.   .   .   .   .

There had been several criticisms of Broadcast Discussions to the effect that because they were scripted and censored they were therefore anaemic and unreal. In order to counter this, it was decided to arrange for an unscripted discussion in the studio between two very experienced broadcasters.

On Monday, 31st August, the discussion began between Holt Marvell (Eric Maschwitz) and S. P. B. Mais on " Living Dangerously ". Both are quick speakers and hard hitters, and soon the gloves were off and no quarter was asked for or given; blows fell thick and fast, each trying to outdo the other in truculence, until it almost developed into a shouting match, and the engineers began to get worried about microphone blasting.

I forget what the upshot was, but whatever it was, the discussion could never have been described as " anaemic and unreal "; it certainly acted as a stimulus to listeners, and made them rush to put pen to paper. Among the shoals of letters and postcards received, most of them uncomplimentary, many saying that we were " preaching revolution ", were two postcards I especially remember. One had only two words on it, printed in block capitals—" YOU SWINE ". The other, after condemning the discussion in no uncertain terms, ended by suggesting (also in block capitals) that the most practical sequel would have been for " MAIS TO STRANGLE MARVELL IN THE STUDIO ".

. . . . .

On 18th October the Sunday night Symphony Concert in No. 10 Studio was devoted to the works of Richard Strauss, conducted by the composer, who came over from Germany to conduct this concert and the Symphony Concert the following Wednesday at the Queen's Hall.

I announced the concert, which included three of his masterpieces—the tone-poems " Macbeth ", " Don Juan " and " Death and Transfiguration ". It was a wonderful experience to be present in the studio and watch this tall, grey-haired, military figure of nearly seventy, this giant of German music, in action, and to note the alertness of the orchestra and the way he produced any desired effect with the minimum of effort, like a virtuoso playing a familiar piece on an instrument.

To me his attitude seemed detached, and remote from what was happening all around him—so unlike that of the traditional great conductor. He moved his stick so little as he beat time, and only very occasionally used his left hand to point a crescendo, or rose from his seat to indicate a climax; yet how finished was the performance of the orchestra, how majestic its depth of string tone. The B.B.C. Symphony Orchestra was certainly one of the finest orchestras in Europe at that time.

When the exhausting programme had ended and the red light went out, the orchestra and small invited audience in the studio rose to their feet and applauded him for several minutes. Only then was there a slight trace of emotion on the stern features of the great man, as he bowed and said, " Thank you, thank you; you were excellent . . . excellent."

. . . . .

The Symphony Concert on 25th November included the first performance of a choral work of outstanding importance—William Walton's " Belshazzar's Feast ". As so often happens in the case of first performances of new works, there was a good deal of doubt about the timing, and the concert took much longer than had been expected. This, added to the fact that it began late, and the cheers and applause and calls for the composer at the end, meant that we were twenty minutes late in starting the talk which was scheduled to follow the concert at 10.25. This talk, entitled " Idle Thoughts ", was to be given by Lord Ponsonby, an excellent broadcaster, who, as it happened, had recently written to *The Times* pointing out that we seldom included in our News bulletins reports of the House of Lords' debates. One of the reasons why we were late in beginning the second part of the concert was because there was a great deal of news about the debate on " Empire economic unity ", and, in view of Lord Ponsonby's protest, the editor was anxious to include a report on an important debate in the Lords.

While I was talking to Lord Ponsonby in the studio, waiting for the concert to end, he grew rather restless and began to grumble about the lateness of the hour, fearing that few people would want to listen to a talk at that time of night. I did my best to explain that it was a musical occasion, that there was some doubt about the timing of the new work, and that there would almost certainly be calls for the composer at the end, then I added, " But that is not the only reason why you are so late in beginning, sir; there was a lot of news to-night, including a long report on the debate in the Lords ". It may have been very tactless of me, but I think he realised that we had acted on the suggestion made in his letter to *The Times*; at any rate all he said was, " Oh, I see."

. . . . .

Sunday, 29th November, was a typical November day, foggy

and cold; the fog, which had not been too bad in the morning, began to thicken in the afternoon and made getting about London difficult. We were broadcasting a performance of the "Messiah" in No. 10 Studio at four o'clock, and though most of the chorus, orchestra and soloists had arrived, there were several people who had not, including some of the soloists and the conductor, Stanford Robinson.

Therefore we could not begin the broadcast at 4 p.m., and I made an announcement explaining that there would be a few minutes' delay. At 4.6 p.m. I made a second announcement saying that the conductor and some of the soloists had not yet reached the studio, adding, "The position at the moment is obscure, but we hope to start very shortly".

Meanwhile I rushed round and managed to find Walton O'Donnell, who at once jumped into his car and made off for the studio to take over the concert, only to find that Stanford Robinson had just beaten him by a short head. We had to re-arrange the order of the solos and choruses because Eric Greene, the tenor, had still not arrived, and, as is well known, two of the tenor solos come at the beginning of the oratorio; he eventually reached the studio just after 4.30 p.m., and the opening solos were put in later.

.   .   .   .   .

Those of you who used to listen to broadcast plays in the late 1920's and early 1930's will remember that there was an actress who frequently took part in them named Lilian Harrison, who had a most charming speaking voice.

On 16th and 17th November she was playing the lead in a play called "Chopin", based on episodes in the composer's life. Important plays and features were then usually broadcast twice, once on the Medium (London) wavelength and once on the Long (Daventry) wavelength.

Miss Harrison, having had a heavy week's work, was experiencing some slight trouble with her throat, and went to a specialist to have it examined and treated. While she was being examined, the small mirror of the laryngoscope most unfortunately became detached— it was about the size of a shilling—and she swallowed it.

The specialist wanted to send her to hospital at once to have it removed, as, naturally, he was very worried about it; but she told him she could not possibly do that, because of her part in the play that night. "Well, to-morrow morning, then," said the surgeon. "No," replied Miss Harrison. "I am in the Children's Hour in the afternoon, and have the second performance of the play to give in the evening."

She did, however, agree to go to hospital to be X-rayed, and arrangements were made for her to be rushed there directly the second performance was over on the Saturday night (17th October).

She played on the Friday night, and gallantly carried on, in great discomfort, all through Saturday, taking part in the Children's Hour and playing in "Chopin" again on the Saturday night. Immediately the play was over she was taken to hospital to be operated on. Fortunately the doctors were able to remove the mirror without much difficulty through the throat, and she was soon up and about again. I was full of admiration for her courage and determination to carry on and play her part; there was no question of an understudy taking over—there was none. She gave an admirable performance, and I very much doubt if anybody outside her own circle of friends knew anything about her mishap, at any rate not until some time afterwards.

    ·   ·   ·   ·   ·

On 12th December Marchese Marconi came to the studio to broadcast on the occasion of the thirtieth anniversary of his sending the first wireless signals across the Atlantic.

He described the difficulties to be overcome and the disappointments he had had on both sides of the Atlantic when storms damaged or destroyed the aerials, and finally his excitement when he eventually overcame all the difficulties and succeeded in sending signals from Poldhu in Cornwall to Nova Scotia. His two technical assistants, Messrs. Kemp and Paget, who took part in the original experiment, were in the studio with us, and each described his anxieties and emotions when success, after many failures, eventually crowned their efforts.

The historic signal sent was the letter "S" tapped out in morse. They brought with them the original tapping key, coil and resistance used exactly thirty years before. I noticed that it was some time before they could get it to work, but in the end it was all right, and listeners were able to hear once again the historic letter

" S " signal, as put out by Marconi himself on 12th December, 1901.

. . . . .

Each 14th November at Savoy Hill we used to celebrate the birthday of the B.B.C. with some kind of party, which was broadcast. P. P. Eckersley, the Chief Engineer, was usually the star talker and entertainer at the piano. All this was very good fun, providing it was not allowed to go on too long. There was also an occasional staff pantomime, which was not broadcast, and in one of these Sidonie Goossens, principal harp of the B.B.C. Symphony Orchestra, was a most attractive leading lady.

In this pantomime there was an early morning scene at Savoy Hill with some dialogue between the commissionaire on early morning duty at the entrance and the charwoman as she scrubbed the floor. This led to her song about the announcers, by Eric Maschwitz, the last verse of which was as follows :—

> " Do announcers make good husbands ?
> Do they gamble, drink or swear ?
> Or linger outside Selfridge's
> Staring 'ard at underwear ?
> Oh, 'andsome is as 'andsome does, the proverb may be trite,
> A man may be a wrong 'un, though 'is accent may be right.
> If 'e leaves 'is teeth in Milton on the lino overnight.
> Oh, are they the same at 'ome ? "

1932

A FURTHER step towards the setting up of an Empire broadcasting service was taken on 4th January, when, in the early hours of the morning, I read the first Empire News bulletin, broadcast on short wave from our Experimental Station at Chelmsford, G.5SW.

We used this station for transmissions for the first time on Armistice Day, 1927, when we broadcast the British Legion Rally from the Royal Albert Hall.

Since then it had been used on many important occasions, and had supplied our engineers with invaluable information by means of observers scattered throughout the world. Now it had been decided to begin broadcasting News bulletins on this wavelength.

I remember that we had to alter our normal News-reading technique a little for this purpose, reading slightly more slowly and hitting our consonants more strongly than is usually necessary. I disliked having to do this, because it broke up the rhythm and distorted the shape of the sentences, but clarity of speech for the listener was the pre-requisite, and it had to be done.

These bulletins were continued all through the year, and ended only in December, when the new Empire Service was inaugurated, and Chelmsford 5SW—or, to give it its full title, G.5SW—having done noble pioneer work, closed down.

. . . . .

When I was about to announce the Sunday night Symphony Concert on 24th January, I saw, and later heard, for the first time a " muted tuba ". I expect it was to Harry Barlow's special design; at any rate he was then the greatest living authority on the tuba. I remember that it gave me quite a shock to see what appeared to be a deep and narrow ladies' hat-box protruding from the bell of this large instrument. The sound produced was most effective, and I should have been interested to hear it used to represent the elephant in the " Carnival of the Animals " by Saint Saens, in place of the usual double basses. I cannot help thinking that the tone

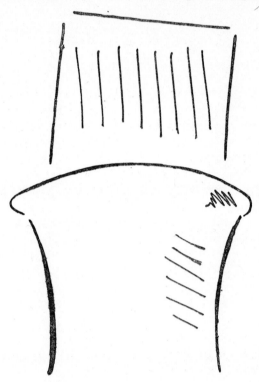

HARRY BARLOW'S MUTED TUBA

would suggest the huge bulk of the pachyderm much more ponderously than the string tone.

.   .   .   .   .

On 19th February, in reading the nine o'clock News rather "against the clock ", as there was a great deal of news, I most unfortunately referred to Bow Street police station as though I were talking about the sharp end of a ship.   Realising my error immediately I had made it, I at once corrected it . . . but it was too late; one of the terrifying things about broadcasting is that a word, once spoken, or a sound uttered cannot be retrieved; it has gone for ever.   I had forgotten all about it by the next day, but the following morning brought this amusing little rhyme, from an old Etonian parson in Surrey, who signed himself, " One who also lives in a glass house " :—

> " A dry-bob bewildered said, ' How
> Can I know what the wet-bobs allow ?
> Does Bow equal beau ?
> Or if that's not so
> Does Bow bow like a tree's bough ? "

. . . . .

On 21st February the tenor John Coats, accompanied by Berkeley Mason, gave a song recital in the studio, one of many admirable recitals, mostly of English songs, given by this superb artist, either in the studio or in the Chenil Galleries at Chelsea.

He introduced each song himself in his own incomparable way, calling attention to the salient points, often adding some witty little remarks, thrown away as it were, just before he gave the signal to Berkeley Mason to begin the introduction—for he had a very keen sense of humour.

A magnificent interpreter of song, he was now getting on in years, and this fact was becoming apparent in the quality of his voice, but, as in the case of Plunket Greene towards the end of his career, his superb artistry, clear diction and strict attention to detail enabled him to carry everything before him, and here he was admirably supported by Berkeley Mason, who always knew what he wanted and how to give it to him.

The mutual understanding between those two was quite remarkable. I had many opportunities of observing it in action, as I turned over the music for Berkeley, and could watch them closely, from a vantage point. This mutual confidence did not, I am sure, come by chance and experience, but was mainly due to prolonged and careful rehearsal and the great care taken in choosing and presenting the programme.

John, of course, did almost everything there was to do; all that remained for me to do was to introduce the two artists, and then he took over. " What can I say to listeners about you two this time ? " I asked him just before the recital began. " Oh," replied John, with a chuckle, " I suppose you can say that we are both known to the police " ! This was typical of his personality;

he loved a joke. But when working he was a strict disciplinarian, and set himself perfection as an artistic ideal, and worked hard to try to attain it.

At four o'clock on the afternoon of 11th March, Jack Payne gave his last broadcast with his band, after having been with us for four years. I well remember his arrival with a small band from the Hotel Cecil. He experimented with this as a nucleus, and gradually enlarged it, until he had built up his fine symphonic dance orchestra, broadcasting most days of the week, and several nights as well.

The Director-General and some of the seniors of the programme staff came to this last studio performance to wish him good-bye and good luck in his new venture, for he was about to begin an extensive tour of the music-halls in London and the provinces. There were a number of Press representatives present, too, so it was definitely an occasion. I made the final announcement, which was as follows :—

"Mr. Jack Payne has been with the B.B.C. for four years, and this is the last time that listeners will hear him conducting his B.B.C. Dance Orchestra. We know that he has entertained many thousands of listeners for many thousands of hours and has carried their good wishes. We wish him and his band the best of good luck in their activities. This afternoon sees farewell to his official connection with the B.B.C., and he is saying it with music "

—a reference to his well-known signature tune.

On 17th March I announced the recital given in the studio by Hüberman, the eminent Polish violinist, and Anne Thursfield, a fine broadcaster, and a most sensitive interpreter of French songs.

I had a difficult time with them at the rehearsal. No. 7 studio, which was high and resonant, and generally used for the Military Band, was too cold for Hüberman, but its resonance and pleasing acoustics delighted Miss Thursfield.

We transferred to Studio 8. This was warmer, but still not warm enough for Hüberman. It was dreadfully dead after No. 7— much too dead for Miss Thursfield, who complained, with some justification, that it was a most uninspiring place in which to sing.

The truth was that with the ventilation plant we then had at Savoy Hill it was difficult to adjust the temperature of any studio to the amount of heat required, the studios served by the plant not being of uniform size. When large studios were just comfortably warm, small ones would be like a furnace. In this case I persevered with the artists, and they saw that I did all that was possible, and were very co-operative, and in the end both gave fine performances, Hüberman's performance of the unaccompanied Bach Chaconne being masterly.

A few days later he was the soloist in Mendelssohn's violin concerto, with our Symphony Orchestra conducted by Percy Pitt.

Now, Percy Pitt was short and tubby, and when conducting he was inclined to bury his head in the score, " coming up now and again to breathe ", as some of the Orchestra used to say. Hüberman had a defect of the eyes, only one of them having central vision, the other being turned outwards, away from the normal axis. During the performance of this concerto Hüberman wished to quicken the tempo of a particular phrase, but could not succeed in attracting Percy Pitt's attention, and the work went on and on like a steadily flowing stream. After the concert was over, Percy Pitt told me that he had found by experience that it was no good looking at Hüberman, because, as he said, " I am never sure if he is looking at me or not ".

.   .   .   .   .   .

On 18th March I made broadcasting history by going to Broadcasting House from Savoy Hill and reading the first News bulletin from there, in one of the small news studios (4A). There were two of these identical studios next door to each other, with a " listening room ", common to both, in between. My first impressions were not at all favourable. I thought it was a most depressing place, the studios being much smaller than I had expected, and rather box-like, with a Reiss microphone suspended in front, close up to the wall, so that when using a fair amount of voice—an essential with this instrument if background hiss was to be avoided—there was bound to be some backlash or reflected echo from the surface of the wall. All the studios are in a central cylindrical tower, with offices and committee rooms on the outside; the lay-out being like that of a ship, with the cabins (offices) on the outside, the engines, boilers, funnels, etc. (studios, control room, etc.), in the centre—in fact the resemblance to the interior of a ship is most striking; even the taps of the wash-basins are of the press-knob type, so familiar to all who have travelled any distance by sea.

On 21st March I announced a programme sung by the Wireless Singers conducted by Stanford Robinson, consisting of Brahms' " Marienlieder " and a Byrd Mass. It was not an easy programme. Several of the regular singers were ill and had arranged for deputies, or had only recently come back to work, and the rehearsal was long and arduous.

Doris Owens, the principal contralto, had laryngitis, and could only just sing; and a few minutes before the programme was due to begin, Gladys Windmill—contralto No. 2—fainted. However, with the aid of some brandy obtained from the host's room we managed to bring her round, and she insisted on singing. When the Byrd Mass had ended, Stanford Robinson, after a pause, thinking the red light had gone out, gave a deep sigh of relief, which, as he was still quite near the microphone, was broadcast.

Directly I returned to my room the telephone rang repeatedly, and various reporters wanted to know what the " yell " was at the end of the programme and what was the cause of it. Such is the power of amplification of a reporter's ear of any incident if he considers there is the slightest chance of a story behind it.

Budget night was on 19th April, and this year a new method of reporting it was tried out : instead of the main provisions being broadcast straight off the tape as they came in, there were only one or two passing references to the Budget in the 6 p.m. News, because it had been arranged for Wickham Steed to broadcast a talk on it at 6.50 p.m., entitled " How the House received the Budget ".

He stayed on in the House until the last possible minute, then rushed to the studio in a taxi, reaching it only a few minutes before he was due on the air. He spoke admirably from a sheaf of notes which he was busily engaged in sorting out when the red light came on. He gave an excellent summary of all the salient points, and some indication as to how each main point was received by both sides of the House. I thought it was a fine piece of red-hot reporting, a precedent which should lead to a considerable extension of actuality work, to the great benefit of the listener.

THE END OF SAVOY HILL
(Goodnight everybody . . . Goodnight)

THE AUTHOR BROADCASTING IN THE NEWS STUDIO (4A)

At 8.20 that night there was a discussion on sculpture by Messrs. Dobson and Casson which, owing to the late finish of the preceding Vaudeville programme, began five minutes late; and it, too, ran over its allotted time, so that I was not able to begin reading the News until 9.12, instead of at nine o'clock.

The next morning Sir John Reith (quite justifiably) was on the war-path because the News was so late. Apparently he had heard neither the 6 p.m. News nor Wickham Steed's summary, and was irritated by the over-run, while waiting to hear the details of the Budget. When someone tactlessly remarked that the main features of the Budget were in the evening papers, Sir John silenced him with, " I never read an evening paper " !

.   .   .   .   .

14th May. This was the day on which we broadcast " The Last of Savoy Hill " programme. It was nostalgic and rather sad, and ended with an announcement by a mystery voice from the new building saying, " This is Broadcasting House calling ", to mark the continuity of the service.

Towards the end of this programme a group of engineers, having closed down the Savoy Hill control-room for the last time, descended the steps leading to the main entrance, talking to one another. They were followed a little later by myself, and listeners could hear my conversation with Oliver, the night watchman, as I sauntered slowly down the familiar staircase, my mind full of memories.

My appearance was Oliver's cue to remove the iron shutter and open the small door in it to let me out into the street. While this was going on, I paused and said to him, " Well, Oliver, I suppose this is the last time you'll be pulling down that old shutter for me ? " " Yes, sir," he replied; " this is the end of Savoy Hill." Poor old chap ! I was sorry for him, as he was very nervous at first, but got it right after a few rehearsals. Then, as I passed through the door, he was to say, " Mind your head, sir "; but he forgot all about it at the broadcast, until I had gone through the door and was well outside. However, it did not matter, because the microphone picked up the sound all right.

.   .   .   .   .

27th June. A hectic evening, chiefly owing to the tactics of

C. B. Cochran, who was due to speak at 9.20 p.m. in the " Rungs of the Ladder " series.

At 7.30 he rang me up to say that he had just received a note from the Talks Director asking him to omit some lines in his manuscript relating to his productions. He strongly objected to this on principle, because it was practically at the last moment, and in any case he did not really want to broadcast at all. I said I was sorry about it, asked him for his 'phone number, and promised to get into touch with Talks Director and ring back later.

Talks Director said he was just going off to an important dinner at the Russian Embassy, and asked me to 'phone Cochran saying that we would accept his manuscript if he omitted the few lines that were crossed out. In the event of further trouble I was to ring Miss Somerville when Mr. Cochran arrived to broadcast, as she would be coming to Broadcasting House to receive him.

Cochran was most affable when I rang again, but absolutely firm, and proceeded to give me an ultimatum : if he could broadcast his talk as it stood, he would come; if not, he refused to come. I thereupon rang the Controller of Programmes, Director of Talks having gone off to his dinner. He seemed reluctant to make any decision, but eventually agreed to my suggestion that I should get into touch with Miss Somerville and if necessary ring Sir John Reith for a ruling. I then 'phoned Miss Somerville, Director of Schools Broadcasting, who proceeded to plead complete ignorance of the facts, so, before ringing Sir John, I decided to consult Gladstone Murray, Director of Publicity. He said that Cochran should not broadcast if he would not conform to our rules. He then rang up Sir John, and after a discussion it was decided to let Cochran talk in any case, because our relations with him were excellent and most valuable; but we were to ask him to delete the advertisements about the whisky and about his shows and the price of the stalls being reduced to ten and sixpence.

I then got Miss Somerville to ring him up, and by asking him to state his objections over the 'phone, she succeeded in inducing him to agree to come to the studio at nine o'clock. I thought this was a clever move, and that she had won the day, but I did not know my Cochran. He, wily bird, came to the studio at nine, bringing with him his wife and Mrs. Robert Lorraine, a friend of

Sir John's. Miss Somerville was outflanked, and we lost the day. After it was over and I was saying good-bye, he was most pleasant about it, and, as a parting shot, smiled and said, " You know, Hibberd, I'm really very easy to get on with . . . very easy indeed . . . but I must have my own way."

.   .   .   .   .

The Royal visit to Broadcasting House took place on 7th July, and elaborate preparations were made beforehand. Admiral Carpendale (the Controller) was in his element completing the plans for this, the greatest day in our history. An " order of the day " was circulated to all staff, ordering an assembly in the concert hall, and confining us all there from 2.15 to 3 p.m.; no one was allowed to use the lifts, all movements having to be made via the stairs. No smoking was permitted in the building between 3 and 5 p.m. We rehearsed the National Anthem, and then sat silently waiting and craning our necks for the sign from H. L. Chilman, the House Superintendent, that the Royal Party was approaching. As the King and Queen entered the concert hall we rose to our feet and sang the National Anthem, and, ably led by Commander Goldsmith, who had been detailed for the task by the Admiral, gave three cheers for their Majesties.

After this the tour of the building began, and we sat silently waiting in the concert hall. Work was supposed to be going on normally, but in reality various " set pieces " had been arranged in the studios, and they were all to be in progress as the Royal Party came round, working to a strict time-table.

As generally happens, not by any means everything went " according to plan ". There were minor mishaps and some last-minute alterations of plans, which may have proved rather confusing. For example, I very much doubt if the Wireless Singers were quite prepared for the cancellation of their order to be singing an Elizabethan madrigal when the Royal Party reached their studio; and to sing, instead, " I want to be happy " !

.   .   .   .   .

On 11th July I announced Mr. George Bernard Shaw, who was making his contribution to the " Rungs of the Ladder " series. He was in terrific form, being quite hilarious and most entertaining. Charles Siepman, Director of Talks, and I watched him through the listening-room window, and roared with laughter at his re-marks as he broadcast. What a superb leg-puller he is ! I had met him officially several times before, on the B.B.C. Pronunciation Committee, and the difficulty then, as now, was to know whether he was being serious or not; and sometimes he *was* being serious.

In this talk he began by referring to his photograph in the *Radio Times* basking in the sun of the south of France, and wearing only a towel and an Anthony Eden hat.

" Now you all know what I look like," he said. " I'm just an ordinary old man with a beard. The only difference between us is that I can write plays and you can't. That's all.

" Now, all sorts of romances are weaved about geniuses—for example, that paragraph in the *Radio Times* which says that my first job was in a Dublin surveyor's office, and that afterwards I was a commercial traveller. I was never in a surveyor's office, and I certainly was never a commercial traveller."

After his talk we told him how much we had enjoyed it, and he chatted away for several minutes, ending with this typical piece of Shavian advice : " If you ever want to criticise people's beliefs, start by telling them something they are bound to agree with, *then* you can set about pulling things to pieces."

.   .   .   .

This year the August Bank Holiday Promenade Concert was a replica of the Prom given in August 1895. It was an interesting example of what the public then regarded as good musical entertain-ment.

The soloists were Kenneth Ellis (bass), Richard Newton (bassoon), Margaret Balfour (contralto) and Robert Murchie (flute), and the concert, which began with the Rienzi Overture, included a Handel aria, Liszt's Second Hungarian Rhapsody and an amusing bassoon solo—really a set of variations—called " Lucy Long ".

It would have been interesting to look up Mr. Bernard Shaw's criticism of this concert, but unfortunately he resigned his post as music critic of *The World* the previous year.

.   .   .   .

The night of 20th August was, I remember, one of the hottest of the year, with temperatures well in the 'nineties, and many of the audience at the Promenade Concert fanned themselves with their

programmes in an endeavour to keep cool.   Several people fainted
or were overcome by the heat and had to be carried out.

On such a night the soloist was the tenor Joseph Heslop, and the
aria he chose to sing was " Che gelida mannina " (" Your tiny hand
is frozen ") from " La Bohème " !

The next night I was announcing an orchestral concert given by
one of the sections of the Symphony Orchestra conducted by Stanford Robinson after the second News.   Shortly after the programme had begun, loud " me-ows " were heard coming from the
direction of the balcony of the concert hall.   They did not greatly
matter while the orchestra was playing, because most of the time
the music drowned them; but when they stopped, and I was about
to announce, the mewing rose to a distinct crescendo—this was the
cat's great moment—and we were all convulsed with laughter :
so much so that I had to go to the microphone and try to explain
to listeners—between my giggles—what it was all about.

Though we could hear the cat's plaintive notes so clearly in the
hall, I doubted very much if her crying was being broadcast, hence
the need for an explanation.   There is nothing more infuriating
than hearing a studio audience—or artists, for that matter—roaring
with laughter at something about which the listener is in complete
ignorance.

Having despatched some studio attendants to evict the offender,
we went on with the concert, but they could not find her, nor was
she, so far as I know, ever found.

" Jemima ", as she was christened—we had assumed it was a
she—was certainly a cat of spirit, to invade what one paper next
day called " that vast mouseless edifice " in Portland Place during
a transmission.

I can testify that it was the first unrehearsed feline studio solo
broadcast—Puss had a golden opportunity, and seized it with both
paws.

Where did she come from ?   How did she get into the balcony ?
One theory was that she was a stray cat left behind by the workmen
when the new Broadcasting House was completed earlier in the year.
It may have been so; I cannot say; I never even saw her.

.   .   .   .   .

Shortly after this incident Sir Thomas (now Lord) Horder was giving a talk in one of the three small studios on the third floor. This was to be followed immediately by a talk to be given by Professor Cornford, Professor of Ancient Philosophy at the University of Cambridge, in the studio next door.

When Sir Thomas had finished and I had collected his manuscript and wished him a hurried good-bye, I handed him over to the host waiting outside and went into the other studio to announce the Professor, but found, to my surprise and alarm, that he was not there.

I took a swift look round the waiting-room and the other studios on that floor, without success, then rang reception in the entrance hall, who said that he had not yet arrived. By this time the red light had begun to flick violently outside the studio door, as it was now past 7.30—the time he was due to broadcast.

I gave the " go ahead " signal to the engineers and went to the microphone and said, " As you know, Professor Cornford was due to give his talk in the series ' Our Debt to the Past ' at 7.30; he has not yet arrived; I expect that he has probably been held up in a traffic jam on his way here from Liverpool Street. We will give him another two minutes before doing anything else."

Still he did not arrive. I therefore told listeners that as I had his manuscript with me, I would begin reading it for him, and if he came in half-way through I would hand over to him. I then started to read his talk, which I soon found was rather difficult, as I had not even glanced at it beforehand. I saw that it contained extracts from Greek and English literature, and I began to have a horrible feeling that when I turned over the page I should be confronted with a quotation from Sophocles or Herodotus in the original Greek, and as my Greek was very rusty, I should at once give myself away.

Fortunately, I was spared that indignity, and was thankful when it was all over.

When I came out of the studio I found a very worried Professor Cornford in the waiting-room. He had just arrived in a taxi from the station. He explained that there had been a signalling fault on the railway, and his train had been held up outside Liverpool Street station, and he could do nothing about it. He was most anxious lest his family, listening at Cambridge, might think that he had met with an accident, and asked me to broadcast a message to them at once.

I told him I could not do that, and reminded him that he could telephone to them, and taking him down to the drawing-room, handed him the telephone, and soon he was telling the whole story to his wife and daughter.

I have often wondered who was the more worried that night : the Professor because he was unable to give his talk, or his deputy because he had to read it at sight.

.   .   .   .   .

The pronunciation of the names of race-horses is an ever-recurring problem, and a good deal of guess-work is inevitable.

There was, for example, Gregalach, and Slavia, once broadcast in error as Saliva (not bad this !). Cotoneaster—named after the shrub —was often, I regret to say, called Coton-easter instead of Cotone-aster. For weeks I referred to a horse named Gonedry as if it were one word, whereas actually it was Gone-dry, written as one word. Sayajirao, Nurmahal and Nasruddin are simple, if you are familiar with Indian names; if not, they can be stumbling-blocks for the unwary. But no matter how careful you are, if you pronounce Las Vegas in Spanish, Douanier in French and Nurmahal in Urdu all correctly, you can be quite sure that the average punter will call them something quite different on the course.

.   .   .   .   .

On 25th October I announced a pianoforte recital given by Professor Tobias Matthay ("Uncle Tobbs" to his friends), a dear old man, with very little hair, only a ring of flowing grey locks at the back. Hilda Dederich, a former pupil, turned over for him, and I believe she came to the rehearsal, too. He played a pro-gramme consisting entirely of his own works, with superb technique. After the broadcast he held a kind of court in the studio. I have never seen anything like it; it was most touching. It was very pleasant, too, to meet many of his former pupils and to see with what great affection he was regarded. Besides Hilda Dederich, Irene Scharrer and Ernest Lush were there, and several others, including Myra Hess, sent their best wishes. Cecile Dixon, who came to the rehearsal but could not stay for the transmission, sent him a buttonhole, which he wore all the evening.

.   .   .   .   .

On the first Sunday in December the Bishop of London (Dr.

Winnington Ingram) came to Broadcasting House to make the Week's Good Cause appeal at 8.45. I looked after him and announced him, and when it was over, at his request I took him round some of the studios.

On the way down from the third-floor talks studios to the concert hall on the lower ground I described the concert hall to him, and told him of the fine organ and of the Gilbert Bayes reliefs on the walls depicting scenes from English country life, and explained that the hall was used for small orchestral concerts, recitals and chamber concerts, but *never* for variety.

Arriving at the concert hall entrance, I threw open the door, and saw, to my dismay, that a rehearsal of a variety act was in progress, the chorus at that moment being put through their paces in a series of high-kicking movements by the producer. Then I saw that they were the ladies of the B.B.C. Revue Chorus rehearsing for the staff show. I said " Oh " (exactly as Maurice Denham used to say it in " Much-Binding-in-the-Marsh " before he added, " I am a fool "). The Bishop grinned, and I hastened to explain that I had forgotten all about the staff revue, " The House Sir John Built ", due to begin the following night.

The Bishop was delighted, and we stayed and watched them at work for a few minutes before going up to the eighth floor, to the Military Band studio, and on to the effects studio in the Tower.

. . . . .

On 14th December a paragraph appeared in the Press announcing that Elgar was writing a new symphony for the B.B.C., to which organisation it was to be dedicated. Surely this was without precedent, a *magnum opus* dedicated to a Corporation ? Sir Landon Ronald, commenting on the news at the annual dinner of the Guildhall School of Music, said, " If Sir John Reith never does anything more to benefit music in this country—which is most unlikely—he will ever be gratefully remembered for making it possible for us to have another work from the pen of one of the greatest symphonic composers of all time." The tragedy was that Elgar did not live to complete it.

. . . . .

At midnight on Saturday, 17th December, G.5SW, the B.B.C.'s short-wave experimental station at Chelmsford, having finished its pioneering mission, closed down, immediately prior to the opening of the New Empire Service—handing over to it, as it were.

It had completed a magnificent piece of work, not only as an experimental transmitter, but also in helping to forge strong links between the old country and English-speaking peoples all over the world.

Beginning on Armistice Day, 1927, it had broadcast all the important national events, and early this year had begun to put out News Bulletins, but its star performer was Big Ben.

Soon, with the advent of the New Empire Service, transmitters with complex aerials at Daventry would be broadcasting programmes and News bulletins day and night, linking up the whole of the Empire. Some of the broadcasts would have to be late at night or early in the morning, as times convenient to listeners are pre-requisites.

There were many engineering and programme problems to be solved before this service could begin. All honour, then, to those who tackled the job under Sir Noel Ashbridge (Chief Engineer) and Mr. (afterwards Sir) Cecil Graves, not forgetting the wisdom and foresight of Sir John Reith and Mr. Whitley (the Chairman) in making the decision to go ahead with the Empire Service scheme at a most difficult time in our history.

. . . . .

On 31st December J. C. Stobart, who had been the B.B.C.'s first Director of Religious Broadcasting, came to the studio to give his last " Grand Good Night " at the conclusion of the " end-of-the-year " programme. Being a very sick man, it is perhaps not surprising that he uttered grave words as he looked back over the year which had just passed. It was a superb and most original effort—a courageous one, too, for he was very shaky, and to me at any rate this seemed to add solemnity to his pungent and carefully-thought-out phrases.

1933

THERE was a controversy going on in the Press with regard to a statement broadcast in our New Year's Eve programme about the " Polish Corridor ", to the effect that Poland was spending 30 per cent of her revenue on armaments.

This statement evoked a protest from the Polish Ambassador, and, later on, comment in an article by " Scrutator " in the *Sunday Times*. He said that though the dispute between the B.B.C. and the Polish Ambassador had been amicably settled, it was hoped that the settlement did not mean any retraction of what had been said on its merits, as an opinion. He then went on to pose the questions, should broadcasting be as free to express opinion as the printed word, or is it always to be the servant of official policy in international affairs ? Should it hold the balance between the parties in domestic politics ? Should its leaning be towards the support of whatever Government is in power, or should it have a mind of its own ? In the light of subsequent events, in peace and in war, such questions were most interesting, and it is perhaps significant to note that " Scrutator's " own view was that, whatever the risks, it would be best to leave the B.B.C. liberty, and a mind of its own.

. . . . .

Most of the S.O.S.s broadcast by us in the past had consisted of messages for relatives of people on the danger list, whose whereabouts were unknown, or police messages asking for witnesses of fatal accidents, and emanating from Scotland Yard or Chief Constables of the counties. On Friday, 13th January, however, we broadcast a message, at the request of Scotland Yard, which was in an entirely different category ; it was the description of a man named Furnace, wanted by the police in connection with the murder of Walter Sprackett.

The following Sunday (15th January) I was again on night duty, when we received a message from Scotland Yard, which I broadcast, saying that Furnace had been arrested. This was the first time that the broadcasting service had been used to assist the police in arresting a much-wanted man.

.   .   .   .   .

Towards the end of the month Sir Landon Ronald was conducting the B.B.C. Symphony Orchestra in a programme which included a memorable performance of Rachmaninov's second Symphony in E Minor. What a fine conductor he was for certain composers—Rachmaninov, Tchaikovsky and Elgar in particular. There had recently been a fuss about smoking in the studio, and a rule had been made that in future there was to be no smoking in any studio. Imagine my consternation when I arrived at the studio and found Sir Landon rehearsing the orchestra with a lighted cigarette in his left hand.

As soon as he had finished I went up to him and, before discussing the presentation of the items, asked him (*sotto voce*) if he would kindly put out his cigarette because there was now a strict rule that there must be no smoking in the studio. As I said this, I noticed that he was smoking a fat Abdullah-type cigarette, with a most pleasant aromatic smell. He smiled and, placing his right hand on my shoulder in a fatherly way, said, " My dear Hibberd, either I smoke my cigarette at rehearsal and during the interval as I always do, and I conduct, or I do not conduct. You must decide which you want." Now it was my turn to smile, and I quickly changed the subject, regarding it then as the only tactical move possible.

Shortly after this incident the ban was lifted, and artists and conductors were again allowed to smoke in studios ; in the case of discussions they were encouraged to do so, in order to make them feel at home and to stimulate the flow of conversation.

.   .   .   .   .

From time to time announcers come under fire in the Press, usually about the quality of speech they use, or certain common errors, such as the intrusive " r ", or, worse still, about the dropping of the voice at the end of a sentence, or the accusation that they are trying to standardise the language, and that soon all dialects will disappear.

The influence announcers have on the spoken word is obviously bound to be enormous, because of the vast size of the listening audience and the number of times they speak in the course of a year; they can therefore never be too careful in striving to avoid common errors or minor affectations.

I do not under-rate the responsibility involved, but I would be the last person to advocate any sort of standard or announcers' English, to the detriment of local colour, and I sincerely regret that in certain parts of the country the fine old local dialects are fast disappearing, much to our loss as a nation. I was therefore very pleased when I read a speech by Sir John Reith on " English as Spoken by the Announcer ", in which he made it quite clear that the B.B.C. has never set out to produce a standard English pronunciation.

I think the accusation that it had done so arose from a misunderstanding of the functions of the Pronunciation Committee, which was appointed to act as a guide to announcers, and indeed to broadcasters in general, in deciding how they should pronounce place and proper names, and, in the case of words which can be pronounced in more than one way, which one to use.

Undoubtedly the people of these islands have become very speech conscious in the past twenty years or so, largely because of broadcasting, but whatever district the London announcer comes from, and be he never so perfect, he can be quite sure that his speech will be anathema to hundreds, if not thousands, of his fellow-countrymen. The main objective, therefore, is to speak clearly and intelligently, whatever the subject, always remembering that, as you have a mixed audience of old and young, you must never let your voice drop at the end of a sentence; if you do, you can be quite certain that thousands of middle-aged and elderly persons will lose the meaning of that sentence altogether.

.　　.　　.　　.　　.

On 16th February, Christopher Stone, the imperturbable, who was due to broadcast a programme of records at 8 p.m., arrived at Broadcasting House at 8.1 p.m., with no programme prepared owing to a misunderstanding. It was only through a chance telephone call from his sister, Mrs. Compton Mackenzie, that he learned that he was scheduled to be on the air. He was also due to broadcast in the Empire Service—North American and Canadian zone— at 1 a.m., and he brought the records for that programme with him. Calmly and methodically, and with complete absence of fuss—so typical of the man—he proceeded to build up a programme as he went along, using the Empire records as a nucleus, supplemented by several more I had brought to the studio, fearing that he was not going to turn up. In this way he gradually and most naturally put over an interesting programme, and I doubt if, excluding the late start, listeners noticed anything at all unusual.

. . . . .

On 22nd March I was faced with a most embarrassing situation as the result of a feeble joke by a comedian in the Vaudeville programme. I suppose he was trying to be both original and topical when he launched this joke on the audience in the studio, and, of course, on listeners in their homes. We had small studio audiences to help the comedians to get the right music-hall atmosphere and the laughs, but it had to be a small audience, or the tempo of the show might be held up and listeners at home irritated. He put his joke in the form of an S.O.S. : " Here is an S.O.S.," he said. " Will Mr. Arthur Arthurs of Surbiton Avenue, Marshpool, Surrey, stop going about with Mrs. James James, as they are not solicitors ? " (the name of the place was not Marshpool but a similar name chosen at random, as a would-be fictitious one). As a joke it fell very flat at the time; the studio audience was obviously not amused, and I thought no more about it until half an hour later, when the telephone rang, and an angry voice, speaking in injured tones, informed me that his name was Arthurs—in fact Arthur Arthurs—that he lived at Surbiton Avenue, Marshpool, Surrey, and that he had just come home after a long and tiring day, and had been told that his name had been mentioned earlier in the evening on the wireless, in connection with a Mrs. James James, a widow lady of his acquaintance, who lived only a short distance from his home.

He went on to explain that he was well known in the district, and a member of the local club, adding that several fellow club-members had rung him up already, asking, " What's all this about you and Mrs. James James, Arthur ? " " The point now is," he remarked emphatically, " what are *you* going to do about it ? " This was a very pertinent question, which led me to consult the Corporation's solicitor before answering it, and impressed upon me the fact that producers cannot be too careful in passing would-be fictitious names in scripts.

The next day was a very busy one, with programmes ranging from Flotsam and Jetsam and singing in the Children's Hour, to announcing James Agate's talk, and reading both News bulletins. During the last programme of the day (Joseph Lewis and his orchestra playing light music) we received a message from Newcastle saying that a large fire was burning only thirty yards from the control room. We made the necessary plans for feeding the programmes to Scotland and the North by another route should this be necessary. It was a good thing we took this precaution, as conditions in Newcastle rapidly became worse, the flames getting to within fifteen yards of the control room before they were put out by the Fire Brigade.

.   .   .   .   .

St. George's Day (23rd April). We broadcast the speeches at the annual banquet of the Royal Society of St. George. The toast of " England " was given by Mr. Winston Churchill; and I sat glued to the loud speaker as he began on a cautious note. (The Corporation had recently refused a request of his to broadcast on the subject of India.)

" To-night," he said, " we are allowed to speak of ourselves as ' Englishmen ', and may even raise the slogan ' St. George for Merrie England '. We must be careful, however, not to presume too much upon the indulgence which has been granted to us. I have to be particularly careful. You see these microphones. They have been placed upon our tables at their own responsibility by the B.B.C. Think of the risk these eminent men are running. Think of their suspense. . . . We can almost see them in our mind's eye, gathered together in that very expensive building, with the questionable statues on its front. We can picture Sir John Reith, with the perspiration mantling on his lofty brow, with his hand upon the control switch, wondering, as I utter every word, whether it will not be his duty to protect innocent subscribers from some irreverent thing I might say about Mr. Gandhi or about the Russian Bolsheviks. . . . But let me reassure him, I have much more serious topics to discuss to-night. I have to speak to you about ' St. George and the Dragon ' " . . . and while not belittling our difficulties, he went on to flay the pessimists, and ended, " We ought, as a nation and empire, to weather any storm that blows . . . and to rejoice at the responsibilities with which Destiny has honoured us, and be proud that we are guardians of our country, in an age when her life is at stake."

Since that day I have announced him several times in the studio —once when he thumped the table with his fist and " boomed " the microphone, and on another occasion when I acted as his target, sitting directly in front of him, at his request. I rather enjoyed this experience of representing his unseen audience, because I could watch him closely as he spoke, observe his gestures, and listen to his superb choice of words and his eloquent phrasing.

.   .   .   .   .

On Sunday, 7th May, the last programme of the evening, immediately before the Epilogue, was a production by E. J. King-Bull of Milton's " Council of the Infernal Peers ", in which the part of Beelzebub was taken by Robert Farquharson, the actor. This was in studio 3A, the largest on the third floor. At the end of the programme Robert Farquharson crossed the passage and went into studio 3E—the religious studio—in order to read the Epilogue.

I wonder if, in all the many parts he has so ably played during a long stage and radio career, he has ever achieved a more violently contrasting quick-change than this !

.   .   .   .   .

On 2nd August, the Chief Scout, Lord Baden-Powell, was in Hungary attending the World Jamboree at Godollo, and we had made arrangements to broadcast a talk by him in the National Programme.

The announcement going over to Godollo was made in the studio in London in the usual way, but unfortunately Lord Baden-Powell had not arrived at the studio there, and after many apologies for the delay, lasting nearly twenty minutes, the Chief Scout's secretary read out a message from him.

I believe that Lord Baden-Powell either had a breakdown in his car or could not succeed in securing a taxi to take him from the country to the studio in time to make the broadcast. Whatever the reason, thousands of Scouts in this country and overseas were extremely disappointed not to hear the voice of their beloved chief.

The announcer in London had a most worrying time trying to cope with a very awkward situation, one which was made more difficult because it was impossible to find out from Hungary what had happened, or how long an interval there was likely to be before the broadcast began.

. . . . .

On 16th August the Director of Programmes—Roger Eckersley —sent for me and asked me some questions about pronouncing the letter " h " : in words like wheat, whale, while, which, etc.—how did I distinguish between " whales " and " Wales " ?   The answer was, of course, that they were both pronounced exactly the same; the context would prevent there being any " homophonic " diffi- culty, as we were never likely to hear of " A school of whales off the coast of Wales ", and I, being a southerner, spoke Southern English, in which the " h " had disappeared from such words.

I told my colleagues about this interview with Roger Eckersley on the subject of aitches, and shortly afterwards Harman Grisewood was almost speechless with suppressed laughter in front of the microphone, at his efforts to put the letter " h " into Whitworth.

Some years later the same criticism cropped up again in a delight- ful letter from a listener living in the North.   As far as I can re- member it read like this :—

> DEAR STUART,
>   Although you have been broadcasting since the year B.B.C.1, you still persist in saying hoo, wy, were, wen, wich, weat, etc., for who, why, where, when, which, wheat, etc.—in short, you are one of that happy band who,
>   Nightly to the air and sky
>   Proclaim your aitchless ancestry."

All this, of course, was true, and expressed so charmingly that I have been most grateful to him, for his letter also states very neatly the fundamental problem of broadcasting—viz., that you cannot hope to please all of the people the whole of the time.

. . . . .

Eric Maschwitz had recently been put in charge of the Corpora- tion's variety programmes, and it was largely due to him that Walford Hyden—for many years Director of Music to Pavlova— introduced to the listening public his Magyar Orchestra, afterwards so popular in the series called " Café Colette ".

Banx's Cartoon of Christopher Stone

IN THE HIGH COURT OF JUSTICE.

KING'S BENCH DIVISION.

COURT No. 8

Special Jury Summons.

To

Arthur James Glew
16, Carrington Road
Rimington.

COUNTY OF LONDON, BY virtue of a Precept to me, the SHERIFF of the County of *London* directed, I hereby summon you to be and appear in HIS MAJESTY'S said Court in the ROYAL COURTS OF JUSTICE, in the STRAND, on Monday the 27th day of March, 1933 at ten of the clock in the forenoon precisely, and so on from day to day, until discharged by the Court, to serve as a Special Juror at the Sittings to be then and there holden

Hereof fail not. Dated this 11th day of March 1933

24, Red Lion Square,
Holborn, W.C.1.

See Notices to Jurors in the daily papers under the heading " Law Notices."

COPY OF A JURY SUMMONS

The Magyar Orchestra was a fine body of musicians led by a Mr. Reilly, and its main task was to play national music of European countries, as played on the Continent, in addition to the ordinary orchestral repertoire. Walford Hyden was a very vigorous conductor, who entered into the spirit of the music, never sparing himself, and going all out to obtain the most sparkling performance possible. One evening he decided to introduce the leader of a famous Hungarian gipsy band, as an experiment, to play some of the Hungarian national airs. The gipsy leader certainly played his native airs and dances with great feeling, but he used no music, playing from memory in his own tempo, regardless of the conductor's beat.

This would not do for Walford Hyden, who shouted at him during the rehearsal, " Watch my beat." But this only made him lose his temper (he was obviously a very highly-strung type), and we had the utmost difficulty in getting him to play at all. He became all " up-stage " and temperamental, and walked out of the building, and only after a great deal of persuasion did we succeed in inducing him to return. In the end the transmission went excellently.

. . . . .

I was most amused, though not surprised, to receive the following charming letter about one of my colleagues in the summer of this year (1933) :—

> " We have heard that Broadcasting House is very warm these hot, sultry summer days, so would you kindly convey our heartfelt sympathy to your announcer who at 3 p.m. to-day expressed his pious wish for a ' thorough ' wash when giving out the order of Evensong at Westminster Abbey ? "

My correspondent was referring to Wesley's well-known anthem, " Wash me throughly from my sin ", which can so easily become a pitfall, " throughly " being read as " thoroughly ".

. . . . .

Saturday, 7th October, was the last night of the Proms, and again this year I was due to announce it. I had the happy idea of going to see Sir Henry Wood about it first of all, and this resulted in the following opening announcement :—

" To-night we are broadcasting the last Promenade Concert of the season from Queen's Hall. Like summer-time, the Proms have now become a National Institution, so much so that we take them for granted, and are apt to forget the immense industry and patience required in their preparation; the planning, the programme-building, the rehearsals, quite apart from the actual performances.

" When I asked Sir Henry this morning if he would like to say anything to listeners before the concert to-night, he replied, ' Yes; I should like you to tell them of the phenomenal repertoire of this fine orchestra [i.e. the B.B.C. Symphony Orchestra]—the phenomenal reper-toire,' he repeated.

" But the marvel of the Promenade Concerts is Sir Henry himself, for to-night he completes the thirty-ninth season of these concerts; not a concert, not a single rehearsal has he ever missed throughout all these years. What a magnificent record ! "

.   .   .   .   .

On 16th October I met my old friend Vernon Bartlett—I have known him since 1915, when we shared a billet in the First World War—and he told me that his talk following the nine o'clock News on Saturday (14th October) had caused consternation at the Foreign Office.

It was spoken, to all intents and purposes, impromptu, following as it did Hitler's announcement, in the News, of Germany's decision to leave the Disarmament Conference and the League of Nations. (This bulletin had included a recording of Hitler's actual words announcing this decision.) In his talk Vernon Bartlett argued that Germany had a strong case, because the Allies had not disarmed, as they had promised to do in the Peace Treaty, and he pleaded for an examination of the case on factual evidence.

The reason why the Government was so annoyed about his talk was that, following immediately after the News containing the official announcement of Germany's decision, such an expression of opinion would, without doubt, appear to foreign listeners as if it were an official pronouncement by the Government, not—as in fact it was—the expression of an individual view by an experienced observer and well-known broadcaster.

No wonder Vernon Bartlett looked tired. He told me that he had had sixty-three telephone calls that night, including a trunk call at one o'clock in the morning from Glasgow, and no fewer than 700 letters this morning! Incidentally, this was still further evidence of the immense power of the spoken word and the swiftness of the reaction to it by the public.

.   .   .   .   .

There was one hectic Sunday in the autumn when I was either rehearsing or broadcasting from 2.30 to 11 p.m. because, owing to illness, we were short-handed, and there were several recitals and concerts on both the National and Regional wavelengths, given in the London studios. Among these, I remember, was a concert given by the Theatre Orchestra and Richard Tauber, with announcements made over music, which had to be carefully rehearsed and timed, a violin recital, a Wagnerian Concert by the Symphony Orchestra, two News bulletins and a recital of English songs by Dora Labbette, a well-known soprano, who also later sang in opera as Lisa Perli.

This artist had a voice of exquisite quality. It was like velvet, and effortlessly produced. Her diction, too, was very clear—a most important point when broadcasting—and she had an extremely attractive personality. In fact to me hers was

> " that melting voice . . .
> Untwisting all the chains that tie
> The hidden soul of harmony."

.   .   .   .   .

The eminent Hungarian composer and pianist, Bela Bartok, gave a recital of works by Bach and himself in the studio in the first week of November. He was a tall, thin, clean-shaven man in the middle fifties, with a rather lined face and a pleasant smile. He began by playing some Bach from memory, then he played a piano sonata of his own, in three movements, and for this he asked me to turn over. This was not too simple a matter, because the music was in manuscript and not very clear, and he proceeded to use the piano as a percussion instrument, and in some of the louder passages lifted his hands so high that it was difficult to get near enough to the music to follow it. It was all very exciting, almost thrilling at times, because the music was full of excitement, but I was thankful when it was all over and I was able to relax once more.

.   .   .   .   .

The 15th November was the birthday of the National Broadcasting Company of America. We had always been good friends of theirs, and we gave half an hour's special programme in their honour, a mixed grill chiefly notable for its variety and the speed with which we switched from place to place.

I put out " Birthday Greetings " to them in my opening announcement, and we then began with the B.B.C. Military Band playing MacDowell's " A.D. 1620 "; then to the Old Vic for the Prologue to " I Pagliacci ", and back to the concert hall for organ music played by Berkeley Mason. From there to Birmingham for Henry Hall and the B.B.C. Dance Orchestra, back again to Broadcasting House for the Wireless Singers in an English folk-song programme, then over to the Queen's Hall, where Weingartner was conducting the B.B.C. Symphony Orchestra in a concert which included Berlioz' " Fantastic Symphony "; back again to the studio for the Wireless Male Voice Choir, and on to the concert hall for the Theatre Orchestra playing Eric Coates's suite " London Day by Day ", and on again, as though the Red Queen were shouting in our ear " Faster, faster ", until we ended with Big Ben and said good-bye.

CHRISTMAS EVE.   THE BELLS OF BETHLEHEM

This was an outstanding broadcast in every way, and a fine piece of organisation by the programme and engineering staffs. I do not think that the majority of people who heard it realised how complex were the arrangements or how many risks were involved. We, in London, were the link between Bethlehem in the East and New York in the West. The programme began at 2000 G.M.T., with announcements made simultaneously in London and New York, for which thirty-two seconds were allowed. Then came the first verse of the hymn " O come, all ye faithful " from Riverside Drive Church, New York, followed by the second verse of the hymn from Winchester Cathedral, and then the bells of Bethlehem.

Here absolute accuracy of timing of the announcements and of the tempo and pitch of the singing of the hymn was essential. We rehearsed and rehearsed. My opening announcement took thirty and a half, thirty-one and eventually thirty-two seconds, and when the broadcast came I was fortunate enough to do it in exactly thirty-two seconds, with the result that a perfect start of the hymn in New York followed; the programme proceeded as planned, the cues being carefully taken up throughout.

There was only one small discrepancy, and I doubt if any listener noticed it. When we returned to New York for the last verse of the hymn—i.e. after the bells and the third verse sung in Winchester Cathedral—instead of hearing the first note of the last verse, as they were a few seconds late, we heard the last note of the third verse instead.

This was undoubtedly one of the most exciting broadcasts in which I have ever taken part, and it was an exhausting one, too !

Here is the opening announcement :—

" This is London.

" The Bells of Bethlehem, a world broadcast telling the story of the first Christmas in relays from London and New York. From Winchester Cathedral, England, and from Riverside Church, New York, where the choirs are singing the Christmas hymn ' O come, all ye faithful ', and from the church of the Nativity, Bethlehem.

" Arranged by the British Broadcasting Corporation and the National Broadcasting Company of America, and broadcast to listeners throughout the world."

Immediately the transmission had ended we had to make our final preparations for the Christmas Day broadcast " Absent Friends ", in which the King spoke so impressively at three o'clock to his subjects both at home and overseas.

1934

ON 6th January we broadcast a birthday concert of chamber music by Dame Ethel Smyth, including her violin sonata in A minor, her string quartet, and two short pieces for oboe, flute and piano.

After the concert Dame Ethel wanted to make a little speech of thanks, but this could not be broadcast, because the programme ran late.

The Press, in reporting the concert, came out with the statement that " her birthday speech had been censored ", making no reference to the fact that, because the music ran over its scheduled time, there was no opportunity for including her remarks. After the red light had gone out she made a neat and witty speech, " to break the sepulchral silence of the evening ", as she put it—referring to my request to the audience not to applaud until the end because we were very short of time. She said she wished to thank the Corporation for broadcasting this programme of her works on her seventy-fifth birthday, and to assure them " that they need not be alarmed at anything she might say into that death's head ", pointing to the microphone.

She was obviously much moved by the occasion, and also thanked Sir Hugh Allen and other musical friends present for suggesting this method of giving her a birthday gift.

      .   .   .   .   .

27th January. H.R.H. the Prince of Wales came to the studio at 6 p.m. to speak about Voluntary Services. He was received by Sir John and Lady Reith and Colonel Alan Dawnay, Controller of Programmes. Once settled in the Talks studio on the third floor— a studio designed to represent a study, with rows of books on the shelves—he was given the usual balance test, and I explained the procedure to him. During the few minutes before he began, he talked to me about broadcasting, and said how much he hated having to make speeches at official dinners when they were broadcast, and that he preferred to come to the studio to do his broadcasting. He referred to the Lord Mayor's Banquet, and to Winston Churchill's superb command of the English language. Then the red light flicked. I announced him and left him alone, remaining in the " listening room " outside until he had finished speaking.

. . . . .

12*th February.* Peter Fleming, author and *Times* correspondent, who had recently returned from the Far East, came in to speak about Manchukuo, the new Japanese-sponsored puppet State, which I noticed he pronounced " Manchugua ", not Manchukuo.

After his talk I remarked how difficult we found the pronunciation of some of the Chinese Generals' names when they cropped up in the News. He smiled and agreed, and then went on, " I don't want to throw a spanner into the works, but the place-names are catches, too. For example, Jehol is not pronounced as spelt, but Rah-hah ! "

We had a good laugh about this, and I explained that in the case of unfamiliar place-names our policy was to give the English equivalent, in order to avoid confusion and enable the man in the street to recognise them when he saw them in his paper in the morning.

This policy was justified many times during the 1939–45 war, when difficult Polish, Czech and Russian names frequently appeared in the official communiqué. As the Russian communiqué only began to come in at 8.55 p.m., and the News began at 9, it meant that it had to be read at sight, and it was comforting to remember that if there were some stiff hurdles to be cleared, one could always " anglicise ". For example, the Polish city of Lodz we pronounced as spelt, though we knew the Polish " L " is pronounced like a " W " and it should have sounded something like " Wush ", not Lodz.

One of the difficulties of broadcast English is that one frequently comes across " homophones "—e.g., sew, sow; Wales, whales; imminent, immanent. Generally, but not always, the context makes the meaning clear.

Another difficulty is that there are alternative pronunciations of words in common use—e.g. acoustics, the second syllable being sometimes pronounced " coo " and sometimes " cow ". Humour is pronounced both with and without the " h "; then there is the fact, so worrying to foreigners, that many words are not pronounced as they are spelt.

A listener once sent me this verse by the late Lord Cromer, which admirably illustrates my point :—

" When the English tongue we speak
Why is ' break ' not rhymed with ' freak ' ?
Will you tell us why it's true
We say ' sew ' but likewise ' Jew ' ?
Beard sounds not the same as ' heard ',
' Cord ' is different from ' word ',
And since ' pay ' is rhymed with ' say '
Why not ' paid ' with ' said ' ? I pray.
' Cow ' is ' cow ', but ' low ' is ' low ';
' Shoe ' is never rhymed with ' foe ',
And in short it seems to me
Sound and letters disagree."

This sentence given me by a colleague is also a good example of some of the pitfalls of the English tongue :—

" A tough-nutted, dough-faced ploughman went cough-
ing and hiccoughing through the streets of Scarborough."

A broadcasting linguistic problem ever with us is the production of sibilants in such a way that they cause little or no microphone blasting. I have known a first-rate script ruined by the speaker because he hissed and whistled his " s " sounds so much that what should have been a serious discourse became, in fact, a comic turn. Sibilant hiss, or blasting, is caused by the initial voiceless rush of air through the mouth before the vocal chords " engage " and produce the word required. If you say to yourself the word SHINE very slowly, you will at once see what I mean. Or, better still, read the following aloud at a good pace :—

" She has a shot-silk sash shop
Full of sura-silk sashes
Where the sun shines on the shop signs ".

I have found that the most satisfactory way of tackling this problem is to speak " s " and " sh " sounds downwards and backwards rather than horizontally and forwards, which is the normal way.

To illustrate this principle, if you take a thin and narrow piece of paper about 2 to 2½ inches long, and hold one end with your finger pressed against your upper lip, leaving the other end dangling free, then say the word " PAT " in a fairly loud voice, the free end of the paper will fly out at right angles to the face, forced outwards by the rush of air. Now, if you repeat this, but instead of saying " PAT ", say the French word " PATTE " (= paw), using the French pronunciation of the letter " p ", the piece of paper remains motionless, no matter how loudly you speak or shout, because there is no forward outrush of air. Apply this principle to " s " and " sh " sounds, and, with a little practice, all trace of microphone hiss caused by sibilants will disappear.

.　　.　　.　　.　　.

On 6th February Bernard Shaw came to broadcast his contribution to the " Whither Britain " series. He was, as usual, in his element when broadcasting, and in answering the question posed by the title seemed to think that Britain was going nowhere in particular—in short, that she was a ship without a pilot, probably heading for the rocks.

Before he began his broadcast I had a long talk with him in the drawing-room, mostly about the English language and pronunciation, e.g. Newfoundland : the new-found-land, I remember, we talked about, the B.B.C. ruling being Nĕwfoŭndlānd, but, in its adjectival form, a Nĕwfoūndlănd dog. Another word we mentioned was Conduit Street, our ruling being KUNDIT Street. But Mr. Shaw said that if he wanted to go there in a taxi he would tell the driver to take him to " KON-DEW-IT " Street ! I wonder where he would land up ?

Mr. Shaw was to have gone on a cruise this month in search of the sun, and it was agreed that his contribution to this series should be recorded beforehand. The recording was made; then America wanted to hear him, but, as the Federal Radio Commission had banned recorded talks, it had to be live or nothing. So a joint request was made by us and the Americans for him to repeat his recorded address live at the microphone. His plans were accordingly altered, and he came to the studio and made the broadcast.

.　　.　　.　　.　　.

6th March. A. J. Alan returned to the microphone with a new story about a High Court case, called " Settled Out of Court ". The *Radio Times* published a copy of what purported to be his jury summons. I understand the editor subsequently received a letter from a solicitor about this, alleging it to be an illegal publication because no record of any man named Arthur James Alan could be found among the list of men who sat as jurors in 1933, the year of the story.

   .   .   .   .   .

13*th March*. I announced a recital given in the concert hall by Harriet Cohen (piano) and Thelma Reiss ('cello). This was an important occasion for me, because it was the first time I used the new ribbon microphone and the first time I met Dr. Alexander, of our research staff, a young D.Sc. of St. Andrews, who had been responsible for its development.

It consists of a narrow piece of aluminium ribbon which moves between the two poles of a strong permanent magnet. It is excellent both for speech and music, and has none of the unpleasant hissing background of the Reiss microphone in picking up weak speech or " piano " passages of music. It does not overload, or " blast ", as it is called; is sensitive on *two* sides—a great advantage in broadcast discussions—and is of robust construction. Crooners will adore it and fondle it lovingly.

   .   .   .   .   .

14*th April*. A wonderful relay of a programme broadcast by the Columbia Broadcasting System of the United States from " Little America ", the headquarters of Admiral Byrd's Antarctic expedition. There was a good deal of doubt about reception conditions from such a vast distance, because tests had shown that sometimes, if conditions were bad, speech was inaudible; at other times it was quite clear. We were therefore very cautious in framing our opening announcement, taking the line that we were hoping for the best, but prepared for a surfeit of atmospherics. As it turned out, reception conditions could hardly have been better, and we heard the voice of the Admiral himself sending us a message, a concert given by some of the members of the expedition, which included songs and choruses with accordion accompaniment, and also the noise of the " huskies " barking—all from a spot some 9000 miles away. Admiral Byrd, the leader of the expedition, was not at the main base, but was spending the long winter 123 miles nearer the South Pole.

The broadcast came to us from the miniature Station K.F.Z. at
" Little America ", which was picked up by Buenos Aires, relayed
to New York, and via New York to Europe. " Little America ",
the expedition's base camp, was situated in the ice in latitude 78°
South, near the Bay of Whales.

This broadcast was a triumph for the engineers—both American
and our own (Post Office and B.B.C.)—and another example of the
way in which distance is being annihilated by radio.

.   .   .   .   .

On 2nd May I announced Edith Penville, a lady flautist who was
a brilliant performer. She played a piece by a Dutch flautist named
de Jong, who once described himself as the " Silly Hollander who
played upon a hollow cylinder ".

The following week I announced the London Music Festival
Concert, given by the B.B.C. Symphony Orchestra in the Queen's
Hall, conducted by Dr. Adrian Boult, with Horowitz as soloist. It
included a memorable performance of the Enigma Variations, and
a terrific performance of the Tchaikowsky B flat minor concerto by
Horowitz and the orchestra. The viola-players, who should have
had a good view, said daylight could be seen between the artist and
the piano stool nearly all the time, so literally was he " on his toes ".

.   .   .   .   .

After a long day's broadcasting I had to take part in a film of the
B.B.C. which was being made in Broadcasting House by the G.P.O.
Film Unit under John Grierson. The technicians could not get
their gear into the studios until after broadcasting hours, and began
to assemble it directly after midnight, when we closed down. Unfortunately, when the cameras were in position a fault developed in
the electric motors driving them, which caused a long delay. Eventually this defect was put right, and I sat in 4A—one of the small
News studios—where I was encircled by arc lights, in boiling heat,
trying to read a News bulletin with an air of complete indifference
to what was going on all around me. Just as we had finished a
rehearsal and were about to shoot, an arc-lamp broke, and we had
to begin all over again. It was 5 a.m. before the " take " was
" in the bag ", and, feeling very limp, we crawled home to bed.

.   .   .   .   .

2nd June. Next week being Derby Week, we decided to ask the

Duke of Portland to come to the studio and talk about his memories of great Derbys of the past.

He was a most friendly and benign old gentleman, who had a twinkle in his eye, and spoke delightfully of some of the famous horses of the past and of the many Derbys he himself had seen. One could tell that he was living every moment of the past over again as he spoke, revelling in the opportunity of passing on to others some of his most treasured memories.

He won the Derby in 1888 and 1889, nearly fifty years ago, and since then had been second in the world-famous race three times, and third twice.

.   .   .   .   .

ELGAR, HOLST AND DELIUS

England lost three outstanding composers in the first six months of 1934. On 23rd February Sir Edward Elgar died, and Sir Landon Ronald, a great friend and a fine interpreter of his works, broadcast an appreciation from the studio.

On 25th May Gustav Holst died, and there passed from among us a most original mind.

Both these men had been orchestral players in their younger days, and both had experienced hard struggles; both were masters of the art of orchestration, and wrote music which was genuinely inspired and has since become immortal.

Elgar and Holst—both of whom I met several times—were examples of greatness linked with simplicity, kindliness and consideration for their fellow men. I remember Sir Walford Davies telling me of a discussion he had with Holst about his " Hymn of Jesus ", and, referring to a difficult and most unusual passage, Sir Walford asked him why he had written it instead of the more usual phrase, which he then played on the piano by way of illustration. There was a long pause before Holst replied; then he said quietly, " Because it did not come to me like that ". As Sir Walford afterwards remarked, " There was nothing more to be said."

.   .   .   .   .

On 10th June yet a third British composer died : Delius, a North countryman who had spent many years of his life abroad, and had recently been living in France.

It was Sir Thomas Beecham, an ardent admirer of Delius, who was responsible for introducing his work to audiences in this country, and for this we owe him a great debt of gratitude.

In the nine o'clock News Freddy Grisewood read an obituary notice of the composer written by Richard Walker, one of the News Editors, and followed it up by playing part of the "Walk to the Paradise Garden" from the opera "A Village Romeo and Juliet".

It was in 1927 that we had broadcast a birthday concert of his works, and I had read out a message of greeting from the B.B.C. to him at his home at Grez-sur-Loing, France.

.   .   .   .

While I was recording Epilogues for use in the Empire Service, with David Tennant and Howard Marshall, the door of the studio opened, and in came the King and Queen of Siam, shepherded by Sir John Reith.

The royal couple were most charming, and seemed to take a great interest in our recordings, but I had never before seen such a ridiculous contrast in size; Sir John, some 6 feet 5 inches, towering above the tiny Oriental King and Queen, and stooping down to speak to them, like a giraffe bending down to toy with the leaves of a bush.

.   .   .   .

In the evening of 2nd August there was a Rumanian studio party with songs and dances to balalaika music, all good fun, boisterous and merry, to get the right atmosphere. The dancer in the red Russian boots, who had flaming red hair, stimulated by the exotic music, began making eyes at me and got very worked up . . . so I went out!

.   .   .   .

9th August. A fine recital by George Parker—my old singing master—who, as usual, brought in some friends to hear him sing in the studio.

Unfortunately that afternoon he had been stung on the forehead by a bee, and his eyes were so swollen that he could scarcely see his music, but this did not appear to affect his singing, and as this was broadcasting, not television, appearances did not matter.

.   .   .   .

During the third week of September, that learned authority on early English music, Sir Richard Terry, was giving a series of illustrated talks in the " Foundations of Music " series, and I was looking after him and announcing him. He was terribly nervous at first, being new to the microphone, but had some most interesting and original material.

He began with " Plainsong ", and, to prove the secular origin of most of the Plainsong modes, he quoted the old music-hall ditty, " Hey, Tommy, who's your tailor ? " This was a good tune, but unfortunately it was rather spoilt by the very solemn way it was sung by some members of Westminster Cathedral choir, who seemed to think they were still in the cathedral, instead of in the studio.

I had a talk with Sir Richard afterwards, and tried to help him to get rid of his nervousness and to present his material simply, clearly and without effort.

The next day he was much happier about it, and most kindly sent me a charming little note of thanks " for the kind courtesy and real help you extended to me in my ghastly ordeal last night before the mike ".

.   .   .   .   .

" Crisis in Spain " was the title of the first English example of the reporting of contemporary events in radio form, broadcast on 22nd August. It covered the sequence of events following the announcement of the municipal elections on 15th March (1931), through the formation of the Provisional Republic on 14th April (1931) and the withdrawal of the Royal Family, to the death in Paris on 23rd April (1931) of the Infanta Dona Isabella. There was no comment, only a factual presentation. I announced it, and attended the rehearsals beforehand, and though I thought it very dramatic in places, it was similar in form to many other features.

I did not realise that by broadcasting the details of this historic occasion we were actually stirring up intense feeling in Spain itself; but such proved to be the case.

Listeners tuning in to Barcelona heard strains of the Royalist anthem—a song banned under the Republic—and immediately the rumour spread that monarchists had seized the Barcelona radio station, repeating the Nazi " coup " of 30th July in Vienna. People listening to the broadcast from Barcelona also heard, to their amazement, references to the Infanta and to the Republican National Anthem.

The explanation was, of course, that the so-called "Royalist" programme had been picked up by listeners to Barcelona in error; what they were really hearing was our Spanish retrospect, "Crisis in Spain". Not since Father Ronald Knox gave his famous "Broadcasting the Barricades" talk in Savoy Hill days—describing an imaginary revolution in London—has there been such an example of mass hysteria unintentionally produced in Europe.

.   .   .   .   .

4th September. Sir Walford Davies told me an amusing story of his first official experience as Master of the King's Musick a few weeks ago.

He was in attendance on His Majesty in the Royal Box at the Royal Albert Hall on the occasion of a celebrity concert, in which both Conchita Supervia and Richard Tauber were singing.

The former came on to the platform most strikingly dressed in a Spanish gown, wearing a mantilla, with a high comb in her beautiful red hair. Her dress had a long train, which, by a series of sharp, swift kicks, she kept moving from side to side, just like Nellie Wallace. She was, of course, a superb singer, a *coloratura* contralto, but this action with her train as she stood on the platform was so comical that everyone in the Royal Box wanted to laugh, and Princess Mary and the others were only just suppressing a tremendous urge to do so when the King gave a deep "snigger" which almost upset the apple-cart altogether.

Then Conchita Supervia began to sing about her native Spain, and at the end terrific applause followed. The King beckoned with his finger to Sir Walford and said rather gruffly, "No encores". Sir Walford then had to hurry round to the back of the stage—and it is a very long way from the Royal Box to the back of the stage—to tell Sir Henry Wood of the King's orders. Meanwhile Richard Tauber was singing, and on Sir Walford's return to the Royal Box he was bowing to the audience, as they rapturously applauded. The King turned to Sir Walford and said *sotto voce*, "I wouldn't mind hearing *that* fellow again"!

.   .   .   .   .

26th September.   At 2.50 we broadcast the launching ceremony by Her Majesty Queen Mary of the new giant Cunarder " 534 " from Messrs. John Brown's yard at Clydebank.

We heard the Queen's voice naming the ship, the sirens from the surrounding ships and the cheers from the crowd as she slid into the water, and we also heard Queen Mary's aside as she said quite distinctly, " Is that all right ? "

.   .   .   .   .

30th September.   After the second News we broadcast the Farewell Concert of Sir Dan Godfrey from Bournemouth, given by the Bournemouth Municipal Orchestra and the Bournemouth Military Band.   Sir Dan had been Director of Music to the Bournemouth Corporation from 1893 to 1934.   After the last item of the concert —Tchaikovsky's 1812 Overture—Sir Hugh Allen made a graceful little speech thanking Sir Dan for his work on behalf of British composers, and then went on to introduce his successor, Richard Austin.

Sir Dan, in returning thanks, was much affected by the occasion, and at one point, when referring to the loyalty of the orchestra, some members of which were now retiring after forty years' service, he almost broke down.   Continuing, Sir Dan said, " We've an old friend with us to-night, Billy Burns ", and he went on to quote a remark of his in describing Sir Dan to a friend, a tribute of which he (Sir Dan) was very proud :—

" Mon, he's hot stuff, but he's just ".

.   .   .   .   .

9th October.   Just after 5 p.m. the news came through that King Alexander of Yugoslavia had been assassinated, M. Barthou, the French President, seriously wounded and two officials killed in the streets of Marseilles.   The murderer turned out to be a Croat named Kalem Petries, who was cut down by one of the Guards.

Lionel Marson read the 6 p.m. News bulletin, which was a difficult one, and while he was reading it, a message came through to say that M. Barthou had died of his wounds.

Plans for the second News were re-drafted, and, after a good deal of discussion, it was arranged that I should do the obituaries following the official announcement of the tragedy, and Harman Grisewood should follow with the ordinary News.   I thought my part

was too long and that we were overdoing it; however, it had to be
read slowly, and I took about seventeen minutes.

. . . . .

16*th November*. The event of the evening was Winston Churchill's talk at ten o'clock in the series " The Causes of War ".
Describing the threatening clouds gathering over Germany, he said
the problem before us, if the storm broke, was the old grim
choice our forbears had to face : whether we should submit, or
whether we should prepare, and he went on to urge that " we must,
without another day's delay, begin to make ourselves at least the
strongest air Power in the European world ". Mr. Churchill came
about 9.50, having first been to consult Sir Milsom Rees about his
throat. He seemed delighted when I assured him afterwards that
reception had been excellent and that America reported 100 per cent
clarity. He was accompanied by his elder daughter and a friend
of hers, and would not have a drink before he spoke. He appeared
to be rather anxious about his talk, and afraid that we would cut
him off, because, though scheduled for fifteen minutes, he could not
complete it in less than nineteen or twenty. I assured him that I
would not cut him off, and agreed, at his request, to sit in a chair in
front of him as a sort of target. Therefore I could observe him
closely as he spoke, and I noticed how he used his hands in making
his points, just as though he were on a public platform. But he did
not speak too slowly and deliberately, as I have heard him in previous
broadcasts. He afterwards told me how difficult it had been to compress into twenty minutes all he had to say, and he also said that before
broadcasting he had had to submit his manuscript to the Foreign
Office.

He had a drink afterwards, lit his cigar and talked for a while,
then he left in a large and rather ancient Daimler car, and I took the
others round the building, and showed them the studios until 11 p.m.

. . . . .

29*th November*. I came in from Chislehurst by the 8.40 a.m. train,
so as to allow plenty of time to be in my place at Broadcasting House
to make the opening announcement for the wedding at Westminster
Abbey of the Duke of Kent and Princess Marina of Greece. The
train was packed, and I had to stand all the way. Crowds already
in the streets, a gala atmosphere everywhere.

H

I rehearsed and timed the opening announcement, which began with an extract from the *London Gazette* : " At the Court of Buckingham Palace, 5th October, 1934, His Majesty was this day pleased to declare his royal consent to a Contract of Matrimony between ", etc., etc.

The broadcast went without a hitch, the bride's " I will " and the word " obey " coming through very clearly; even the slight confusion over her husband's name was all that it should have been.

It was a triumph for the engineers, overcoming all operational difficulties from their headquarters in the crypt of the Abbey, and for Gerald Cock, Outside Broadcast Director, and his commentators.

The programme was broadcast in many languages, and had probably the largest audience of any transmission in the history of broadcasting up to that date.

.   .   .   .   .

2nd December. Josef Hofmann, the eminent pianist, came and gave a recital in the studio. His agent insisted that he should bring his own piano, in spite of the excellent Steinways and Bösendorfers we had in the studios. The reason was that he has small hands, and uses a piano which has been specially made for him, with notes narrower than the normal size; Ernest Lush found that on it he could " stretch " ten notes quite easily (i.e. an eleventh !) Hofmann played superbly, skating over the difficulties of Liszt's Hungarian Rhapsody No. 12 as though they were non-existent.

That week I also announced the " Melodies of Christendom ", directed by Sir Walford Davies in the concert hall of Broadcasting House. The carols were exquisite. One which he gave me to read out before the Wireless Singers sang it so impressed me that I made a note of the words : —

> " Into this world of sorrow,
> Into this valley of rue and sadness,
> Came Christ, our dear Consoler,
> And brought men gladness.

> " Now is the time of His coming,
> Now are our hearts with joy replete,
> But, to lead men to Heaven,
> He bread of tears did eat."

It was set to music by Percy Buck.

.   .   .   .

25th December. The Christmas Day programme at two o'clock was a family affair called " Empire Exchange ", ending with the introduction of H.M. the King by the grand old shepherd of Ilmington. It was a stroke of genius on the part of the producer to find him and put him in the programme; there must have been many people with lumps in their throats as he announced the King.

For this far-flung programme D. H. Munro was at the control panel, a specially constructed outsize model with a sliding seat to cope with its great width.

As usual, for a week afterwards Munro could only speak in a whisper—not that he had had to shout at anybody, but such was the effect of the great nervous strain on the man in the key position.

THE future of India being a subject much under discussion, the Corporation decided to broadcast a series of talks by eminent men with experience of that vast country with its teeming millions of many races and creeds.

On 8th January Sir George Schuster, a former Finance Minister of the Government of India, spoke; on 11th January Lord Lloyd of Dolobran, who was Governor of Bombay from 1918 to 1923, gave his views, and on 29th January Mr. Winston Churchill made his contribution.

Mr. Churchill had always held strong views on India and all that nearly three centuries of the Pax Britannica had achieved for that country, and he could speak from first-hand knowledge, having himself served with the Malakand Field Force in 1897.

He spoke resolutely and convincingly, using a good deal of emphasis in making his points, at times thumping with his fist on the arm of the chair, and causing some anxious moments for the engineers. It was fortunate that he did not thump the table, as the microphone was standing on it, insulated only by a thick piece of sponge rubber. (A few days later I noticed that the engineers had decided to remove the microphone from the table and suspend it from the ceiling.) The staff photographers came in afterwards to take a photograph of him sitting in front of the microphone. He did his best to induce Sir John Reith to be photographed with him, but Sir John politely but firmly declined the invitation.

.   .   .   .   .

G. K. Chesterton's book-talks were invariably a joy to listen to. He was a delightful person to work with, and always so cheerful, but on 31st January I observed that it seemed a great effort for him to broadcast. I had not noticed this before.

When I asked him how he was, he replied very slowly, "I am quite well, thank you, except for a little mental decay." Apparently he had mislaid his spectacles at the rehearsal, but fortunately his wife, who was with him, found them in time.

.   .   .   .

At about this time the new Maida Vale Studios had been taken into regular use. The largest was a fine studio designed to accommodate an Orchestra of 100 or more players and a choir; there was also a Balcony for a small audience. It was decorated in dark green and "Battleship" grey, and gave the impression of spaciousness. There was plenty of height, too, an ideal home for the Symphony Orchestra.

On 2nd February I was to announce a concert given by the B.B.C. Orchestra and conducted by Julian Clifford. Five minutes before the concert was due to begin, the Orchestra were in their places in the Maida Vale Studio tuning up, but, to my surprise, there was no sign of any conductor. Eight o'clock came, and the red light began to flick, but still there was no conductor. I signalled to the Orchestra to carry on with tuning, and whispered to Marie Wilson, who was leading, that I would give Clifford one more minute, after which she would have to conduct, if he had not arrived.

This she flatly refused to do, deputing Manus O'Donnell, her number two, to do it for her, explaining, "He's used to it; he has an orchestra of his own".

In the end it was not necessary, because Clifford, very out of breath and full of apologies, then came into the studio, and we began the overture at 8.2$\frac{1}{2}$.

He told me later that his car had refused to start, and when it eventually did so, he flew along, regardless of any speed limit. He was most upset about being late, and came to see me afterwards seeking my advice as to how best to make his peace with the Music Department.

.   .   .   .

5th February. At 10 p.m. I announced Mr. Baldwin, who was broadcasting in the series of talks on India. Sir John Reith brought him along to the studio, and he gave a first-rate talk on the subject, which, as everyone knows, bristles with difficulties.

After the talk was over, in discussing some of the previous speakers in the series, Mr. Churchill's broadcast was mentioned, and Mr. Baldwin said, "There were two things about which Winston did not agree with us in the Conservative Party—Air and India. In each case he went round to the *Daily Mail* to try to find out if he had their support before he did anything else. Winston is like that. One thing I hope I shall be given credit for in the years to come; that is that at the beginning of the General Strike in 1926 I put Winston on to the *British Gazette*."

.   .   .   .   .

10th February. I was the narrator in Honegger's " King David ", a work which contains some marvellously clever writing of barbaric music (such as the " March of the Philistines "). I found the narration over music full of pitfalls, the words being written, not with any time values, as in an ordinary vocal score, but the rise and fall of the voice having to coincide with certain phrases played by the orchestra, and certain places in the " Lament of David for Jonathan " had to be reached by both voice and orchestra at the same time. The calling up of the soul of Samuel by the incantation of the witch of Endor (at the request of Saul) is a brilliant piece of dramatic writing, but as it was a studio performance, being among the orchestra, and not on a stage above it, I found the volume of sound around me almost overwhelming.

.   .   .   .   .

In the middle of February I went to Blackheath to do some studio shots of the B.B.C. Film. There I had a long talk with John Grierson, the Director of the G.P.O. Film Unit, a vivid personality, a live wire, and full of ideas. We talked about films, radio and television. He thinks that the advent of television will be a godsend to the film industry, because it will mean that they and the B.B.C. will have to work on similar lines.

At the moment, in his opinion, film-producers really have only one type of film to sell; but with the advent of television they will have to think again. The use of actuality television programmes in the cinema may revolutionise everything.

That same evening I announced a recital given by Bratza, the Yugoslav violinist, and Jovanovitch, his fellow-countryman. Both wore black velvet suits and both brought with them a small but most beautiful ikon in a gold frame, which they placed on chairs nearby while they were giving their recital.

.   .   .   .   .

It was always refreshing, after reading fourteen minutes or more of solid official News (and what heavy going this can sometimes be !), to end with something, if only a few lines, in lighter vein, and editors eagerly seized upon any opportunity that offered.

The second News on 22nd February was an example of this, and it took the form of the following story :—

Magistrate to deaf defendant, speaking close to him and very slowly and deliberately : " Can you hear me ? "

Deaf defendant : " Excuse me, sir, but your stud has come out."

On the same day I received a letter from my old House Master, R. R. Conway—a perfect " Mr. Chips "—saying how much he had enjoyed the broadcast of the play that bears the name of that famous character, but adding two criticisms : the congregation sang " Amen " at the end of the first verse of the end-of-term hymn, and they did not drag. Not much misses his critical ear, in spite of his being almost eighty.

. . . . . .

20th March. I announced the Symphony Concert from Queen's Hall given by the B.B.C. Symphony Orchestra. This was an outstanding musical occasion, because the soloist was Jascha Heifetz, the world-famous violinist, and he was broadcasting here for the first time; his playing of the Mozart Concerto No. 5 in A was a sheer joy. The concert also included some symphonic excerpts from the opera " Lulu " by Alban Berg, composer of " Wozzeck ". Freddy Grisewood and I were alone in the announcers' room, and after having revelled in the Mozart, we began to listen to " Lulu " and the strange atonal effects that followed. May Blyth was battling gallantly with the solo part, which, as far as one could gather, had nothing to do with what the orchestra was playing—like two parallel lines which travel along together but never meet. After a while I felt I could stand it no longer, and made a wry face, whereon Freddy, taking it as his cue, at once switched over to the Regional, where Harman Grisewood, reading the News, said, " And the Gendarme opened fire ". " I'm not surprised," said Freddy.

Next day I was explaining this coincidence to Arthur Wynn, who was formerly an announcer at Savoy Hill and now spends his life booking artists for concerts or turning down applications of would-be artists, as the case may be. He is a most attractive personality, with a great sense of humour and a story to hand to illustrate any situation. He played the part of Lockett in " The Beggar's Opera " in Sir Nigel Playfair's production at the Lyric, Hammersmith, and I always remember his rebuke when I introduced him to a friend as " the original Lockett ". " No, Stuart," he said, " not the 1728 one, if you please " ! As usual, he had a story to tell me. It was about a drunken man wandering disconsolately and very unsteadily down Piccadilly, dragging behind him a long piece of string to which nothing was attached. Presently he sees a policeman, goes up to him and, taking off his hat, asks him most politely, " Officer, can you please tell me if you have seen the Invisible Man ? Because he has stolen my dog."

. . . . .

On Sunday, 5th May, a special service in preparation for His Majesty the King's Silver Jubilee was broadcast from the concert hall, the Archbishop of Canterbury (Dr. Lang) giving the address. He looked a most imposing and venerable figure in his scarlet gown; but why use the Symphony Orchestra to accompany the choir, when the fine concert-hall organ played by Dr. Thalben Ball would have supplied all that was necessary ?

. . . . .

6th May. The Silver Jubilee. This was a long and rather tiring day, but a gloriously hot one—the King's weather.

I arrived at Broadcasting House at 9.30 a.m., and, after checking over all our plans with the engineers, and a short rehearsal at 11 a.m., I announced the broadcast of the celebrations in this country and throughout the Empire.

I began by giving a summary of our plans for the event, and ended by announcing the service in St. Paul's Cathedral at 11.30 a.m. I listened to this service, which was most impressive, and to the commentaries on the scenes along the route of the procession and outside the cathedral.

After lunch I had a rehearsal with Lawrence Gilliam for the feature in the evening, and at night I announced the Prime Minister, who spoke from the studio, and was followed at 8 p.m. by a superb broadcast by the King from Buckingham Palace. Finally I did the

Jubilee News, during which we went round the provinces, to see how they were celebrating the Jubilee.

The broadcasts of the Jubilee celebrations overseas were highly successful, and everyone seemed very pleased about them.   These lines from a Press article stand out in my memory :—

> " Broadcasting has been born during the King's reign, and it is fitting that by its aid, the remotest portions of the Empire should have been brought within the sound of the King's voice."

.   .   .   .   .

Saturday, 11*th May*.   Last day of Jubilee week.   I was on duty in the afternoon and evening.   I had arranged to go home by the 10.41 train from Charing Cross, and with great difficulty reached there in time to catch the train.   The crowds which had come to see the flood-lighting were enormous and most good-humoured. When at length I got into a carriage in which six persons were already standing, suddenly all the lights went out, and nobody knew what had caused this or when we should start.   After half an hour's wait the authorities told us that there had been a fire on Hungerford Bridge, just outside the station, and presently they shouted, " All passengers proceed to Cannon Street—no more electric trains." This was much more easily said than done, and soon I was in the thick of a seething mass of people in the station yard, some trying to get into the station, others trying to get out.   It took me over a quarter of an hour to reach the gate into the Strand.   Villiers Street was impassable, a solid phalanx of humanity, but eventually I struggled down the Strand to Trafalgar Square, and laboriously made my way to Whitehall, en route for Westminster, where I got a District train to Blackfriars, and so a train to Bickley, reaching home at 1 a.m.

.   .   .   .   .

A superb recital by Segovia, the world-famous Spanish guitarist, was broadcast from the studio on 2nd June.   He played Bach and even John Dowland, as well as Spanish music.

What a wonderful broadcasting instrument the guitar is !   One can hear every note and every gradation of tone and colour.

Remembering that Segovia liked the studio on the warm side, " It is not for me, it is for my instrument ", I had a word with Pedro

Morales, the Spanish conductor, who has lived in this country for years, and who was looking after him. He asked that the studio might be warmed up for Segovia. I therefore saw the heating engineer at eight, and by nine oclock we had raised the temperature by twelve degrees.

Segovia kept on rehearsing until just before the recital began at 9.20; at 9.15 he took off his coat. "Ah, that is a good sign," said Pedro; "he is quite happy now." The result certainly justified our efforts to make him feel comfortable and enable him to concentrate on the music.

.   .   .   .   .

3rd June. After an absence of five years, Toscanini returned to London to conduct the B.B.C. Symphony Orchestra at the Queen's Hall in the London Music Festival—an event of the greatest musical significance. What a season this was for listeners! First Heifetz, then Segovia, and afterwards Toscanini.

It was a triumph both for the orchestra and for the great man himself, who seemed delighted with the playing of the orchestra and the applause he received from the audience.

"I am very, very happy, very pleased and satisfied with everything," he said after the concert had ended.

.   .   .   .   .

On 21st June I went to the headquarters of the G.P.O. at St. Martins-le-Grand to act as one of the judges in the competition arranged by the Post Office to choose from among telephone operators the most suitable voice for announcing TIM, the new Talking Clock.

There were nine candidates, and the judges included Sybil Thorndike, Mr. John Masefield (the Poet Laureate), Mrs. E. D. Atkinson and Lord Iliffe. We had agreed to a stiff test, and listened to all the voices in turn, and did not finally decide on our choice—Miss E. W. Cain of West Croydon—until nearly two o'clock. Then we adjourned for lunch, when we met several of the G.P.O. senior officials, the Postmaster-General (Major Tryon), Sir Donald Banks, Sir G. Bennett and Sir Stephen Tallents. I returned to Broadcasting House soon after 3.30 p.m., where I had to set to and write up an account of it all for the News. I think I probably created a precedent by reading the News, which included a paragraph about the TIM competition, and then going on to give an eye-witness account of the proceedings.

.   .   .   .   .

22nd June. A programme of light music was given by Fred Hartley and his orchestra, with Brian Lawrence, the Australian vocalist, appearing for the first time with this combination. Hartley is a gifted and resourceful pianist: no wonder Sophie Dixon calls him the Toscanini of Light Music.

Later, in reading the nine o'clock News, I lost some of my accustomed morale, when I found myself incapable of pronouncing the word " Mohammedanism ", which occurred twice in the bulletin. Bernard Shaw is right when he says that in order to pronounce the word Mohammed as the Eastern peoples do, you really should be able to neigh like a horse. Why not call them Moslems, or Mussulmans, and the religion Islam, as is done in India ?

.   .   .   .   .

This being British Week at the Brussels Exhibition, it was arranged that a visit should be paid to the Exhibition by the London Philharmonic Orchestra with its conductor, Sir Thomas Beecham, and that we should broadcast part of the gala Sunday night concert from the Palais des Beaux Arts.

We knew that the British Ambassador and members of the Belgian Government were to be present, and therefore, in the presentation, took the greatest care to stress the importance of the occasion. Imagine our disappointment when, just as I was all set to announce it, a message came through to say that, owing to an unforeseen delay, it would begin late. I had to explain this to listeners and to substitute a programme of records, which continued for nearly half an hour. When at last we learned that they were ready to start in Brussels, we were naturally eager to hear what followed my opening announcement. After the usual applause for the conductor, and the playing of the British and Belgian National Anthems, the concert began. As Freddy Grisewood and I listened to the loudspeaker in the announcer's room, I at once realised that there had been an alteration in the programme. I had announced the symphonic poem " The Garden of Fand " by Arnold Bax as the first work to be played, but it was quite clear that, whatever the music was, it was not "The Garden of Fand". The music seemed familiar, but we could not give it a name. I said to Freddy, " It sounds like something the Military Band plays—some kind of overture." He agreed, and knowing that Leslie Woodgate was in his office, rang him up and asked him what it was. " The Overture to ' The Wreckers ', by Ethel Smyth," he replied. " Of course," I said, and at that very moment the telephone rang.

Now, I have heard that Arnold Bax was not particularly fond of Ethel Smyth's music. Whether this is true or not, I do not know, but what I do know is that Arnold Bax objected to this overture being announced as " The Garden of Fand ". He was too incensed to ring through himself, the voice at the other end of the telephone being that of his secretary, who said, " Dr. Arnold Bax wants to know what you mean by saying that this is his music now being played in the programme from Brussels. Please put out a correction at once."

Freddy Grisewood, who answered the 'phone, politely explained that we had not been informed of any change in the programme, and, while we regretted the error, we certainly could not interrupt the concert now that it had begun, but we would apologise at the end—which we did.

We afterwards found out that the cause of the trouble was the holding up of the orchestral scores by the Customs at Ostend. Sir Thomas Beecham decided to alter the programme at the last moment, announcing the change of programme in the hall before the broadcast began, but not telling *us* anything about it.

. . . . .

On 10th August I put out an S.O.S. in the National Programme at 11 p.m., which we afterwards heard was almost immediately successful, in spite of its being for a person on holiday in Sweden. It was for Mrs. F. C. Shelmerdine, wife of Colonel Shelmerdine, Director-General of Civil Aviation, asking her to go to a Truro nursing home, where her mother, Mrs. Haskins, was dangerously ill. This is what then followed :—

Saturday, 10th August, 11 p.m. S.O.S. broadcast from London.
12 midnight Mrs. Shelmerdine told of the S.O.S. in Sweden.

Sunday, 11th August,   3 a.m.   Went by train to Malmö, Sweden, flew to Amsterdam, then on to Croydon. Caught a train to Truro, Cornwall, reaching there on Monday morning, a journey of 1,100 miles.

.   .   .   .

The death of the B.B.C. Chairman, Lord Bridgeman, was announced in the News on 14th August. That night I had a long obituary notice about him to read—some four pages in all. I found this difficult to sustain and no little strain to read.

.   .   .   .

17*th August*. Announced Sir John Reith, who came to the studio to broadcast an appreciation of Lord Bridgeman and his work for the B.B.C. He told me that he had heard me read the obituary notice on Wednesday, 14th August, while on board his yacht off the island of Mull. He had returned from leave specially to attend the funeral to-day.

.   .   .   .

An unusual thing happened in the Proms on 28th August, a very hot night, with the usual crowded house at the Queen's Hall. Alec Whitaker was taken ill while playing the oboe obligato before Noel Eadie began singing the Bach aria, " Sighing, weeping ". We heard the tone-quality getting worse and worse, until it finally gave out altogether, and we were just able to hear Whitaker say, " Sorry . . ." After about a minute's pause, Sir Henry stopped the orchestra, and went on to the next aria. Then he went back to the aria " Sighing, weeping ", Terence McDonagh playing the obligato. At the end of the concert, just before the News, we put out an announcement explaining that Alec Whitaker had suddenly been taken ill.

.   .   .   .

On the last day of August I met Gipsy Petulengro, a most interesting person, who came in to broadcast a talk about some of the unusual things that gipsies eat : the greatest delicacy with them seems to be hedgehog pie.

I remember that when I was serving in Waziristan (the hinterland between India and Afghanistan) in 1920, one of our sentries shot a porcupine. The Pathans (who are Moslems) were delighted, and skinned it and ate it with great relish, after roasting it over a wood fire. They told me it tasted like chicken hearts. Certainly the meat looked white, like that of chicken. In talking to Petulengro, I noticed how many Hindustani words he used to describe articles in general use in this country—e.g. *nimmak* = salt; *pani* = water; *lal* = red, etc. Strong evidence of the Eastern origin of the gipsies.

On 1st September Dr. Temple (Archbishop of York) broadcast a memorable talk on " The Christian and the International Situation ". His authority and breadth of vision are most impressive; an altogether outstanding personality, and a fine broadcaster. It was a strange and melancholy fact that the Epilogue, following within a minute of such a brilliant talk on this subject, should begin with the words " Nation shall rise against nation ".

The Second News on 3rd September was full of the details of Queen Astrid's funeral, and after it had ended I broadcast an S.O.S. to doctors about a swab sent through the post to the Royal Institute of Public Health without any information as to its origin :—

> " A throat swab with no particulars of identity was received at the Royal Institute of Public Health, Queen's Square, W.C., yesterday. The culture of the swab was positive. Will the doctor who posted the swab to the Institute communicate with Terminus 4788 or Hampstead 1261 ? "

The swab was found to bear diphtheria germs, and the postmark was believed to be a London one—though this was not clear. Later in the evening we heard that the S.O.S. had been successful.

On Sunday, 8th September, I announced a hymn recital given by the Wireless Singers directed by Geoffrey Shaw, who was one of the earliest of the broadcasters to schools at Savoy Hill in the 1920's. He is a first-rate broadcaster, with a vast store of knowledge on his subject and a keen sense of humour. He talked to me about those early days when J. C. Stobart was beginning experiments in broadcasting to schools and he was an H.M.I. at the Board of Education. He also told me that he used to try to teach Sir

John Reith to play the piano when he was a small boy, adding, "He was the most argumentative boy I ever met"!

. . . .

On 4th October, Alec Templeton, the blind pianist who plays in Jack Hylton's band, and who is shortly going to America, gave a most original and entertaining programme in the studio. He has a prodigious memory and a brilliant technique, and can improvise extensively on any theme one cares to give him.

He told me that he forms a mental picture of each person he meets directly he hears him speak, and this he can express in music, just as a good portrait-painter can suggest the personality of his subject as well as his actual physical appearance. I had two friends with me in the studio, and before the broadcast, much to their delight, he at once reeled off a few chords, followed by some fast-moving passages which sounded very cheerful, and then turned to me and said, "There you are, that's you!"

. . . .

At last we have found the right person for the "Men Talking" series—a Commander Campbell, R.N.R., a man with a good broadcasting voice and a collection of sailor's yarns which must be unrivalled—spun not by the yard, but by the mile.

He was certainly most entertaining, and spoke quickly and well, without a note, and without any hesitation throughout: it was quite the most natural performance in this series as yet. He had evidently kept his eyes (and ears) open when on his travels, and profited from the experience gained in carrying out one of his former duties—that of entertaining the passengers during long evenings at sea.

. . . .

On 31st October I went to have tea at St. Dunstan's with Sir Ian and Lady Fraser to discuss the Talking Book, recordings of speech reproduced on slow-running discs, continuing for half an hour before any change of record is necessary, an invaluable aid for blind people, and an invention which has since proved very useful to us from a recording point of view.

The way Sir Ian has triumphed over blindness is wonderful. He walks about St. Dunstan's unaided, putting his hand on a rail here, a familiar wall there, without any apparent effort. He is very keen on the Talking Book, realising what a boon it would be to the blind. He wants to use voices with experience in broadcasting, and asked me to read some of the Books of the New Testament. They have their own recording studios and control room in St. Dunstan's.

.   .   .   .   .

2nd November was a disastrous evening, all the trouble being caused by bad timing : when will programme-builders learn to time their material accurately ?

It all began with permission being given by the night P.A.—programme authority on duty—allowing an orchestral concert in Maida Vale to run two and a half minutes over its scheduled time. This in turn meant a three-minutes-late start to the variety programme which followed. After the variety programme came the News Summary at 9.30 p.m., which I was to read. Will Hay was at the top of the bill, and while waiting in the studio for the signal to go ahead, I was listening to him on head-'phones and thoroughly enjoying it, when, to my horror, he was suddenly faded out, and the engineers gave me the signal that they were ready for the News. I felt so dreadful about it that I tried to make the best of a bad job by making a rather lame apology before beginning the News. The Press the next day were up in arms about the fading out, and that afternoon we published a written apology to Will Hay for the unfortunate mistake.

THE ANNOUNCER'S SPECIAL

On Saturday, 9th November, after a long day at Broadcasting House, ending at midnight, with the help of a waiting taxi I managed to get to Charing Cross station about a minute before my train was due to leave at 12.10 a.m.; and I walked past the barrier on to Platform 4, above which was displayed a board marked " Orpington and Chislehurst ". The train was not standing at the platform, but, as it was a Saturday night, when trains are sometimes a little late, I thought nothing of that. When at 12.13 I went up to the ticket-collector and asked him what had happened to the Chislehurst train, he answered with surprise, " It left from No. 2 platform on time ". This rather shook me, as of course I knew it to be the last train, and I also knew that the Orpington and Chislehurst board had been over the entrance to Platform 4 when I passed the barrier. There were five or six other passengers there bound for Orpington, who now came up and, in no uncertain terms, corroborated what I had said. As they raised their voices, along came the Inspector. They were furious with him, saying, "How are we to get home?" "We've all been fooled," "I'll report you," and that sort of thing. Realising that this would get us nowhere, and knowing that there was a train from London Bridge to Bromley about 12.45, and that I could, if necessary, walk the three and a half miles from there, I got into a train then leaving for London Bridge. While in this train I did some quick thinking, and remembered that London Bridge was the Divisional Headquarters of the railway. Arriving there, I went straight to the inspector's office and told him what had happened, beginning in a rather casual tone of voice, "Nice game at Charing Cross to-night, Inspector. Your men put up the Orpington train-board on No. 4, and then ran the train out from No. 2; and as it was the last train, I look like being stranded, unless I walk home from Bromley." He was incredulous, and said, "You must have made a mistake." No, I assured him, I had made no mistake, and, what is more, I warned him that he had better be prepared for the other angry passengers dropping in at any minute, who would not relish the walk from Bromley to Orpington at one o'clock in the morning. At this he opened his eyes wide, began to look very worried, but was obviously reluctant to take any action to put things right. I paused for a moment or two; then decided to play my trump card. "It isn't as if I had been out enjoying myself at the theatre or something," I said. "I'm B.B.C., and have been broadcasting on and off all the afternoon and evening, and am pretty tired. . . ." The three magic letters B.B.C. did the trick, and he at once decided to ring up the night controller on duty. At that moment, as I had warned him, a bunch of angry passengers from Charing Cross burst in to demand retribution. I explained that I had already forestalled them, and that the inspector was now talking to the night controller about it. We had to wait ten minutes or so while he checked up, then he sanctioned a special train, which drew into London Bridge station just after one o'clock. The guard did not seem at all pleased about this extra piece of duty. We ran non-stop to Chislehurst, and when we got there the signalman in the station box had to come down to the platform to let me out.

. . . . .

On 13th November I spent the whole afternoon going through the lists of names of the election candidates and constituencies and noting their pronunciation, obtained from official sources.

The next day was polling day, and after recording my vote, I went to Broadcasting House early for a voice test, the Controller ruling that " no one with a cold is to give out election results ".

From 10 p.m. we broadcast light music played in turn by the Victor Oloff Sextet, the Parkington Quintet and Reginald King and his orchestra, fading out of this and going over to the News studio as the results came in, and then back again.

I made the announcement about procedure at 10 p.m., and immediately afterwards results began to come in, the first being Cheltenham. Four of us—F. H. Grisewood, Harman Grisewood, Alvar Lidell and myself—did half-hour spells. A buffet was provided on the fourth floor to keep us going.

From 12 to 1.45 a.m. there was a spate of results, and Freddy Grisewood fed me, checking up the names from our official list beforehand—a great help. Then we changed places and I fed him. After about 2 a.m. things quietened down and then petered out. I caught the 3.13 train home from Blackfriars, travelling with Fleet Street men reading the first editions of the morning papers.

. . . . .

On 24th November John Barbirolli was the guest conductor of the B.B.C. Symphony Orchestra in a studio concert, which included a performance of the Concerto No. 3 in G for violin and orchestra by Mozart, the soloist being Eda Kersey.

The work was given a fine performance, and I was particularly struck by the long and difficult cadenza, which was obviously not written by Mozart. I had a word with Eda Kersey afterwards about it, and she told me that " though it may sound difficult, as a matter of fact it is quite violinistic; Albert Sammons wrote it for me ".

. . . . .

In this Jubilee year the title of the main Christmas Day programme at 2.30 p.m. was " This Great Family ". I had the honour of announcing His Majesty, who was speaking from Sandringham. He spoke superbly, being so homely, simple and direct; it was a most moving talk from the Head of " this Great Family ".

1936

*I*ST JANUARY. Letter from an old friend, a journalist, who knows Canada and America well, and is now the editor of a famous paper. He listened to the Christmas Day broadcast, and wrote to me in glowing terms about our efforts, and went on to say "The King's age is now most noticeable in his radio voice, but he retains the touch".

. . . . .

THE KING'S ILLNESS AND DEATH

15th January. Official announcement from Sandringham broadcast in the News that the King had a cold due to the severe wintry weather, and was confined to his room.

17th January. First intimation that the King was ill—i.e. that it was something more than a cold. First bulletin issued from Sandringham broadcast, which referred to "bronchial catarrh, and signs of cardiac weakness . . . regarded with some disquiet".

18th January. Read second General News, which contained more serious news of the King . . . "anxiety persists", said an official statement. Sir John Reith, C. G. Graves (Controller of Programmes) and Lindsay Wellington (Director of Programme Planning) all decided to remain standing by over the week-end; special arrangements made for "shifts" of announcers to be available for broadcasting bulletins.

19th January. During the afternoon and evening, bulletins were broadcast saying that there was no change in His Majesty's condition. Sir John Reith ruled that a prayer for His Majesty should be included in the Epilogue, and that Dr. Iremonger (not myself) was to read it—"It must not be done by a layman", he said. Sir Walford Davies took charge of the music of the Epilogue.

20th January. The morning bulletin about the King was: "A more restful night; no substantial change to report". We repeated this prior to all programmes until just before the News at eight minutes to six, when a new bulletin came in—which was broadcast at once—stating that " the condition of His Majesty shows diminishing strength ". An obvious warning to be prepared for the worst.

This bulletin was repeated from 6 p.m. onwards; later, in view of its gravity, we cancelled the variety and all similar programmes.

At 9.25 came the gravest bulletin of all. This was broadcast at 9.38, after a warning announcement at 9.35 that it was coming. The bulletin ran : " The King's life is moving peacefully towards its close ". Then I repeated it, and added, " We invite you to join

RUSH KING.

9.25 FULL BULLETIN.

"THE KINGS LIFE IS MOVING PEACEFULLY TODWARDS ITS CLOSE

SIGNED FREDERIC WILLANS, STANLEY HEWETT, DAWSON OF PENN"

THE 9.25 P.M. BULLETIN AS IT CAME OVER ON THE TAPE MACHINE

in recollection and prayer for our King ". I repeated this bulletin each quarter of an hour until midnight; then I read a special announcement saying that the B.B.C. would remain open, Big Ben going out at the quarter hours, any announcements to be made to be given out then.

At 12.10 we had the sad news, and at 12.15 Sir John Reith made the final announcement, as follows :—

> " It is with great sorrow that we make the following announcement : King George V is dead.
> " We voice the grief of all the people of his Empire, we offer profound sympathy to Her Majesty the Queen, and the Royal Family. With our fellow-citizens at home and overseas, we affirm our loyalty to the Crown."

The following official bulletin came in only a minute after Sir John's announcement :—

> "Death came peacefully to the King at 11.55 p.m. to-night, in the presence of Her Majesty the ·Queen, the Prince of Wales, the Duke of York, the Princess Royal and the Duke and Duchess of Kent."

At about 12.30 a.m. a Sidcup listener rang up and offered to drive me home to Chislehurst—a very kind thought.

. . . . .

21st January. I was so tired the next morning that I did not wake up until after nine o'clock. I did not go to Broadcasting House until the late afternoon. Meanwhile normal programmes were suspended except for the Service and Weather Forecasts, and Big Ben, which was broadcast every quarter of an hour until 9.30. To London in the late afternoon to read special News bulletin later at 8 p.m., including messages from the new King to the three Services, and details of the funeral arrangements. At 9.30 I announced the Prime Minister, Mr. Baldwin, who spoke superbly about the late King. He began :—

> "After he had served his own generation, by the will of God, he fell asleep and was laid unto his fathers ".

His talk was followed by the Epilogue.

. . . . .

25th January. News full of descriptions of the vast queue at Westminster Hall, and the lying-in-state.

. . . . .

26th January. At 7.15 I went to see Dr. Iremonger about the announcement of the memorial service in the concert hall at 7.55 p.m., and found him arguing with Sir Walford Davies about a setting of some of Milton's words, which Vaughan Williams had specially written for this service, to be sung by the choir before the Dead March.

> "Nothing is here for tears, nothing to wail . . .
> . . . nothing but well and fair
> And what may quiet us in a death so noble."

Sir Walford said Vaughan Williams insisted on my reading the words before they were sung, or else cancelling them. Iremonger, with an eye on the clock, said the reading would take one and a half minutes. To clear up the *impasse* I eventually found Graves (Controller of Programmes), who said, "Go ahead". Despite under-rehearsal, the programme seemed to go reasonably well. (There was an audience of 500 in the concert hall.) The Archbishop was superb, very impressive, and the Wireless Singers, under Sir Walford, surpassed themselves.

On 27th January I announced "King George V in Memory", a tribute in poetry and music arranged by R. Ellis Roberts and produced by Robin Whitworth, which was simple, dignified and graphic. To quote just one sentence :—

" He spoke and the people listened, for his words were
homely words, spoken from the heart to the home."

28th January. The King's funeral. Left Chislehurst for London at 8 a.m. There were twenty-two people in my carriage from London Bridge to Charing Cross. Huge crowds everywhere on the route. I announced details of the broadcast at 9.15 a.m. The Pipes at St. James' Palace were most moving. What a tug they can give to one's heart-strings !

I also put out an announcement at 12.45, saying that the royal train was half-an-hour late, and again at 1.15 p.m., when we heard that it had reached Windsor. The final announcement was at 2.33 p.m., stating that " broadcasting will cease until to-morrow morning, except for the Shipping Forecast at 11 p.m., and for Big Ben at 6 p.m. and 9.30 p.m."

29th January. I read Queen Mary's " Message to the Nation " in the Regional News at 9 p.m., and again later in the National News Summary.

15th February was memorable for Bob Bowman's brilliant commentary on the Ice Hockey International, Great Britain *v.* America, at Garmisch-Partenkirchen. Bob is a Canadian who was lent to us for a few months by the Canadian Broadcasting Cor- poration. He knows the game backwards, and put out a quick-fire commentary of this, the fastest game in the world, with amazing efficiency, and with most amusing descriptions of the fearless tackling by both sides, the "upper cuts and rib-roasting" which went on in front of the British goal. He certainly knows how to put over concentrated excitement, and is never at a loss for the name of a player or a picturesque phrase to describe the play, however fast it rushes along.

. . . . .

On 18th February I announced Ernst von Dohnanyi, the eminent Hungarian composer and pianist, and learnt from his own lips that when pronouncing his name the stress is on the Doh.

He played Mozart, Beethoven and his own Rhapsody in C, Opus 11, No. 3, a work requiring immense technique. I had not heard him for some years, and I got the impression that the programme was almost too much for him. This was borne out by what he himself said later on : " I am always asked to play my own works," he said, " but I do not like to do so now; they are so difficult " !

. . . . .

On 24th February another great artist, Charles Tournemire, the French organist, gave an effortless exhibition of organ-playing in the concert hall of Broadcasting House. He is famed for his improvisations, and it was arranged that he should be asked to improvise on a theme by Sir Walford Davies, given to him during the recital. I explained what was going to happen. He would be heard opening the sealed envelope near the microphone, and would then play the theme named. After a pause, he began to improvise brilliantly on this theme, and I noticed, to my surprise, that his assistant, who was there to turn over for him, did all the setting of the stops—he walked from side to side, pressing a coupler here, a group of stops there, while the great man played. Never had I seen such a practical example of " Two minds with but a single thought ".

. . . . .

On Sunday, 22nd March, I announced " Melodies of Christendom " in the concert hall, given by Sir Walford Davies and the Wireless Singers (now the B.B.C. Singers), with Dr. Thalben-Ball at the organ. It was a splended Sunday night programme, which ended with some of the St. Matthew Passion music by Bach, finely sung by the B.B.C. Singers. Such was Sir Walford's passionate desire to achieve as near perfection as possible, that even this performance did not satisfy him, and as he said good night he added, "And I do wish it had been better". All meant, of course, in the spirit of the true artist; but the singers, after their strenuous evening, were not pleased.

William Byrd's music was being sung that week in the Foundations Series, by the B.B.C. Singers. The words of one work were so simple and beautiful that I made a note of them :—

> "How vain the toils that mortal men do take
> To hoard up gold that time doth turn to dross,
> Forgetting Him who only for their sake
> His precious blood did shed upon the Cross.
> And taught us all in Heaven to hoard our treasure
> Where true increase doth grow above all measure."
>
> (From Byrd's "Psalms, Songs and Sonnets", 1611.)

On 8th April Lord Macmillan was giving the National Lecture at 8.15 p.m., taking as his subject "Law and the Citizen". He was speaking at a meeting of the Royal Philosophical Society of Glasgow, and it was announced as an Outside Broadcast from that station.

Soon after he had started speaking, the quality of his speech began to deteriorate, and became worse and worse. After about five minutes the broadcast ended abruptly, and we in London could not find out the reason for the failure. Eventually, with the help of the Post Office line engineers, our own engineers rectified matters at 8.33 p.m., following an apology for the break, put out by me, explaining that the delay was due to line trouble.

It was unfortunate that a National Lecture, given by a speaker of such eminence as Lord Macmillan, should be interrupted in this way, as, though one picked up the thread of his argument later, far too much was lost at the beginning; no doubt many listeners switched off during the break and did not switch on again. The moral at that time seemed to be to try to avoid long land-line connections to the transmitters when broadcasting an important speech.

The following week I took part in an interesting radio experiment—a programme written by Herbert Farjeon and produced by M. H. Allen, entitled "London Calling 1600", described by the author as "an impression, a conjecture, a shot in the dark at what listeners might have heard had broadcasting been invented in the reign of Queen Elizabeth ". One heard " Greensleeves " instead of jazz; the News, including the latest report about the fall of the Earl of Essex; discussions in Elizabethan prose—great care having been taken about Elizabethan pronunciation—about tobacco, about precautions to avoid the plague; songs to lute accompaniment, a running commentary on a bear-baiting, and an Outside Broadcast of " Twelfth Night " from the Globe Theatre.

A critic wrote later, " Surely this was one of the occasions when radio, with triumphant success, was doing one of the things it does better than the stage, the film or the novel, completely and uniquely stuff for its own medium ". As far as I know, this programme has never been repeated.

.   .   .   .   .

An announcers' meeting was held at 4.45 on 22nd April to hear an address by Professor Lloyd James of London University, who for some years has been our adviser in phonetics, and was also Secretary of the B.B.C. Pronunciation Committee on Spoken English. He was recently returned from America, where he had been on University and B.B.C. business, and he gave us a most instructive account of his three months' tour in that country. He made one startling point, when he told us that the American Universities regarded broadcasting in America as having no cultural value at all, but looked upon the programmes put out by the various networks solely as instruments for selling goods.

.   .   .   .   .

Early on the morning of 24th April Lord Mottistone was due to take part in a special Lifeboat Feature programme to the Empire. At 11 p.m., feeling rather tired after a long rehearsal, he came down to the drawing-room for some refreshment. Unfortunately, he had been told some years ago by Lord Dawson of Penn—who was frequently mentioned in the conversation that followed—that it was extremely injudicious for him to drink spirits before speaking in public, and presumably this advice also held good for broadcasting. In consequence, Lord Mottistone was unable to accept the Corporation's proffered hospitality in the form of whisky or brandy, and asked if some port could be obtained.

Now, this was a slightly embarrassing position, but after some difficulty, a bottle of port was procured from the Langham Hotel, half-an-hour elapsing before the bottle *and* the corkscrew materialised.

In the meantime his lordship was becoming more and more in need of sustenance, and even offered to pay for the port himself or, alternatively, to go over to the Langham and fetch it in person. Both offers were, of course, politely declined on the grounds of courtesy and in the major interests of the Corporation.

The suggestion that port is good for the throat is evidently not a pure fairy story, and perhaps, after Lord Mottistone's experience, in future a decanter of port will always be available in the drinks cupboard for distinguished guests.

. . . . . .

26th April. Yesterday being the twenty-first anniversary of the landing at Gallipoli, we broadcast a commemoration programme compiled by Val Gielgud from the official History of the War and contemporary writers. It was a tribute to the memory of

" Those who died before Byzantium
To save the fishy straits of the sea;
Men swift in the work of war."

. . . . .

On 4th May I announced a recital of songs by Gretchaninov, sung by Tatiana Makushina, which was to have been accompanied by the composer, but, as his wife was taken ill, he was unable to come.

It was a most interesting collection of songs about the Russian countryside, superbly sung in Russian, but it ended too early, and I had to go to another studio to fill up after Madame Tatiana had repeated one of the songs.

I had hoped to hear from the composer's lips how he pronounced his name, but as he did not come I asked Madame Tatiana where the stress fell. This was her reply : " Some say Grĕtchănĭnōv, some say Grētchănĭnŏv, and others says Grĕtchānĭnŏv "—which was not very helpful.

Some two weeks later I announced a song recital given by one of the great names in music—Madame Blanche Marchesi, famous as a singer and as a teacher of singing. What personality this old lady had, what vivacity, and what skill ! Edwin Evans, the music critic, who introduced her, told listeners that she was seventy-three.

Though she had not much actual voice left, what there was, was of excellent quality and most skilfully controlled. To be able to sing a recital of songs ranging from the sixteenth century to the present day (including "Amarilli" by Caccini, a song that takes a great deal of singing when one is young and has plenty of breath to spare), at the age of seventy-three, and to phrase properly, as she did, was a triumph.

. . . . .

22nd May. We broadcast the departure of R.M.S. *Queen Mary* on her maiden voyage to New York, a superb piece of outside broadcasting. The stentorian tones of her siren could be heard as she left the dockside, and the cheers and shouts of "Good luck" from the thousands who had gone down to see the great ship leave.

. . . . .

The Sunday Orchestral Concert at 9.30 p.m. that week, conducted by Dr. Adrian Boult, included the rhapsody "A Shropshire Lad", by George Butterworth, the brilliant young composer who, to the great loss of English music, was killed in action during the First World War. It is a particular favourite of mine, as is the song "Loveliest of Trees", on which it is based. It is a work that breathes the spirit of the English countryside in a most wonderful way.

A lone figure sat at one end of the balcony that night; it was the composer's father, who had come up from the country especially to hear this performance of his son's masterpiece.

. . . . .

Having completed ten years' service with the Corporation, I was given three months' grace leave, and seized the opportunity of taking my wife on a short visit to Canada and America.

I had determined to try to forget all about Radio, but having arrived in Ottawa, I was discovered by the Station Director, the studios being on the top floor of the great Chateau Laurier Hotel, where we were staying. He asked me to come upstairs, and kindly showed me the studios and explained some of their problems, the most serious being competition from American stations; some of these were very powerful, and broadcast programmes of excellent quality. Then there was the problem of the vast distances to be spanned, and the consequent differences in time, which were most complex. They were then broadcasting a Dominion Day programme from London, which came over well, and as it ended

I heard Dance Music announced coming from the Banff Springs Hotel in the Rockies. I remember how impressed I was by the Director's statement that it was farther from Ottawa to Banff overland than it was from London to Ottawa, a journey which had just taken me a week in a Cunard liner.

.   .   .   .   .

We approached New York from Albany by paddle-steamer on the Hudson river, which gave us fine views of the pleasant rolling countryside and the Catskill Mountains; we also passed West-point Military Academy and the famous Sing-Sing prison en route.

Arrived at New York, I went to Radio City, Headquarters of the National Broadcasting Company, a very imposing building, sixty-four stories high, with most impressive arcades of shops on the ground floor, but, in spite of the size, at that time the National Broadcasting Company was occupying only the first ten floors, the remainder being let.

I was welcomed most cordially by the Programme Director, given tickets for the Radio City Music-Hall, and later taken round the studios, all of which were ventilated with an elaborate " conditioned air " system, as in Broadcasting House, the walls being made of glass, to enable visitors being conducted round the corridors to watch broadcasts in progress.

A series of exhibits were on view showing the history of development of radio in America, including models of transmitters and some of the early apparatus. All day long parties were conducted round the exhibits and studios, because, as nearly all the programmes are sponsored, everyone was a potential purchaser of time-on-the-air. I noticed that the studios were mostly on the small size, all effects used being produced in the actual studio, not, as in Broadcasting House at that time, in a special effects studio, there being a mixer-unit in the Listening Room outside. The conditioned-air unit, with its sixty-four large dials, was as impressive as the system was efficient ; I was told that it was possible to raise the temperature of a studio eight degrees in as many minutes, if required.

The large auditorium studio was very fine, with its extensive stage flanked by huge red curtains, the whole being most tastefully decorated. The microphones were the only indication that it was designed principally as a broadcasting studio, and not as an ordinary concert-hall. It, too, was surrounded by glass sound-proof walls, so that parties being escorted round could watch without actually going inside.

Later, after going to the top of the Empire State Building, 1248 feet high, feeling it sway slightly in the wind, and admiring the superb view of the city below, I visited the Columbia Broadcasting System's Headquarters, and was shown round by Mr. Baruch, one of the announcers. I met several of the programme staff and engineers. Only ten studios were then in use on twenty floors of a great building, the lay-out being similar to that of the National Broadcasting Company.

. . . . .

On 4th October I went to the Maida Vale studios for the first time since I came back from America, and found the large Orchestral studio (No. 1) completely transformed. Instead of all members of the orchestra being on the studio floor, a tiered staging had been erected, as in the Queen's Hall. This proved of great help to the conductor and ensured a better balance of the instruments. An Elgar concert given by the London Symphony Orchestra was being conducted by Dr. Adrian Boult, with W. H. Reed leading and Henry Holst playing the violin concerto. I spoke to Willy Reed about the concerto, knowing him to have been the friend and confidant of the composer, but he was not very helpful, stressing the enigmatic way in which Elgar always spoke about his own works.

. . . . .

During that week there was included in the News a comic paragraph about an American bird I had never heard of before—the " yellow-bellied sap-sucker " of Utica, New York. The bird in question is apparently slowly but surely pecking down a man's house. The house is a wooden-frame one, and the sap-sucker has pecked holes clean through the wall. He is a small black-and-white bird with a yellow belly—not a wood-pecker, mark you, but a sap-sucker.

. . . . .

On 20th October I spoke at a luncheon at Stationer's Hall in the City. When I returned to Broadcasting House, I found a telephone message awaiting me asking me to ring Inspector Rawlings at Tottenham Court Road police station. Everyone was filled with inquisitiveness. "What have you been up to, Stuart?" they asked. I could think of nothing at all exciting that had happened to me recently, so I rang Inspector Rawlings to find out what he wanted. He was most pleasant and apologetic, and said that he had rung up on a routine check, because they had had two inquiries from the Brighton police to the effect that a woman, who said she was my wife, had ordered a fur coat costing forty guineas at a local store, and had told them to " send the bill to my husband, Stuart Hibberd, at Broadcasting House ". The same woman had also been staying at an hotel there, and had referred the management to me when it came to settling the bill.

"Is that all right, sir?" asked the Inspector.

I said : " All right? No, it is not all right. You had better ask my wife at Bickley what she thinks about it. A fine trick to play on a man ! I have never been to Brighton in my life, and know nobody there. Please ask the Brighton police to put a stop to it at once."

Luckily, the local firm had not parted with the fur coat; but what happened in the case of the hotel I never heard. Some days later I learned from the police that the poor woman had been taken in an ambulance to a mental home. I had my leg pulled unmercifully about this incident. My friend Barbara Godwin, who joined the Programme staff about the same time as I did, said, " What a fine idea ! I think I shall now order a fur coat and tell them to send the bill to the Director-General."

.   .   .   .   .

A note appeared in an evening paper on 10th November about the test held to choose two new London announcers. There were more than a thousand applicants for the job, and this number was reduced to twenty, all of whom were candidates at the test.

It was a severe examination under studio conditions before a microphone, the Board being presided over by Professor Lloyd James. The two successful candidates later went to the Staff Training College for a general course, following which, after special tuition by Professor Lloyd James, they joined the London announcing staff.

.   .   .   .   .

On the 23rd I heard that Harman Grisewood was shortly leaving us to become an assistant to the Director of Programme Planning. A most depressing piece of news for me, as he was one of the best announcers we had ever had, most talented and experienced, with a fine voice, and a good brain, too.

I know of no person who can compare with him in certain aspects of broadcasting, such as the reading of a Shakespeare sonnet, or fine prose in serious vein.

I felt so strongly about this, after years of spade-work building up a first-class team, that I decided to take the matter up and protest about it. It seemed to be farcical that, on the one hand, we should go to endless trouble to comb the country in an endeavour to find new announcers of merit, while, on the other, having got a first-class performer—a real artist in words—we calmly let him leave the microphone to transfer to an office job. For every four hundred men who could do the office job, planning, administration, etc., etc., I very much doubt if you would find one with the voice, personality and brain—note the order in which I refer to these three things—of Harman Grisewood.

If he is so good—as I maintain he is—why not reward him with a salary commensurate with his worth—pay him twice the salary I am receiving, if you like, as long as you keep him at the microphone—rather than let him go to become a back-room boy ? Such, briefly, was my argument. But it was of no avail; I was over-ruled and we lost him. (He is now—1950—Controller of the Third Programme.)

.   .   .   .   .

30th November. During the reading of the nine o'clock News a report came in, and was rushed to the News studio and put in front of me, just off the tape, that the Crystal Palace was on fire, and burning fiercely.

Having broadcast this report, we added a caveat, asking people not to go near the fire, because of increasing the difficulties of the police and firemen. In spite of this warning, huge crowds soon gathered to see the conflagration, seriously hampering the firemen in their work and badly congesting the roads. The fire was at its height about 8.30 p.m., and went on burning for hours. Later in the evening we broadcast further accounts of its progress, and finally an eye-witness description from a house nearby.

LORD REITH

VICE-ADMIRAL SIR CHARLES CARPENDALE
(The Controller)

This is yet another example of how swiftly a broadcast announcement can produce a mass psychological reaction.

· · · ·

When going up to London the following day by train, my eye caught the headlines of an illustrated paper which two girls opposite to me were reading : " King wants to marry Mrs. Simpson ".
This was the first time I had seen that lady's name mentioned in print in this country. When I got to London I found the evening papers had her photograph, with this news, on the outside page. But nothing was mentioned about her in our News bulletin.

· · · ·

On 4th December I read several News bulletins, one of which included the Prime Minister's statement made to clear up misunderstandings—viz., that if His Majesty married Mrs. Simpson she would be Queen. Everybody seemed to be talking about the crisis. The Archbishop of Canterbury made a statement, pleading for no reference to the crisis from pulpits on Sunday.

· · · ·

7th December. There was still no news about the crisis, except a statement made by the Prime Minister, which I put out in the 6 p.m. News, that the King had not yet come to a decision, and one from Mrs. Simpson stating that she was willing to withdraw from a situation which had become unhappy and untenable.

· · · ·

THE ABDICATION

The papers on 9th December were full of rumours of abdication. Harman Grisewood rang me just before lunch to say that it was obviously abdication, and asked if I would come in and put out a statement at 4 p.m. Arrived at Broadcasting House, I found all my department waiting in our common room on the fourth floor, listening for the expected statement. The timing had been put forward, and it was read by Alvar Lidell at 3.30 p.m., all stations joining us for it.
A special bulletin was issued at approximately a quarter to five—which I read—giving Mr. Baldwin's speech and the King's statement. The bulletin took almost half an hour to read. Freddy Grisewood read the 6 p.m. News, I read the 7 p.m. bulletin (forty-

one minutes of it), and Freddy the 9 p.m. News, which took nearly an hour.

Large crowds gathered in Downing Street and outside Buckingham Palace and 145 Piccadilly, the home of the Duke and Duchess of York.

.   .   .   .   .

11*th December*. Abdication of King Edward VIII announced in the Press. *The Times* said, " Don't call it Romance; call it rather Grand Drama."

That night at 10 p.m. the King spoke from Windsor Castle, Sir John Reith introducing him as follows : " This is Windsor Castle. His Royal Highness Prince Edward." He sounded very worn and sad, and spoke with difficulty for about seven minutes, ending : " And now we all have a new King. I wish him and you, his people, happiness and prosperity with all my heart. God bless you all. God save the King." After this, following a long pause, I closed down.

.   .   .   .   .

KING GEORGE VI'S ACCESSION

All ordinary programmes were altered, and we broadcast the proclamation of the new King from both St. James's Palace and Canada. I did the linking announcements, on a cue from the producer, as all three points of origin were linked to the panel. We then went over to de Lotbinière (O.B. Director) in Hyde Park. He was excellent. His timing was marvellous. He always managed to sandwich in his comments so that they began directly after one gun had fired and ended just before the next, ten seconds later. From Hyde Park we went over to Ottawa to hear the proclamation read by the Prime Minister, Mr. Mackenzie King.

.   .   .   .   .

13*th December* (*Sunday*). At the service in the concert hall the Archbishop of Canterbury gave the address, stating concisely and frankly the Church's point of view about the crisis. It was a memorable occasion, and I can see him now in his scarlet gown, a venerable, motionless figure, sitting at the desk reading his address (I was on the platform above him), and can hear the rise and fall of his voice as he repeats the words : " The pity of it ! oh, the pity of it !" He also included a tribute to the Prime Minister, who, " with great courage, took the whole burden on himself ".

.   .   .   .   .

25th December. The main programme was " Music for Christmas " at 9.20 p.m.—Christmas fireside music from many different parts of the British Isles. We went round the Regions from Wales to Scotland. It was all quite good and well thought out, but for Christmas night I felt I wanted something much more light-hearted —say ten minutes of Tommy Handley or Leonard Henry—in the middle to liven things up.

.   .   .   .   .

Boxing Day. Frank Bridge conducted a concert in Maida Vale studio No. 1, which included the " Songs of the Sea " by Stanford, sung by Harold Williams and the B.B.C. Men's Chorus.

The position of the choir was unusual. They were facing the soloist and the orchestra, the conductor having his back towards them, as he faced the orchestra, with the result that there were virtually two conductors—Harold Williams conducting the choir, and Frank Bridge the orchestra. No doubt the reason was that in this way it was possible to obtain a really good balance. The broadcast went well, in actual fact, but it might have been anything but satisfactory.

.   .   .   .   .

29th December. I received a pathetic letter from an Essex widow, who wrote to me from a sick bed, saying that she had been seriously ill for three weeks, and, having no pension, had nothing to live on except what the relieving officer allowed her, plus the few shillings her out-of-work son of eighteen was able to earn doing a temporary job as a van-boy. They both appeared to be in a bad way, with very little food, the boy being most depressed, and threatening to take his life. She wrote to me, as I was announcing " Unto Us", asking, " Does anyone care ? I have yet to find anyone who does."

I rang the district nurse, who at once went along to see her, and wrote two days later to tell me that the British Legion were going to look after her. Thank Heaven for the British Legion ! A very sad case.

1937

IST JANUARY. I began the year by receiving a most amusing anonymous letter, which shows that to some members of the community, announcers (male variety) have a utility value of a very special kind. This is what it said :—

> "We often wonder if you realise what a unique position you fill in a thoroughly female household (even the cat and dog are female). It is nearly that of husbands—we cull many of our ideas from you—and though at times it is excruciatingly tantalizing not to be able to argue with you, we feel you are positively our own—of the family.
>
> "It is devastating to go to another female's household and hear you holding forth, in just the same semi-affectionate way you do at home; it seems positively *unfaithful*, but we try to forgive and forget. You are admirable substitutes for husbands, in fact models; never late, never worrying if dinner is late, always at home in the evening, never bad tempered, generally fairly cheerful and delightfully Victorian. Anyway you have two quite devoted and grateful friends whom you can never hear. We always say, 'Good night . . . Good night' to you.
>
> "Wish I could sign my name, but after this frankness . . . excuse me ! "

.   .   .   .   .

On 10th January at 4 p.m. John Hilton gave the first of a series of talks on gambling. He was one of the few really outstanding performers at the microphone; a good brain, a ready wit, he put into practice *all* the basic rules of good broadcasting, being completely natural, and blessed with a clear, well-modulated speaking voice, which he used cleverly to praise or censure, as the case might be. He had a great fund of human sympathy, and a readiness to hold out a genuine helping hand to those down on their luck or in need.   He always treated the microphone as if he were speaking to a person or a family seated opposite him in the studio, and there was never any mass psychology behind his approach.

On this occasion, under the title of " Why I Bet ", he put himself in the position of the ordinary man-in-the-street, and analysed the reasons for betting, and the motives behind them.   He was so human and forthright.   There was never any nonsense about him, and his advice was always sound.   He was a most lovable person who never spared himself, because he was too busy trying to help other people, and consequently was generally badly overworked. Mary O'Farrell told me she adored him, so, doubtless, did thousands more.

.   .   .   .   .

This week we lost another of our regular staff, also a first-class performer.   Freddy Grisewood was seconded to do special work for music, outside broadcasts and television.   In view of what I wrote about the profession of announcing when his cousin Harman left us the previous year, the remarks of a well-known Radio critic are worth noting.   There was, however, one saving grace in Freddy's case : he is still heard by listeners—he has not become a back-room boy.

"I cannot understand [said the critic] the B.B.C.'s policy about announcers.   With one voice they profess to attach great importance to the whole theory of announcing, yet with another they make it impossible for the best men to keep the job, when they have become expert at it.

"Is announcing either important or difficult ?   In my opinion it is both.   A good announcer can make or mar a programme, and it is not easy to speak an English which will satisfy without irritating; to be multilingual; to be a monument of tact; to be capable of dealing with all sorts of emergencies; to be satisfied with getting no credit, little thanks and inadequate pay.   The Americans go to the other extreme, and allow their announcers to earn fabulous salaries—and yet why not ?   If they can attract listeners, why not encourage them to do so ?   The effect of present policy will inevitably be to discourage the best

type of man from ever attempting announcing as a career;
if he does it at all, it will only be as a stepping-stone to
other jobs."

.   .   .   .   .

It was early in January 1937 that British music sustained a great
loss in the sudden death of Harold Samuel, the pianist. He was
only fifty-seven when he died from heart trouble, worn out from
overwork and almost continuous travelling. I had known him for
many years as a fine pianist, a man with a well-stored mind and a
great sense of humour. He was most good-natured, and knew
everyone in the artistic world, and was, I am sure, generally admired
and respected by all with whom he came in contact.

A superb Bach and Beethoven player, with a monumental
memory, he was a tremendously hard worker, who obviously
enjoyed life and took a delight in giving pleasure to other people.
I shall always remember him chatting away to me in the Military
Band studio in Broadcasting House just before a recital, playing the
big C sharp minor fugue from the first Book of the 48, while the
engineers were checking up the balance. He turned towards me
and talked, not appearing to be concentrating on what he was
playing, but doing it automatically, and yet all the time that glorious
music was pouring forth from the piano. The engineers, having
satisfied themselves that there was nothing wrong with the balance,
were enjoying both the music and his stories.

I was so glad to see that some years after his death Herbert
Howells included in his charming book of musical portraits,
" Lambert's Clavicord ", a musical picture of him, called " Samuel's
Air ", a living memorial to a great artist.

.   .   .   .   .

At the request of de Lotbinière (" Lobby " to all his friends),
Director of Outside Broadcasting, I agreed to help him in his
broadcast of some of the attractions at the Olympia Circus, by having
my hand read by a lady palmist in one of the side shows. She was
not told who I was, but was requested to read " a man's hand " and
tell the listeners what she saw in it. " Lobby ", in another corner
of her tent, on a separate microphone but out of earshot, had told
listeners what was going to happen and who the victim was. At a

given signal he switched over to our microphone, and the broadcast started.

She asked me for my right hand, and, taking it and looking at it for a few seconds, began by saying that I had had three careers, two having been interrupted—the third was the one I was now in; that I had surgeon's hands, and asked if I had ever studied medicine ? (I had read Physiology amongst other things at Cambridge ; at the end of my second year came the war, and I joined the Army.)

She then went on to say that I had a good life and protection line, and that I should stay on in my present profession until my middle fifties, when I should take up a hobby I had always wanted to do. She said that I was happily married—much more so than I should have been had I married either of the other two—that I had no family and was fond of outdoor pursuits.

Now, all this was so true that I began to wonder what was coming next. She seemed to know more about me than I myself remembered, or cared to remember; and now all this was public property.

The broadcast was considered to be a great success, if a bit of an ordeal for me, and after it was over I relaxed and went round the fun fair and enjoyed myself.

I believe Madame X (or whatever she calls herself) stertill advises the fact that it was *she* who was chosen to read my hand, and broadcast what she saw in it to the great British public, at the Olympia Circus of 1937.

.   .   .   .   .

It was in January that I announced two famous Frenchmen in one week, the first being Bètove, the comedian, who gave a most entertaining show with the Theatre Orchestra. He sat down at the piano and began mimicking artists singing in different languages, imitating them and making fun of their tricks. Then he did some of his well-known " pastiches ", à la Wagner, Rossini, etc. The Rossini one, in which the speed of the " William Tell " motif at the end was terrific, was extremely funny.

The second Frenchman was M. Stèphan, a great teacher and an inspiring broadcaster, and an old and very dear friend. Generally the gentlest of men, he held forth about the Talks Department having turned down his manuscript for Madame de Bioncourt on " Les

Revendications de la femme française" at the last moment, after having sat on it for no less than six weeks

"I will go out and get drunk to-night," he said furiously, speaking with great emphasis. The very last thing I could ever imagine him doing.

. . . . .

On 16th February C. C. Gaddum, talking to schools in the "Round the Countryside" series, was most interesting about Brock the badger. He told us how shy badgers were, and how, in order to observe them, he once climbed a tree above a badger's holt and waited for Brock to come out. After a long wait he was eventually rewarded, but things did not go according to plan. Brock came out and looked nervously round, sniffed the air and then began to dig up a bees' nest at the foot of the tree, with the result that the bees angrily flew out, and took vengeance on the wretched Gaddum sitting in the tree, and stung him in six places. He managed to stick it out by taking off his coat and wrapping it round his head and shoulders, but it was a most uncomfortable half-hour or so. This all took place near Bracknell in Berkshire. I knew that Brock was mainly a vegetarian, but I did not know how fond he was of honey.

. . . . .

Just before 4.30 p.m. on 28th February I put out this S.O.S. for assistance to be sent to a vessel in distress off the Yorkshire coast :—

"Vessel in distress N.N.E. off Huntcliffe, East Yorkshire. Impossible to communicate with life-saving authorities. Will any person hearing this message in the neighbourhood of Saltburn, East Yorkshire, inform the coastguards and life-saving authorities?"

The message had come from the coastguard station at Blyth, Northumberland, which had been unable to get into touch with the Saltburn coastguards, because of telephone-line trouble. Many people hearing the S.O.S. rang up the Redcar lifeboat station, and the ship, a Spanish vessel, was eventually taken in tow by two tugs.

. . . . .

Early in March I went to the Imperial Studios, Wardour Street, to do some speech-recording on four reels of the film "Our Royal

Heritage ". When I arrived, I found John Reynders and his orchestra in the stuffy little studio rehearsing. The atmosphere was dreadful, and the heat appalling. I had to speak in a small box, with Millar, the camera-man, at my side watching the film and giving me cues when to speak and when to stop—the orchestra playing in the studio the whole time. It was just like being in the control-room telephone-box in Studio 1, Savoy Hill, in the old days—a box within a box, in fact. We began at 9.20, and did well to get all four reels finished by 2.45, by which time I was quite ready for lunch.

. . . . . .

1st April. I announced the concert of the Royal Philharmonic Society at the Queen's Hall, given by the London Philharmonic Orchestra, leader David McCallum, and the Philharmonic Choir, conductor Sir Thomas Beecham.

The concert included the first performance of " Flourish for a Coronation " by Vaughan Williams, and in Part Two, Elgar's Symphony No. 1.

The programme began five minutes early, because the Duke and Duchess of Kent arrived at 8.25, but in spite of this Sir Thomas was twenty minutes late at the end of Part 1, and the concert continued to run twenty minutes late until the end !

. . . . . .

On 9th April there was a most interesting outside broadcast from Carshalton in Surrey, consisting of a demonstration of fire-walking, as carried out in India. Harman Grisewood was down there, and described first the preparations, and afterwards the fire-walking by an Indian named Ahmed Hussein. He told us how a narrow trench had been dug and filled with brushwood, which was then set on fire. After it had been burning for some time, all the burning wood was removed from the surface, leaving the trench filled with a level layer of red-hot wood embers. Then excitement rose to fever-pitch as the actual fire-walk began. Hussein did his job quite effortlessly, walking on his bare feet over the red-hot embers calmly but swiftly, with head erect. A subsequent examination showed no trace of any burning of the flesh. The demonstration was arranged by Harry Price for the University of London Council for Psychical Investigation. Harman gave an excellent account of it all, but, having a portable " mike ", and no doubt having to dodge in and out of the crowd, he seemed to be rather out of breath.

. . . . .

On 4th May I did the presentation of a programme of quite original design, arranged by George Walter, and played by the Orchestre Raymonde, conducted by him. He called the programme " Accelerando ", and it began with a slow Oriental song. Then, as the title suggests, it gradually got quicker and quicker until it culminated in the " Flight of the Bumble Bee ". It was just as though the Red Queen had been at his side saying " Faster, faster " throughout the whole of the programme, consisting as it did—in the words of the White Knight—of " all kinds of fastness, I assure you ".

It was great fun, and went well—a successful experiment which I hope will be repeated before long.

. . . . .

12th May (Coronation Day). I announced the Coronation at 10.15 a.m., beginning :—

> " This is London. To-day, in the hearing of an innumerable congregation of their subjects, and of millions of listeners all over the world, Their Majesties King George VI and Queen Elizabeth are to be crowned at Westminster Abbey. . . ."

The Coronation ceremony came through very well. The King and Queen were both excellent, as were the Archbishop and Dr. Iremonger. The solemnity of the service, the acclamation of the congregation shouting " Long live the King ", the singing of the choir and the magnificent music of the Abbey organ, all combined to make it a never-to-be-forgotten occasion.

The commentary on the Procession, too, was finely done, lasting for several hours, and entailing many weeks of careful preparatory planning by the engineers and Outside Broadcast Department. In spite of poor visibility at times, television also, with Freddy Grisewood acting as friend and guide to viewers, had a veritable triumph. I can vouch for this myself. Being confined to Broadcasting House, I was able to follow most of the events, sitting quietly in the Television studio.

The Corporation kindly gave all those retained on duty in Broadcasting House a luncheon in the Council chamber. Sir Stephen Tallents, who was responsible for Public Relations, and who sat next to me, was delighted at the smooth way everything had gone, and I think listeners were pleased too.

.   .   .   .   .

I was at Broadcasting House all day on 20th May, and made the announcement of the Spithead Review in the afternoon The commentary was good, but the quality from H.M.S *Nelson* was poor. I was at home in the evening when the description of the illuminations was broadcast at 10.45 and Lieut.-Commander Woodroofe began his famous commentary with, " The fleet is all lit up " ! It went on for only a bare five minutes, before it was faded out, during which time he told us, " It is like fairyland; the ships are covered with fairy lights ", Then, after a pause, he repeated, ". . . covered with fairy lights." Then another pause, followed by, " Even the destroyers are lit up . . . they are all outlined." He mentioned the American ship *New York* as being particularly brilliantly lighted. Then there was an interruption due to some talking nearby, when I heard him say, " Shut up ". An apology, and yet another pause. Finally he said, " The lights have been switched off. . . . It has all gone . . . there is nothing between us and Heaven. . . . No magician ever waved his wand with greater acumen . . . the Fleet has disappeared."

Then came the fade out, and the announcement from London, " That is the end of the Spithead Commentary ". Hundreds of telephone calls were received at Broadcasting House asking why the commentary had been cut, but the Corporation had no statement to make. Just before midnight, however, a statement was issued saying, " The B.B.C. regrets that the commentary was unsatisfactory, and for that reason it was curtailed ". The next day Woodroofe was severely reprimanded by the authorities, but it must not be forgotten that he was a first-class commentator, and that the commentator of to-day owes much to him for the pioneering work he did.

.   .   .   .   .

On 2nd June I went to Toscanini's rehearsal of our Symphony Orchestra in the Queen's Hall, and spent a most interesting and instructive morning. He was rehearsing the Pastoral Symphony—the Symphony No. 6 by Beethoven. To watch him at work was to see a man who was the inspiration of all the players, a man who existed only to interpret the music as written by the composer. He conducted the whole of the time without music, and absolutely electrified the orchestra. Only once did he open the score on his desk, to check up on some comparatively small point. He used no extravagant gestures, but we all knew that every movement, every change of facial expression had a definite meaning, and they evoked an immediate response. A truly wonderful conductor. And nearly seventy years of age !

.   .   .   .   .

On 30th July I was in charge of the evening programmes, and had a busy time, first, because we had to fade out the relay of Act 2 of " The Magic Flute " from Salzburg before the end of the act, and secondly because of an unfortunate " aside ", consisting of the words " that bloody man " spoken with great emphasis, broadcast after the Minister of Health's talk in the Regional News Summary.

Lionel Marson was reading the 10.5 Regional News Summary, which had to begin on time because of the Minister's talk on the " Extension of State Pensions ", and also because we had to go over to America at 10.20 for a talk on the America Cup. Most unfortunately, Salzburg began ten minutes late.

I did all I could to see that the opera was faded out artistically, getting Alvar Lidell to follow with the score and to fade it out at an appropriate place, and apologise, using the emergency microphone.

No sooner had I got back to my room—a central listening point—after watching Lidell carry this out admirably, than the telephones began to ring. Having dealt with a few of these calls, I told the operator what to reply to the others, when the line was suddenly cleared and a priority call came through from the Chief Engineer, telling me of Marson's *faux pas*, which he had just heard while listening at home, and about which, of course, I knew nothing.

I sent Lidell off to find out the facts, while I told the telephone operators and Pat Smithers, the Press Officer on duty, that we were making inquiries about the offending words, and would put out an official statement later.

Now, it so happened that a few weeks previously Sir Kingsley Wood had come to Broadcasting House to broadcast, and, owing to an oversight, no senior official was there to meet him, and he was kept waiting for some time before being taken to the studio. Apologies were afterwards made to him, and on this occasion not only was the Controller of Programmes there to receive him, but he was taken to Sir John Reith's room, and the Director-General himself accompanied him to the studio and saw that the usual hospitality reserved for distinguished guests was offered to him after the broadcast. It was doubly unfortunate, therefore, that, in spite of all the efforts of the Corporation Chiefs to assist him in his broadcast and make him feel at home, this lapse should have occurred.

The Controller of Programmes (Cecil Graves) came into my room after saying good-bye to Sir Kingsley, and between us, on Lidell's return, we pieced together the chain of events and drew up the official statement. Marson explained that while Sir Kingsley was speaking in one of the Talks studios, he, in the News studio on the floor above, was discussing with the News Editor what items of news they should include in the bulletin after Sir Kingsley Wood had finished speaking—knowing the approximate duration of his talk—with a view to going over to America at exactly 10.20 p.m.

They had looked over several items, some of which the News Editor said he would like to go in, when they came to one about a poor unfortunate man whose name had been before the public recently, and who was now trying to earn some money by going into a lion's cage in a circus. Marson asked the Editor, " Why include that man ? " to which the News Editor replied, " Because he's still news ". " What, that bloody man ? " said Marson, and, most unfortunately, at that instant Sir Kingsley Wood's talk ended, and the man on the panel-control position faded up the News studio, but omitted first to put on the red light warning Marson that the studio was live, and the last three of his words were broadcast, sounding as if they were meant to refer to Sir Kingsley.

At 11.30, before the Late News Summary, we put out the official statement as follows :—

" We wish to make an apology to Regional listeners. At the end of a talk by Sir Kingsley Wood in the 10.5

News Summary to-night part of a conversation in another studio was inadvertently transmitted. We wish to apologise to listeners for the terms of this conversation, and to explain that it had, of course, nothing to do with the preceding programme."

Meanwhile, what did Sir Kingsley himself think about it? He thought nothing about it, because he knew nothing until he got home, when he seemed highly amused. " I did not know it had happened," he said. " I simply made my speech and came away."

.   .   .   .   .

Shortly after this I took part in a broadcast with Julius Bing on the subject of Shakespeare in German. It was not an easy task, but after some rehearsing with the producer, Paul Bloomfield, and some tips from Lionel Gamlin, the " To be or not to be " soliloquy went fairly well. The translation of the English was admirable. I remember it began : " Sein oder nicht sein, das ist hier die Frage ". Listening to this made me realise what an ideal medium for the soliloquy broadcasting is—thoughts crystallised as words being heard and understood by millions, effortlessly, in a moment of time.

.   .   .   .   .

The following letter appeared in *The Times* to-day (20th October) from Prof. Dover Wilson :—

" *HAMLET* ON THE WIRELESS "

Sir,

One so often hears the announcers of the B.B.C. criticised—generally unjustly—that I should like to voice the admiration I am sure must have been felt by all who were listening to the National Programme at 6.25 p.m. on Friday, for the beautiful rendering of the " To be or not to be " soliloquy in *Hamlet*.

Yours faithfully,
J. DOVER WILSON.

.   .   .   .   .

Towards the end of November I went to Denham to take part in a film. It was quite a small part—a shot of a B.B.C. announcer broadcasting an S.O.S. from a studio. The name of the film was " Storm in a Teacup ", and I was received by Dalrymple, the

Assistant Director, who took me to his office, where we went through the script together. After one or two slight alterations, made on my suggestion, we went into the studio to meet Victor Saville, the producer, who was busy supervising the shooting of some scenes.

Savile waved me to an empty chair next to him, and I watched with great interest the scenes being shot. He then introduced me to the cast, including Cecil Parker, Vivien Leigh and Ursula Jeans, and decided to give them a rest and complete my scene.

He sent for his camera-man, who brought the make-up expert with him. On my being introduced to the camera-man, he took one quick glance at me; then, turning to the make-up man, jerked a thumb in my direction and said, " George, no eyebrows. Put them in, will you ? "

We all had a good laugh about it, and Saville hastened to explain that because I was fair and my eyebrows almost white, unless they were touched up they would not be photographed by the camera at all.

.   .   .   .   .

I suppose it is because their consonants are so difficult to pronounce that the Russians make the finest linguists. After their own language, any other is almost child's play. That fine artist Tatiana Makushina gave a recital on 12th December, in which she sang songs in no fewer than five languages, and all so effortlessly, too. She sang Easthope Martin, German Lieder, Rachmaninov, Medtner, and a song, called " In mezzo al Mar ", by an Italian composer whose name I have forgotten, which made a great impression on me, because it was a picture of a storm at sea, with the waves mountains high.

That evening was memorable also for the first broadcast performance of a work by a young British composer whose name was new to me—Benjamin Britten. It was called " A Boy was Born ", and was included in the " Music for Worship " Series. It consists of a number of choral variations based on a sixteenth-century theme of that name. It was most effective; difficult to sing, and modern in its idiom, but obviously an outstanding piece of choral writing.

.   .   .   .   .

23rd December. A most enjoyable family party was held in the Children's Hour in a bakingly hot studio in the sub-basement.

Mabel Constanduros, as " Grandma ", introduced each one of us in turn. We had a percussion band, in which I helped to make noises with a mouth-organ; there were two pianos and various other noises off. Both Marson and Gamlin were in good form. The *pièce de résistance* was Grandma's story of Alfred and the Cakes. . . . I literally ached with laughing.

．　　　　．　　　　．　　　　．

Christmas Eve. Both the " Service of Nine Lessons and Carols " from King's College, Cambridge, in the afternoon, and carols from St. Mary's, Whitechapel, sung by the B.B.C. Singers accompanied by the Military Band, conducted by Leslie Woodgate, have become traditional on Christmas Eve. The broadcast from King's College, Cambridge, is quite outstanding for its excellence. That marvellous building, which does not contain a single pillar, is the perfect setting for the superb singing by the choir which we are accustomed to hear year by year. When, after I had made the opening announcement, the boys began with the haunting phrase, " Once in Royal David's city ", it always brought a lump to my throat.

St. Mary's, Whitechapel, was an ancient and beautiful church, with one of the few remaining outdoor pulpits in England. The Rector, The Rev. John Mayo, an old and dear friend of mine, who was the first person ever to broadcast a sermon in this country, always gave between the carols a most homely three-minute chat on the theme of Christmas.

Christmas Day began by being a glorious winter's morning, frosty and very cold, but clear and sunny. A little later it suddenly changed and became foggy, and this eventually developed into one of the worst London fogs we have experienced for years. I was broadcasting at 10 a.m., had another programme at Maida Vale at 1 p.m., and was due back in Broadcasting House to announce the main programme at 2.45. The fog, though bad in Portland Place, was reported to be only slight at Maida Vale, so I set out in the car, and almost immediately got stuck in a very thick patch. After a dreadful journey I eventually arrived at Maida Vale six minutes late for my programme.

I did not risk a return journey by car, but came back by tube— much simpler and much quicker in a fog. I went straight to 4B, the News studio, where I was to announce the King. Just as I was

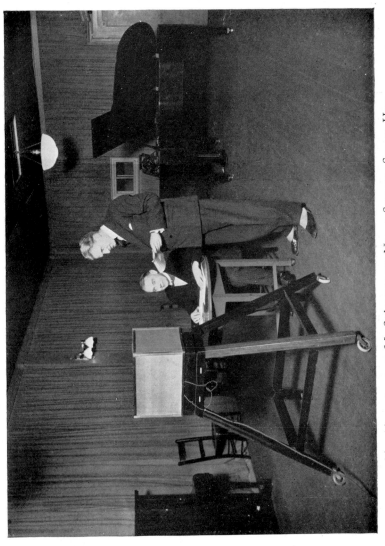

The Author and M. Stéphan in No. 3 Studio, Savoy Hill
(Note the " Meat-safe " Microphone)

A FAMILY PARTY IN THE CHILDREN'S HOUR

(From left to right: "Sophie" Dixon at the piano, the Author, Derek McCulloch, Tom Fanon, George Dixon, Barbara Sleigh, Dennis Freeman and Freddy Grisewood) waiting for my light cue at three o'clock, my attention was suddenly diverted by a woman's face, then a man's appearing at the window, peering at me in the studio. I furiously waved them away. As they went I saw that it was one of the News staff, who was evidently showing a friend round the studios. But what a day and time to choose!

This was His Majesty's first Christmas Day broadcast since he came to the throne. He was speaking from Sandringham, broadcasting a Christmas message to the Empire at Home and Overseas. It was a short message, lasting only about four minutes. He began by referring to his father as the " head of a great family whose words brought happiness into the homes and hearts of listeners all over the world". Then, saying that he could not aspire to take his place, he went on: " But, as this is the first Christmas since our Coronation, the Queen and I feel that we want to send you all a further word of gratitude, for the love and loyalty you gave us from every quarter of the Empire, during this unforgettable year now drawing to its end." Then, after speaking of the " immortal message of Christmas ", he ended, " We send our Christmas greetings and wish you, under God's blessing, health and prosperity in the years that lie ahead."

I took all my cues on a green light in 4B, the News studio. After the National Anthem, following the King, sung by the B.B.C. Chorus, there was a minute's silence; then I announced the B.B.C. Military Band playing the " Folk-song Suite " by Vaughan Williams, which begins with, " I'm seventeen come Sunday", and is in several parts. This suite was to be followed later by a selection from the " Yeomen of the Guard ". The " Folk-song Suite " had not been going on long when I was astonished to receive a green light cue to announce. I thought it was much too soon, but I had no score, and had forgotten how many movements there were, and, being six floors away from the band, I could not check up with the conductor. I therefore decided, after a slight hesitation, to announce the " Yeomen of the Guard ", only to hear on the head-phones the band continue with another section of the suite! Such are the pitfalls of the panel—the human element only too easily creeps in; that and the fog were the only two blemishes in an otherwise excellent Christmas Day's broadcasting.

1938

UNDER the exchange scheme I went up to Edinburgh for a month to take over the presentation there, Aidan Thompson coming down to London in my place. We stayed at the Roxburghe Hotel in Charlotte Square, which had formerly been a private house, and was close to the B.B.C.

After reporting to Melville Dinwiddie, the Scottish Regional Director, and meeting Andrew Stewart, his Programme Director, and the rest of the staff on 4th January, I attended a Press conference in the afternoon, and replied to questions fired at me by reporters. Burnett, the Public Relations Officer, was an admirable chairman, and largely due to his tact and good humour, and possibly to my telling them some stories against myself (mainly to do with mispronouncing Scottish place-names), it went off well, and they were all most friendly. There are obvious advantages in a Region as a working unit, as compared with Head Office. Here everyone meets for coffee at 11 a.m., a period which is strictly limited to fifteen minutes, whereas in London you can go three months without seeing any of the Seniors, so large is the unit.

On 5th January I announced my first programme in Scotland, a concert given by the B.B.C. Scottish Orchestra, conducted by Ian Whyte, and distinguished myself by ringing the fire alarm, instead of giving the usual " go-ahead " signal to control room. This caused some surprise, and no little amusement, but I was reassured when I was told that I was by no means the first person to have pressed the wrong bell; I made a note, for future reference, that the fire-buzzer was painted red.

On 6th January we dined with Ian Whyte and his wife at their house in Pitt Street, and after dinner we discussed various topics, including speech, football, music and ghosts.

Ian is a brilliant musician, and can read and play with ease from any full score. How we got on to the subject of ghosts I do not remember, but it resulted in his telling us the following startling experience he and his wife had had when staying at Glentanar Castle in the Highlands.

The castle is haunted by the ghost of a piper who betrayed his lord to the enemy, by giving them a certain signal played on the pipes. He was later captured, imprisoned, and had both his hands cut off, before being put to death.

Unknown to Ian and his wife, they were given the haunted room, which was above the moat. Apparently the amputated hands of the piper were subsequently buried under the hearthstone in this room, and the body thrown into the moat below.

In the middle of the night both of them woke up quite suddenly, feeling very cold and hearing the sound of water dripping from the ceiling—drip . . . drip . . . drip . . . it went—and there in the corner of the room, coming very slowly towards them, was a filmy apparition in the shape of a man. At first they were too scared to move, and watched the unearthly figure slowly approaching them to the sound of dripping water. On each side of the body there were blobs of light where the hands had been cut off.

Ian got up, and found that he could pass his hand through the figure. He turned on the lights, and could still see it dimly, and hear the dripping sound. Eventually it slowly retreated the way it had come, and gradually disappeared.

The next morning at breakfast Ian described their frightening experience to their host, who only laughed and said, " Oh yes, that was our ghost all right—the piper who betrayed his lord. He is quite often about in that room."

I was not at all surprised to learn that Ian and his wife insisted on changing their room before the next night.

. . . . .

On 12th February the B.B.C. Singers sang madrigals by John Willbye, 1574–1638, and I was struck by the magical beauty of the lyrics of those days.

For example :—

> " Thou art not young, thou sayest,
> And Love's delight thou weighest not.
> O take time while thou mayest,
> Lest when thou would'st thou mayest not."

Did not Robert Herrick, a little later on, say the same thing very neatly in :—

> " Gather ye rosebuds, while ye may,
> Old Time is still a-flying;
> And this same flower that smiles to-day,
> To-morrow will be dying " ?

Then there is this gem :—

> " April is in my Mistress' face,
> And July in her eye hath place,
> Within her bosom is September,
> But in her heart is cold December."

. . . .

John Snagge, who was rapidly making a name for himself as the " stunt-merchant " of the B.B.C., that night tried his hand as a diver, going down in 14 feet of water in Siebe Gorman's training-tank in Westminster Bridge Road. He described his sensations as he went down into the water, what it felt like when he had reached the bottom of the tank, and what he could see there. His account of his efforts at sawing a piece of wood and hammering nails into the wood down there was very funny.

. . . .

On 6th March Lord Sankey came to the studio to talk about the Bible in England in connection with the fourth centenary of the Open Bible. As no producer was available, I did my best to help him with one or two suggestions at the rehearsal, and he seemed most grateful.

After the rehearsal, and while waiting for the broadcast to begin, he talked to me about those well-known personalities, Ramsay MacDonald, Philip Snowden and Stanley Baldwin. He told me that Mr. Baldwin was very ill with arthritis and depression, and could walk only with the help of a stick. After he had left I went to Maida Vale to announce a piano recital given by that great artist Edwin Fischer in the large studio there. Before the recital began, he played to us for nearly half an hour. Afterwards I went back with him to Addison Road in a friend's car, returning to Maida Vale in time to read the Epilogue.

The following day I received a charming letter from Lord Sankey thanking me for "my great encouragement" and saying that he had waited up especially to hear my Epilogue.

. . . . .

During the week 12th–19th March we in this country heard of :—

(*a*) Hitler's triumphal march into Vienna as he annexed Austria.

(*b*) Sir Samuel Hoare's speech on A.R.P. requirements.

(*c*) Barcelona devastated by bombs, hundreds killed and injured.

(*d*) Dr. Mess's broadcast on " Can progress be traced in human history ? "

How ironical that this subject, chosen weeks before, should have been included in the programmes for this week !

. . . . .

On 15th March I announced John Watt, who was introducing his clever radio adaptation of " Snow White and the Seven Dwarfs ".

Talking to him afterwards about the sense of frustration which he and his Department experience from time to time, various suggestions being turned down by the " powers that be ", he said it was all done by " Sno' Use and the Seven Controllers ".

. . . . .

Admiral Sir Charles Carpendale retires from the Corporation. He was " the Controller " when I joined in 1924, and for some years he had been Sir John Reith's right-hand man as Deputy Director-General. He had stayed on for a few years beyond the normal retiring age by special dispensation, and now the time had come for him to make way for a younger man, though I must hasten to add that both mentally and physically he seemed to be exactly as when I first met him. He had done a magnificent job of work, not only as an Administrator in the Corporation, but also as President of the International Broadcasting Union, a body whose main task was to promote the interests of broadcasting in the international field. A fluent linguist, he was extremely popular on the Continent, and every year he went to his beloved Switzerland to ski.

A large farewell party was held in the concert hall, many of the Regional Directors and Programme Directors coming to London specially for the occasion. I saw " Carps ", as he was affectionately known, for a few moments, shook hands with him, and wished him every happiness in his well-earned retirement. He always revelled in a party, and was in great form. How all the girls adored him !

Later the floor was cleared, and Percy Edgar, the Senior Regional Director, and the Admiral mounted the platform, and both made short and amusing speeches, the latter being obviously much moved by the occasion. Then followed a surprise, as though a magician had waved his wand, six naval ratings and two buglers suddenly appeared out of the blue, sent by the " Lords Commissioners of the Admiralty " and the Admiral was piped ashore. This was a most impressive little ceremony, and a great honour both for the Admiral and the B.B.C.

. . . . .

On 4th April Droitwich long-wave transmitter went down with a fault at 6.9 p.m., during the first News, just as I was about to begin reading the report on Arthur Greenwood's speech in the Commons Debate on the Vote of Censure. Shortly afterwards a man rang up and tried to make out that the breakdown was intentional. It was no easy matter to persuade him to the contrary.

. . . . .

It was during the second week of April that my old friend Derek McCulloch (Uncle Mac) was badly injured in a head-on collision between a Green Line bus and a lorry on Banstead Downs near Epsom, while on his way home from London—his home is in Banstead. He sustained a badly fractured ankle and suffered from shock, but in spite of this, by hopping on one leg, he managed to help another injured passenger out of the smashed bus. Poor Mac ! as if he had not been through enough already, with some seventeen or eighteen operations as the result of war wounds.

(Eventually his leg had to be amputated below the left knee, and he had a great deal of trouble with it before the artificial limb settled down.)

I announced a recital given in the concert hall by Irene Scharrer, one of many I have announced by this most sensitive artist. She liked subdued lights in the studio and no movement at all while she was playing—nothing, in short, that could possibly disturb her concentration on the music.

As it was Good Friday, she played a movement from Bach's Organ Concerto in C, and Chopin's " Barcarolle ", most beautifully. She brought two American friends with her, and after the recital I took them round the studios which were not in use, and also showed them the model of Ariel moulded, so Miss Scharrer said, on her daughter's face—a fact I did not know before.

. . . . .

On 26th April I had a part in " Scrapbook 1928 ", and spent the whole morning rehearsing with the cast, resting in the afternoon ready for the evening's transmission, as long hours spent in stuffy studios can be very tiring. I was particularly interested in this year, because Leslie Baily, the author of the script, had drawn on my diary for certain details about Savoy Hill.

Looking back ten years can be a melancholy business. The international outlook was then " set fair ", and there was a feeling of optimism in the air. The Kellogg Pact renouncing war as an instrument of policy had been signed that summer, and it was depressing now to be reminded of it.

. . . . .

During the first week of May we were broadcasting the First Act of the Opera " Der Rosenkavalier " from Covent Garden, when, shortly before the end of that Act, Lotte Lehmann, who was singing the part of the Princess, was taken ill, and we had to leave the Opera House and come back to the studio, making an explanatory announcement as to what had happened.

Some fifteen minutes before the end of the First Act, Lotte Lehmann suddenly paused in her action, threw up her arms, and said, " I can't go on . . . finish ". She then turned and walked slowly off the stage, the curtain being lowered. I filled up with some stand-by records while trying to find out what the position was, but after twelve minutes with nothing definite from the Opera House I realised that we should not now be able to go back, as the nine o'clock News was due in about ten minutes. I therefore explained this to listeners, and carried on with my records, dictating an apology to go out at the beginning of the News at 9 p.m., which I gave to the News Editor.

Meanwhile, what was happening at Covent Garden ?   Madame Hilda Konetzni, who had been busy rehearsing " Elektra ", was in a box at this performance, and agreed to take Mme. Lehmann's place, which she did, in due course, most successfully.   Interviewed about it afterwards, she said, laughingly, that the main reason for the delay was the difficulty she experienced in getting into Mme. Lehmann's clothes.   " I had to use many, many safety-pins."

.   .   .   .

The following week Wing-Commander Pope, when talking about his flying adventures, told us of a crash he once had in a country district and the sequel to it.   He said that he was dazed, and so pinned down by the machine that he could not move.   After what seemed to him more like hours than a few minutes, some locals and the village constable came up, not expecting him to be alive under such a mess.   However, one of the locals suggested cutting open the fabric with a pen-knife to have a look.   They took a little time to cut through it, and when at length they did so, the blade of the knife only just missed Commander Pope's eye as it jerked through the fabric.   The policeman then looked in and saw him move. " Blimey, Bill ! " said the policeman, " he's alive !   He winked at me ! "

.   .   .   .   .

Sir Kingsley Wood announced in the House on 14th June that Sir John Reith was shortly leaving the B.B.C. to become the new whole-time Chairman of Imperial Airways, a post worth £10,000 a year.   A sad day for the Corporation, to lose the man who really was the B.B.C., and who had been mainly responsible for its creation. A man of vision, a fair man, a man who knew what he wanted and knew how to get it, a statesman of the first order, a disciplinarian with a sense of humour, a shy man, who combined a stern expression with a leaven of sweet reasonableness, a much-misunderstood man, a born leader of men, a doughty fighter, a man with an iron will, but a lonely man—at least that was my impression—but a human being and a most loyal friend.

The announcement came as a great shock to us all at Broadcasting House, as the appointment had been a well-kept secret. " Let us hope," I wrote in my diary, " that our loss will be Imperial

Airways' gain, and that the country and Empire will never forget how much they owe to him for his public service conception for the B.B.C."

.   .   .   .   .

Many fine artists who never use music on the concert platform, use it, or have it handy, when broadcasting from a studio.

Early in July I was announcing a recital of French music given by an old friend of mine, who was about to play a suite by Ravel. As he went to the piano he turned and whispered, " I really know this music by heart, but as it is in the studio, please sit behind me with the score, and be ready to put it in front of me if I turn round and give you a blank look."

Luckily for me, this was not necessary, but I was kept so busy counting bars that I paid very little attention to the quality of the performance.   I do not remember having been asked to do such a thing before.

.   .   .   .   .

On 19th June the appointment of the new Director-General was announced in the News; a person I had never heard of before, but, from his record, evidently a fine man—Professor Frederick Ogilvie. He was described in the Press as " a man of wide cultural background and deep social sympathies, having a forthright Scots independence and integrity of mind, who cannot be brow-beaten or cajoled ".

.   .   .   .   .

Saturday, 6th August, was the opening night of the forty-fourth season of the Promenade Concerts.   I announced the first concert and Sir Adrian Boult's introduction to the series before it, then, later on, I went to the Queen's Hall to announce Sir Henry J. Wood (he always preferred to be announced like this, not just as Sir Henry Wood—I believe there was once another Sir Henry Wood?).   At 9.35, during the interval, Sir Henry was making an appeal for the Jubilee Fund to endow hospital beds for orchestral musicians.   It was a hot night, the temperature on the Air Ministry roof being 83° at 6 p.m.   I found Lady Wood fanning him in the conductor's room when I arrived.   He had been much affected by the wonderful reception he had been given by the audience, and I was conscious

of this as he pleaded with listeners to respond liberally to his appeal
for this splendid cause.

.   .   .   .   .

In view of the international situation, the Corporation had been
pressing the Government for some time past to make up its mind
about what we should be required to do in the event of a national
emergency.   On 19th August I heard that information had been
given to us in general terms, but that no details had yet been worked
out.   At 5 p.m. I attended a meeting convened by the Controller
of Programmes (B. E. Nicolls), who traced the history of events
leading up to the Government decision and indicated the probable
trend of immediate action.   It was all very nebulous and vague, and
of course secret, but, even so, it was a useful meeting, and helped to
clear the air.

The next day one of the more sensational of the daily papers
published a statement that the King had banned the broadcast of the
Royal Command Performance.   This was untrue, and in the late
afternoon I had a telephone call from His Majesty's Private Secretary,
Sir Eric Miéville, then at Balmoral.   This led to our broadcasting an
official statement in the 6 p.m. News that the Press statement was
false.

.   .   .   .   .

Towards the end of September I returned from a holiday in
Devon to find everybody very glum about the international situation.   I read through the secret emergency action file to make myself up-to-date, and this was not exactly cheering either.   So many
people were talking loosely about the situation, referring to "a
surrender to the Dictators".   One friend of mine, an ex-regular
with a fine record of service, actually went as far as threatening to
take out Mexican papers, because he said that Mexico was the only
country prepared to make a stand against the totalitarian States.

Soon after this I went to Alexandra Palace to take the place of
Vernon Bartlett in a television programme, as he had had to go
abroad at very short notice.   I rehearsed the script with Mrs.
Adams, the producer, and Horrabin, the artist, who was to draw
maps of Central Europe illustrating the international situation in
terms of frontiers.   I found the surroundings very strange, with
glaring lights above, and groups of people standing around in the

studio during rehearsal. I was also affected by the uncanny action of the slowly moving camera and its crew, creeping silently towards me on its rubber-tyred trolley, and all the time one had to sit there and try to be natural, as though nothing was happening anywhere near.

Poor Horrabin was new to it, so was I, but my broadcasting experience helped me, and I had been filmed before. He was extremely nervous, and once or twice I had to step in and come to his rescue. His drawings were very clever and clear on the screen. Subsequently he became one of the television star turns.

. . . . .

AT THE HEIGHT OF THE MUNICH CRISIS.

During the afternoon of 26th September I listened to the broadcast of the launching of the *Queen Elizabeth* by the Queen at Clydebank. I afterwards heard, though I did not know it at the time, that the launch took place too soon. Lord Aberconway, in pointing out the press-button to the Queen, accidentally touched it with his finger, and away went the ship, Her Majesty having the presence of mind to say her piece just in time.

In the course of her speech at the launching ceremony she gave the nation a message from the King. " The King bids the people of this country be of good cheer. . . . He knows well that, as ever before in critical times, they will keep cool heads and brave hearts."

That night at Broadcasting House I was in charge of the programmes, and also announced the Prime Minister at eight o'clock (he spoke from 10 Downing Street), the last words of the announcement being : ". . . his speech will be heard all over the Empire, throughout the Continent of America, and in a large number of foreign countries ". It was an historic broadcast, and was followed by translations in German, Italian and French.

. . . . .

27th September. Impressive appeal by Roosevelt to Hitler for peace. " The present negotiations still stand open. They can be continued if you give the word." This should give Hitler the chance of saving face. Will he seize such a Heaven-sent opportunity ?

Frank Phillips read extracts from the Prime Minister's speech in the House of Commons very well. It was interspersed with records,

Phillips having to read it bit by bit, as the News Editors assembled it from the tape-machines. After he had been doing this for about half an hour, the dramatic announcement came through that a message had been received from Hitler agreeing to suspend mobilisation for twenty-four hours and calling for a conference in Munich to-morrow between Chamberlain, himself, Daladier and Mussolini.

Marson was at the German Embassy when Hitler's message came through from the Counsellor's brother at the German Foreign Office. He was fitting gas-masks at the time, and the Counsellor at once wrote a note to the Prime Minister. It was this note which was handed to him during his speech, and which was read so dramatically to the House a little later.

.   .   .   .   .

On 30th September we broadcast the terms of the Munich settlement, which had been signed at 1.45 a.m. They appeared to be very stiff indeed.

All programmes were altered to meet the needs of the situation, there being only one programme on the Regional wavelengths, with Foreign News bulletins following the Second News at 8.15 p.m. for about an hour.

I announced the outside broadcast of the arrival of Mr. Chamberlain at Heston, where he had a good reception, but it was nothing in comparison with the tumultuous reception he was given when later he returned to Downing Street from Buckingham Palace.

There was a lull at Broadcasting House after the tension of the past few days; everyone seemed to be busy discussing the terms of the settlement, many people thinking that the Prime Minister had sold the pass. I could not agree. Certainly the price was a high one, but I was not prepared to say that it was too high, until I had faced up to the alternative—war, and the loss of innumerable British lives—and I was not at all sure that we were in a position to wage war.

.   .   .   .   .

On 3rd October I read the 7 p.m. News, which included a full report of speeches in the Commons Debate, including Duff Cooper's resignation speech and the Prime Minister's on the Munich Agreement.

.   .   .   .

10th October was the date of the opening recital in the new series of organ recitals in the concert hall, the artist being Gunter Ramin, organist of Bach's old church, St. Thomas', Leipzig.

I announced this recital, and was most impressed by Ramin's brilliant technical performance. I have heard the great Bach D Minor Toccata and Fugue played dozens of times, but never have I heard it so alive as this man made it.

Sir James Jeans and his wife (Susi Hock) were both there. She was a fine player herself, and they had an organ in their Dorking home. Gunter Ramin was staying with them, and seemed a very pleasant man, but, like so many great artists, he was highly strung, and he had no English at all.

.   .   .   .   .

31st October was Reginald Foort's last day with the Corporation, and I was due to take part in his farewell programme, with Campoli, George Melachrino and Ivor Dennis, in the evening, before he began his tour of the country. It was a glorious autumn day, and my wife and I took our lunch out in the car to the woods beside Keston ponds in Kent, where the colours, especially the beech and birch reflected in the water of the lake, were most beautiful in the sunshine.

While there I decided, if John Watt agreed, to try to end the programme in an original way, writing a couple of verses after the folk-song " Spanish Ladies " and singing them to that tune. John Watt and the Director of Talks both agreed, if Reginald Foort had no objection. After some hesitation he did agree, and we proceeded to rehearse it, with Reggie Foort at the organ and Ivor Dennis at the piano.

Here is the piece of doggerel I eventually sang at the end of the farewell programme :—

" Farewell and adieu to you, dear old Reginald,
  Farewell and adieu to you, Reginald Foort,
  For you're on the trail for to go round old England
  And we hope that your journey will not be for nought.

  Now let every man drink off his full bumper,
  And let every man now drink up his port.
  We'll sing and be jolly and drown melancholy,
  With ' Here's to the Health of our Reginald Foort.' "

Foort himself seemed delighted; he had several 'phone calls and heaps of telegrams. I had my leg thoroughly pulled about the doggerel: was this the action of an official B.B.C. announcer on duty? Lionel Gamlin said I ought to leave the Corporation at once and join forces with Foort: he would!

.   .   .   .

On Armistice Day, Sir Fabian Ware, Vice-Chairman of the Imperial War Graves Commission, spoke finely about " The Nation and its War Dead ".

While he was speaking I left him alone in the studio, and as he ended, and I came in again to make the closing announcement, he began talking to me before the red light had gone out. Realising that his words would have been heard, I replied in the ordinary way, but control room, hearing " conversation ", took the studio out before I had a chance of making my closing announcement.

All he said was, " Twelve minutes ", and I replied, " Yes, sir, just about ", but one of the daily papers came out with a large heading : " A. S. H. gongs the General! " By such simple processes do molehills become mountains in the Press.

.   .   .   .

On 24th November Sandy Macpherson, the new B.B.C. Theatre Organist, joined us, and was introduced by John Watt. Sandy is a Canadian who made his name over there with the Metro-Goldwyn-Meyer group of theatres.

As Sandy comes, so Joe Lewis goes. Joe joined us in the very early days, and was with Percy Edgar in Birmingham as Staff Conductor before coming to London.

A pupil of Granville Bantock, he specialised in choral work, and I well remember the first time I met him, when he came down from Birmingham to conduct a performance of Bantock's " Pilgrim's Progress " at Covent Garden.

Subsequently I announced many of his studio programmes, in particular those of sacred music : " Comfortable Words ", " From the Oratorios ", etc. I shall always be grateful to him for introducing me to Berlioz' " L'Enfance du Christ ". It was a studio performance, with some most beautiful singing by Isobel Baillie and Stanley Riley, especially Miss Baillie's singing of the carol " Lullay lullay ".

" Joe ", as he was known to a host of musical friends, had a wonderful way with a chorus or orchestra, having a fine sense of humour, an inexhaustible supply of stories to fit all tastes, and the great gift of repartee. He always managed to get people to work for him willingly and without fuss.

. . . . .

On 7th December the lights failed in the concert hall while the Richard Crean Orchestra was playing. The players gallantly carried on for some seconds, then, as they had no music, the sound died away and I apologised, explaining to listeners what had happened, and telling them that a fuse had gone. In only two or three minutes the house electricians had replaced the fuse and we went on with the concert. I noticed a paragraph about it on the P.A. tape-machine when I went up later to read the News.

. . . . .

A white Christmas this year, plenty of snow in the country districts around London. On Boxing Day, John Masefield, the Poet Laureate, who was due to take part in a programme, rang me up from Boar's Hill, Oxford, to say that the roads were impassable and that he could not come.

. . . . .

On the last day of the year a listener sent me a cutting about Juliana Berners, a fifteenth-century writer, warning people against using nouns of multitude promiscuously. Among a long list of what she called " correct terms " she included the following :—

" A congregation of people, a host of men, a bevy of ladies, a herd of deer, swans, cranes or wrens, a sege of herons, a muster of peacocks, a watch of nightingales, a flight of doves, a clattering of choughs, a pride of lions, a gaggle of geese, a skulk of foxes . . . " and may I add to that list a new one : a mumbling of announcers.

1939

ON 1st January, 1939, we broadcast President Roosevelt's speech in full, forty-one minutes of it, instead of approximately thirty, as we had been told. He attacked the policy of the Dictator States in no uncertain terms; and as I listened I thought I could detect the old Puritan spirit breaking through.

On 23rd January Christopher Stone returned to the microphone in "Birthday Party", a variation on the theme of "In Town To-night". In it was Anna Lee, who was a great success. She told us that she had one baby and hoped to have lots more. When, a little later, Ann Maritza told her that something wonderful was going to happen to her next year, Christopher Stone wickedly said, " Hello, twins ! "

.　　.　　.　　.　　.

Early in February there was a tea-party in the room of the Director of Programme Planning (Charles Siepmann), and we were introduced to one of the Governors, H. A. L. Fisher, the historian, who had especially asked to meet us. We had an interesting talk together about our work and kindred problems, and the meeting was a pronounced success. He was the only Governor who had ever asked to meet us as a body; it was he, too, who sent us such an encouraging telegram after the crisis last year.

.　　.　　.　　.　　.

On 15th March I received a most pleasant letter from Mr. J. Thompson—who had recently taken part, with Professor Lloyd James, in the broadcast on " Announcer's English "—telling me that, according to a poll taken by a Northern paper after the debate, we won easily.

" Little did I know how much the British public loves its announcers ", he said. " Ladies from Maida Vale forgot they were ladies. One of them analysed my voice so completely that I felt I must tell her that she had got everything but the smell. These

168

MR. MIDDLETON

women defended their announcers with the ferocity of a tigress defending its young."

.   .   .   .   .

SEQUENCE OF EVENTS FROM 17TH MARCH TO 30TH APRIL

The Prime Minister denounced the German invasion of Czecho-slovakia in a speech broadcast to Europe, America and the Empire on 17th March. Was this the end of an old adventure or the beginning of a new one?

France and America, too, condemned Hitler for the invasion. Sir Nevile Henderson was recalled.

In the middle of such critical times, two amusing topical slips by News-readers are worth noting: (1) Fragrant *démarche*; (2) a reference to Hitler as "thrice-purged traitor".

.   .   .   .   .

We broadcast an important statement by the Prime Minister at 4 p.m. on 31st March, saying that "in the event of any action which clearly threatened Polish independence, and which the Polish Government considered it vital to resist . . . H.M. Government would feel themselves bound, at once, to lend the Polish Government all support in their power".

.   .   .   .   .

On 5th April I attended a long meeting with the Programme and Engineering Staffs about emergency plans, and the next day, in a tense international situation, the Polish Pact was signed. This was on Maundy Thursday, and on the following day, Good Friday—of all days—Italy invaded Albania. I announced this in the News at one o'clock and later at 4 and 6.20 p.m. Alas! poor Zog.

A few days later B. E. Nicolls, the Controller of Programmes, came in to see me, and seemed to be most pessimistic about the world situation. He thought war to be inevitable. He told me that he was busy trying to arrange for more publicity for A.R.P.: in his opinion things were not moving half quickly enough. Recruiting, too, was only fair, not good to excellent, as it should have been.

.   .   .   .   .

On the last day of April I had lunch with Mr. Middleton. What a lovable personality, so human and forthright. And how he enjoyed a joke!

Give him his head at the microphone and leave him alone, and he would talk as long as you liked on almost any country subject, and always in a most attractive and interesting manner, and I guarantee he would end exactly when you asked him. But worry him and go into unnecessary detail, and you would upset him, though I doubt if listeners would ever have known it. The only time I ever saw him put out was once when an over-zealous producer had been bothering him about petty details. When the producer had gone, and only he and I were left in the studio, he turned to me and said, "Fussy old hen!" How right he was!

He spoke to me of the immense publicity he had had as the result of his broadcasting, and the numerous offers he had to turn down. He told me that he had been quite overwhelmed by offers and inquiries. By no means all of them had any connection with gardening. One was an offer to appear at a famous music-hall in London at £200 per week! With a wicked twinkle in his eye, he said, "But I'm a gardener, not a comedian; I could not do such a thing". Middleton had a most wonderful gift of making scenes and characters come to life by chatting about them in a homely and simple way. I remember a talk he once gave about his native village and the people in it he knew so well as a boy. He went on to contrast those times, not unfavourably, with the present. When he had ended, I felt that he had been introducing me to all his old friends in turn, so finely was it done.

. . . . .

On 7th May I went to the rehearsal of the Empire Day programme with Lawrence Gilliam, the producer, and was amazed to hear him speak first to Glasgow, then to Cardiff, and afterwards to Toronto, Belfast and Manchester, one after the other, as though they were, if not in Broadcasting House, at any rate in the London area.

Edward Ward, who was then an announcer and News-reader, is a most gifted artist, and sketched on the back of a B.B.C. programme a portrait of Campoli, the violinist.

. . . . .

During the last week of May I announced a concert played by the Symphony Orchestra conducted by Sir Hamilton Harty. When discussing the programme with him beforehand I showed him the

announcement of the John Field Suite, and he smiled and said,
" Is it too much to say that he died happily of drink ? "

Later, when referring to the Tschaikowsky " Romeo and Juliet "
Fantasia, he said that he remembered how a certain famous conductor once pulled up the orchestra at rehearsal, and said, " Gentlemen, gentlemen, 'ave pity on poor Ophelia " !

. . . . .

On 9th July I met Ruth Draper, and rehearsed with her for
almost an hour until the transmission at 7.20 p.m.   What a talented
person she is !   Like all good artists, she was very nervous, this
being her first broadcast over here.

I soon saw that the microphone was not a help, but a handicap.   The fact that it was a fixed point meant that she had no
freedom of action, having to restrict all her movements to the
small arc of a circle in front of it.   Then, too, she missed the laughs,
with which she was so familiar.   This added to the difficulties of
her performance, but, in spite of this, it was a fine piece of work.
The Kerry woman's character sketch came over especially well;
" showing the garden " was not quite so good, for the reasons already
stated.   She seemed delighted that we were pleased with her
efforts, but she took a lot of convincing that her performance really
was good from our point of view—being most self-critical, a sure
sign of a great artist.   I noticed that when talking to her in the
studio one could tell at once that she is an American, but when she
is acting a non-American role there is no trace of an American
accent.

. . . . .

Frank Phillips, who was in charge of the evening programmes on
14th July, had a hectic time.   The Droitwich aerial was struck by
lightning, and the aerial wire which stretches between two 700-feet
masts was burnt up.

Our resourceful engineers soon got the old Daventry 5XX long-
wave transmitter going again, in spite of it not having been used for
five years.   This put out the programmes until the close, while
emergency squads of engineers worked like slaves to erect a substitute aerial at Droitwich.

I wonder how many people sitting snugly in their homes realised
what a job of this magnitude meant.   The engineers worked at it

all through the night, with the aid of A.R.P. searchlights, to enable transmitting to be resumed at the usual time in the morning. In fact, the incident acted as an A.R.P. exercise, as 5XX was to be held in reserve permanently for any contingency of this kind. It must have been eerie work erecting a new aerial 700 feet up, in the dead of night, in the glare of searchlights. Hats off to the engineers !

· · · · ·

The death of Sir Dan Godfrey, the man who did so much for music in Bournemouth, and who did all he could to encourage young musicians, both composers and performers, was announced on 20th July. The Bournemouth Municipal Orchestra under his direction was famous not only in this country, but also on the Continent. I owe him a great deal for the many happy hours spent in the old Winter Gardens at his Symphony Concerts, when the augmented orchestra consisted of about sixty-five players.

Frank Phillips, Sir Dan's son-in-law, told me that he had recently been in poor health and became bored, because his life-interest was music, and lately he could not make any.

When he retired in 1934 he had conducted no fewer than 2,000 Symphony Concerts—a magnificent record.

· · · · ·

On 12th August I met Mr. Kaltenborn, the Chief News Commentator of the Columbia Broadcasting System, who spoke about " How America Receives News from Europe ". He is intimate in style and has the important gift of sustaining interest in the subject-matter throughout, so that his material is alive. One is compelled to listen to him through the sheer force of his personality, every word being winged. Ed. Murrow tells me that he has been broadcasting comment of this excellence for seventeen years.

· · · · ·

When in the tube on my way to Broadcasting House on 21st August I was dismayed to see in the headlines of the *Evening News* of the man next to me the announcement of the death of B. Walton O'Donnell, or " Bandy " O'Donnell to his many B.B.C. friends.

It was so unexpected because I had not even heard that he had been ill, but I had not seen him for some time, as he had lately been in Belfast.

It was he who raised the Wireless Military Band in 1927, coming to us from the Royal Marines at Deal. In a few years he had converted it into the world's most famous military band.

Ten years later he handed over the conductorship of the B.B.C. Military Band—to give it its new name—to his elder brother, Major Percy O'Donnell, also of the Royal Marines, to take up the post of conductor of the B.B.C. Northern Ireland Orchestra. He will be greatly missed by his many friends, particularly those in the B.B.C. and Royal Academy of Music.

In the old days King George V often listened to " Bandy's Band ", as we used to call it. When he visited Broadcasting House, and the senior members of the Staff were being presented to him, lined up in the entrance hall, he looked at them, and then, turning to the Director-General, inquired, " Where's that fellow Walton O'Donnell ? "

.   .   .   .   .

The following is the sequence of events as recorded from official sources, from the announcement of the Russo-German non-aggression pact, to the declaration of war by the Prime Minister, and the events of the subsequent few days after the declaration :—

The News on 23rd August included the bombshell announcement of the conclusion of a non-aggression pact between Russia and Germany. That night I wrote in my diary :

" This may, of course, mean nothing—it may be ' grandstand play ', as the Americans say; on the other hand, it may be of vital importance to every one of us. Italy has nervous indigestion and Japan the tummy-ache as the result. Does this mean a new alignment of the Powers ? "

In the 6 p.m. News, which I read, was an announcement that there would be a railway strike on Saturday, just to add to our difficulties. A special Cabinet communiqué was issued at 8.30 p.m. calling up more men, renewing our pledge to the Poles.

.   .   .   .   .

24th August. Details of the Russo-German Pact signed on August 23rd, published in the Press. The Germans appeared to have got all they wanted. Germany was increasing her pressure on Poland. The Prime Minister's speech at 3 p.m. showed how serious things were, but the country was united and determined.

The stage seemed set for a " flare up ", Germany trying to persuade Turkey to remain neutral by threatening her with Russian pressure.

The entrance hall of Broadcasting House looked like King's Cross on Christmas Eve. The advance party was preparing to leave—the first move in the dispersal scheme on an emergency No new message came from any Government Department, except one from the Admiralty to repeat the message about the " seldom seen buoy ". This showed that the Government was taking no risks in a perilous situation.

On 25th August all leave was cancelled, and everyone was busy taking black-out precautions. The Polish–British Agreement had now been signed. All possible precautions were taken in Broadcasting House, even to fixing gas-doors in position on the lower floors. That evening about 10.30 p.m. Phillips rang up to tell me that the first warning had come in, and that I was to report at 9.30 a.m.

At 9.30 a.m. I attended the conference with the Director of Programme Planning, in which we went through the details of our emergency plans. Later I went to another demonstration of the emergency equipment by Dryland, afterwards returning home to check up on precautions there.

On the 29th the crisis was still acute, but there appeared to be a distinct swing in our favour, Turkey remaining firm, and Yugoslavia being busy putting her house in order. Here everyone seemed to be taking things calmly and quietly, the order being " business as usual ", in so far as the situation permitted. There were further conferences in the late afternoon, at which I noted that things seemed to be " getting more and more complicated ".

On the last day of the month the News was full of the increased provocation in Danzig by the Germans. At about 10.30 p.m. Hitler issued a statement laying down the sixteen points he required to be fulfilled for a settlement. Later it transpired that Poland had never been allowed to see these sixteen points.

· · · · ·

1st September. At breakfast Richard Walker (" Foreign Editor ") told me that Gauleiter Forster had offered Danzig to the Reich, and that Hitler had taken over and issued a proclamation, saying he knew that his army would fight well. The balloon was up.

· · · · ·

2nd September. I stood by at Broadcasting House all day; virtually no news. Berlin was pretending that the military operations in Poland were not really war, but only "to rectify the eastern frontier". No reply was received to our ultimatum of yesterday.

We kept broadcasting statements to this effect. People were beginning to get restive; whispered questions were going round, such as "Are we ratting?" "Is it the French?"; and then, as no news came in, not a question, but a statement, "The French are not ready".

A glorious summer day. Why is it that at this, the most lovely time of the year, men should start thinking about killing their own kind? In the evening reports came in showing that the House, too, was restive, and at midnight we learnt that the Cabinet was sitting, and that a bad thunderstorm was in progress!

.   .   .   .   .

3rd September (Sunday). I stood by to go to Downing Street at 8.30 a.m., but did not go, Lidell, who was spare man, going instead. At 10 a.m. he put out an announcement from there saying :—

> "Following the midnight meeting of the Cabinet, the British Ambassador at 9 a.m. this morning gave the German Government *two further hours* in which to decide whether they would *at once* withdraw their troops from Poland. This ultimatum expires at 11 a.m. The Prime Minister will broadcast to the nation at 11.15 a.m."

No reply came from the Germans. Therefore at 11.15 the Prime Minister, speaking with great pathos, announced a state of war with Germany, and this for a second time, with so few years in between.

France's ultimatum was presented at 12.30, and expired at 5 p.m., after which she, too, was once more at war with Germany.

I recall the closing words of the Prime Minister's speech :—

> "Now may God bless you all. May He defend the right. It is the evil things we shall be fighting against— brute force, bad faith, injustice, oppression and persecution; against them I am certain that the right will prevail."

I read the one o'clock and several other bulletins which included the Prime Minister's speech. As I was reading one of the evening bulletins the sirens sounded. I remember how difficult it was to concentrate; automatically my mind was trying to picture the scene outside; but it was not an actual raid, merely a tryout, and the " All Clear " soon went.

After tea I walked up to Regent's Park to get some air and to see the balloons. The sky seemed full of them. I looked at the lorry securing one of these R.A.F. " monster fish ", and noted that there was a large earth-pin nearby. Dozens of men and women were hard at work filling sandbags to provide shelter for the R.A.F. balloon crew. I went back to Broadcasting House to listen to the King's broadcast at 6 p.m. " In this grave hour, perhaps the most fateful in our history, I send to every household . . . this message . . ." He was magnificent!

The News followed, read by Marson. It included a statement that France was now at war with Germany, and that the Cabinet was being reconstructed. Mr. Churchill going to the Admiralty— a move that will give the country great confidence.

I stayed up after midnight with the Duty News Editor on emergency duty. We had an air-raid warning at 3 a.m. It was uncanny to hear the short blasts of the police whistles, with a background of wailing sirens.

Soon after this we received the news that the *Athenia* had been torpedoed off the Hebrides. Very slick work. The submarine must have been in position long before the declaration of war. What fools the Germans were, she was full of Americans going home! Ed. Murrow of the Columbia Broadcasting System was with us, working in the News Editor's room most of the night. A fine fellow who knows his job and is a general favourite.

. . . . .

The autumn flowers in the gardens are now at their best—golden rod, helenium, asters, etc.—and in the sky balloons floating lazily, basking in the sunshine. What a contrast to London after dark, so strange and eerie, yet with an unsuspected beauty, the buildings on either side of Portland Place rising like the steep sides of a Norwegian fiord.

. . . . .

6th September. Wakened by the sirens at 6.50 a.m. in Broadcasting House, I scrambled into some clothes and went to the concert hall, now being used as the main shelter for those on duty. One end of it had been converted into a dormitory, in which twenty or thirty people were asleep. The other was filled with people sitting and standing around in groups, dressed in all sorts of garments : girls in dressing-gowns of various hues, some thirty or more charladies, some with their mops and buckets, and engineers and programme staff on duty, like myself.

We sat there for two hours before the " All Clear " went; then there was a stampede to the canteen for breakfast, and of course nothing was ready.

The R.A.F. busy dropping leaflets on Germany, and the Poles having a bad time—Germany having an enormous air superiority.

There was a good naval story going round about this time.

> *Lt.-Commander* (2nd-in-Command), coming briskly on to the bridge of a destroyer, to Captain : " The ship's engines have stopped, sir."
> *Captain* : " I know. There's an enemy submarine about."
> *Lt.-Commander :* " Are you going to depth-charge her, sir ? "
> *Captain :* " No, I'm sending down a diver with leaflets ! "

. . . . .

7th September. Programmes resuming a more normal shape now that the orchestras, Drama, Schools and Variety are being broadcast from Bristol. We have received some encouraging letters from listeners about our handling of the crisis. I had an exceptionally fine one from Sir Seymour Hicks, written from the Garrick Club.

> DEAR SIR,
>
> There are thousands like myself who are deeply grateful to you and your comrades who—hour after hour—perform a most difficult and, beyond words, tiring work. I hope you will not take it amiss that I write to you. I should only like you to know that an ordinary member of the public—who earns his living by serving his country—appreciates to the full all that you are doing, and thanks you wholeheartedly.
>
> Yours,
> SEYMOUR HICKS.

. . . . .

On 9th September the early morning bulletins included the first news of our Expeditionary Force in France, and also indicated that the French were doing well and that the Poles were making a stand at Warsaw. They stated, too, that the R.A.F. had already been in action.

Being on early morning duty, I decided to go up to the roof of Broadcasting House to see the dawn. As the sun came up I had a most wonderful view of St. Paul's Cathedral, Westminster Abbey and the new London University Tower. In contrast, I could not help thinking what a hideous place St. Pancras is. The top of Broadcasting House was like the boat-deck of a ship; only the funnels were missing to complete the picture. This resemblance to a ship is also true of the inside of the building, the offices and committee rooms on the outside corresponding to the cabins, while the central tower housing the studios corresponds to the engines and other machinery in the centre of a ship.

If one listens silently for a minute or two in any of the studios it requires little effort to imagine that the " purr " of the air-conditioning plant is the distant noise of the engines.

In the sub-basement, three floors below ground, this " purr " is occasionally drowned by a deep-throated rumble which comes and goes—the sound of a tube train passing not so many feet down below.

. . . . .

INVASION OF POLAND BY RUSSIA

Now we were at war again, I suppose it was inevitable that we should be told about some of the minor horrors and how to deal with them, as well as the major ones. I was therefore not surprised to see that I was down to announce Professor P. Buxton, the entomologist, whose subject was " The Louse ". Before the 1914 war we attended the same lectures at Cambridge, and I remember him as a familiar figure in a Norfolk jacket and red tie, who, though very wide awake, often appeared to be fast asleep during the lectures. He was an expert on all kinds of moths, bugs and beetles, and spent many of his vacations in North Africa or on the Continent collecting foreign specimens, which included a praying mantis. He once brought back a scorpion from Africa, which escaped from his rooms in Trinity College, much to the horror of his bedmaker. It was eventually found in the Court.

While I was at Cambridge, one day Pat Buxton was sitting next to me when Sir Arthur Shipley, the Master of Christ's, made one of his rare appearances in the lecture theatre. Sir Arthur was a distinguished zoologist specialising in the invertebrates; he was also an authority on food and drink, and a great raconteur. At that time he must have been in the early sixties, and was decidedly plump, even tubby. He stood in front of a kind of lectern, on which he placed his notes, and, when pausing to look at them, had first to put on his glasses—folding pince-nez which he kept in his waist-coat pocket.

On this occasion, having glanced at his notes, he dropped his glasses on to the floor when in the act of putting them back on to the lectern.

Now, the idea of Sir Arthur bending down to pick them up so tickled our fancy that a titter went round, followed by a guffaw from Buxton beside me. Sir Arthur paused, looked in our direction, and then carried on undismayed, as if nothing had happened. After a few minutes, when he again wished to consult his notes, he looked blankly down at the glasses lying on the floor, glanced up at his audience, paused again, and then, with perfect timing, leisurely and solemnly put his hand in the other waistcoat pocket, and pulled out another pair of pince-nez and adjusted them on his nose, as we cheered him to the echo. He then smiled an acknowledgment, and the lecture proceeded. As far as I know, nobody saw him pick up the first pair of glasses—they were still on the floor as we all trooped out at the end of the lecture.

.   .   .   .   .

1st October (Sunday). National Day of Prayer. At 9.15 Mr. Churchill spoke finely on the first month of the war. "Hitler," he said, "decided when the war should begin; but it is not for him or his successors to say when it will end. It began when he wanted it, and it will end only when we are convinced that he has had enough."

.   .   .   .   .

Lionel Marson is delighted that he has got his Army job and will soon be in uniform again—he is going to the Small Arms School, Hythe, at the end of the month.

. . . . .

On 2nd November I travelled up to London with Heddle Nash, the tenor, who lives near me. He was full of woes, lamenting lost work and opportunities because of the war, in particular a cancelled tour of New Zealand. I had not realised how much artists had been hit in this way. It must make life very difficult for them.

Arrived at Broadcasting House, I found I had to tackle a crisis. W. R. Mathews, "the Amateur Handyman", was held up by a failure on the Underground, and I had to read his talk for him. It was no joke having to read out, at sight, complicated instructions on the care and maintenance of lavatory cisterns.

. . . . .

On Armistice Day we broadcast the Service and Silence from Westminster Abbey. In the evening I was due to announce the Queen, but I received a message from John Snagge from the Palace saying, " Please do not announce the Queen, because the last time the King was upset by the flicking of the red light, and he would prefer that the announcement should be made there by the Director-General." John then added that he had been busy the greater part of the morning rehearsing the Director-General in preparation for this. The Queen, as always, was superb—a most natural broadcaster. The " Testament of Beauty " which followed was an excellent production, and went well until near the end, when a catastrophe occurred. They were using St. George's Hall, and the line went dead between there and Broadcasting House. Val Gielgud was heartbroken about it, and later I broadcast an apology.

. . . . .

On 23rd November I had to read nearly three pages about the Venlo incident, in which two British subjects, Captain Best and Major Stevens, were kidnapped by the Gestapo on Dutch soil.

In view of the importance attached to this piece of news, I should like to have seen it beforehand, but on important occasions such as this, last-minute telephone calls are often made to the Government Department concerned. In this case it was the Foreign Office, and I had to read it all at sight.

. . . . .

The Variety Boys were doing a fine piece of work keeping up our spirits and making us laugh, the Western Brothers in their song "George Washington Goebbels", and Arthur Askey and "Stinker" Murdoch in "Band Waggon", playing the fool in my "flat" at Broadcasting House. This week they made a Christmas pudding. And what a pudding!

On Sunday, 24th December, on returning from leave, I was on duty during the day, and taking part in a programme given by the Military Band, called "Pictures in the Fire", one of a series started by Lionel Marson before the war. Unfortunately it was spoilt because of the insertion, prior to the programme at two o'clock, of a long Admiralty message, lasting some seventeen minutes, about a new minefield. Mr. Middleton's talk was cut by five minutes, and we began at 2.29 instead of at 2.15, and were faded out at 2.45. This was most annoying, but of course we all realised that the important notice of the minefield had to take precedence.

Christmas Day. The main programme was "Round the Empire", which I rehearsed in the morning, and announced at 2.15, the linking being done by Howard Marshall. It ended with the King's Christmas message to the peoples of the Empire at 3 p.m. (from Sandringham).

It began with my sending greetings to the British Isles, the British Commonwealth overseas, to France and Poland and to all our listeners. Then came "The Empire's Greeting", a programme of Christmas scenes and messages. In his speech, the King, after emphasising that it was their love of peace that had given them a unity unknown in any previous war, said : "We feel in our hearts that we are fighting against wickedness, and this conviction will give us strength from day to day to persevere, until victory is assured".

1940

IN the first week of January we were busy making plans for the opening of the new British Expeditionary Force programme, and on 7th January we discussed and carefully worked out the opening announcement with Professor Lloyd James and John Snagge. Having finally settled everything, I found that I had to make some irritating last-minute alterations, because the engineers wanted five minutes in which to make the change of the wavelength, and we had forgotten all about this essential point. At 11.30 a.m. on 11th January I made the announcement which began : " This is the B.B.C. calling on 342 metres ", the new B.E.F. call sign ; and so another B.B.C. service was born.

On the 18th Alan Howland came back to us, after a long spell as a free-lance artist in radio and films. Alan was a first-rate Newsreader and Radio story-teller, one of the clearest readers at speed I have ever known; and when one considers that the News Editor has to compress into fifteen minutes all the salient points of the contents of a whole newspaper, it will be appreciated that, though gabbling must be avoided, clear, crisp reading at speed is a great asset, and few can do it effectively.

Each person has a natural optimum rhythm, which best suits his own particular style, and it is not always easy to alter this to a slower or quicker pace, as I myself recently discovered when broadcasting a talk to schools for Lloyd Williams, the producer. He insisted on my speaking much more slowly than my normal speed, because I was talking to children, and this meant breaking up the natural rhythm groups of the sentences. The following week we had a meeting with Professor Lloyd James, in which we discussed future plans. I made a note of the Professor's actual words at this meeting. " We must envisage ourselves," he said, " News, and Empire and Overseas News, a self-contained unit, in the future.

While we are establishing the nucleus of this Unit, with Miss Miller, our fully qualified phonetician, on the spot to help, we must think out, collaborate and plan for our future requirements in the new building " (he was referring to the projected extension of Broadcasting House to at least double the present size).

He then went on to make this interesting point, posing a question and answering it himself. " What is to be the future of Reuters ? " he asked. " Probably *you* will be—the typewriter and the teleprinter will go, and the word will be spoken directly into people's homes."

It will be interesting to see how this works out in the years to come, but, personally, I do not think the spoken word will ever replace the written word, however excellent the service offered to the public, because I am certain that one is complementary to, and not a substitute for the other. One can easily tire of listening to the spoken word, and the time comes when it is a relaxation to switch off and pick up the paper or a book.

The fact that our News bulletins consist of objective, factual news, with little comment or expression of opinion, means that, far from taking the place of the papers, and so reducing their sales— as indeed was thought probable in the 1920's—it creates a demand for newspapers, in order to read comment, social and gossip columns, advertisements and other tit-bits for which we do not cater.

.   .   .   .   .

Two days later I listened to Mr. Churchill's fine speech broadcast from Manchester. There were two interruptions during the introductory speeches, when voices were heard shouting, " We want Mosley," or something of the sort; then, with one's ear glued to the loud-speaker, a whispered conversation was audible between Mr. Churchill and the chairman—presumably the result of a suggestion to throw the hecklers out. " No," I heard Mr. Churchill say—" no, let me deal with them. I've had forty years' experience of this kind of thing." It was a situation in which he revelled, and at the end he was given a tremendous ovation.

.   .   .   .   .

What strange and unexpected things can happen in war-time. As I ended a programme called " The Naval Crown ", given by the B.B.C. Military Band, on 10th February, I met Lionel Gamlin, who told me that at 11.50 the previous night, as he was about to read some Edward Lear in the studio, to quote his actual words, " I found a naked controller just about to go to bed."

" What did you do ? " I asked.

" Oh," said Lionel, " I sent him out to brush his teeth for ten minutes."

In several of the studios there were emergency beds for the staff, and apparently Sir Stephen Tallents, the controller on duty, was on the point of retiring, not suspecting that there would be a studio transmission at so late an hour, when he met Gamlin going in to broadcast.

.   .   .   .   .

On 17th February I read the midnight News, which included the exciting story of the seizure of the German prison-ship *Altmark* by H.M.S. *Cossack*. The *Altmark* was carrying 300 British seamen battened down below; these men were the crews of merchantmen sunk in the South Atlantic by the *Graf Spee* before Christmas, and were now being taken back to Germany.

The *Cossack* tracked down the *Altmark* off the coast of Norway, and came up to her in the darkness in a fiord, capturing her after a short, sharp fight. The prisoners down below cheered on hearing the sound of British voices shouting, " It's the Navy ! The Navy is here ! "

Earlier, after the nine o'clock News, a midshipman from H.M.S. *Exeter* spoke admirably about the River Plate action, *Exeter* having got back to Plymouth to-day, where she was officially welcomed by Mr. Churchill and Sir John Simon.

.   .   .   .   .

On 18th March I announced Viscount Cecil of Chelwood (who wrote on my announcement sheet, " My name is pronounced SISSLE "—in case I should mispronounce it), a most delightful, courtly old gentleman; one of the old school. He is rather deaf and has a pronounced stoop. Being a tall man, I suppose this is inevitable at his age—eighty. He has such a pleasant voice and smile, and incidentally is a first-rate broadcaster. I could not help thinking of a remark of my father's, made to me when he was about the same age as Lord Cecil, " No, sir, I am not deaf, but my hearing is a little dull "—a fine distinction !

.   .   .   .   .

CAMPOLI
(A sketch by Edward Ward)

SIR ADRIAN BOULT

28th February. Frederick Allen joins us from Manchester, where he has been helping out on the unestablished staff. He has a good, clear voice. I understand that he has been a professional singer and that is why his voice is clear and easily produced. He is a much older man than I thought, having listened to him over the air. Broadcast voices can be most deceptive.

. . . . .

I had a long talk in the studio with Norman Birkett, the eminent K.C., before I announced his " Onlooker " talk on 5th April.

We were discussing the use of the voice in broadcasting and public speaking, and he stressed, as I have often done myself when discussing the qualifications of announcers, the importance to public speakers of acquiring a singing technique. Here are his actual words :—

> " How grateful I am that I had singing lessons years ago, and so can produce my voice easily and without effort, in contrast to so many of my colleagues, who are often the victims of throat trouble and hoarseness. I never use a glass of water, however long I may be speaking."

I should like to hear those words quoted in all places where the human voice is extensively used, be it law court, stage, screen, pulpit or studio.

. . . . .

The Invasion of Denmark and Norway and Afterwards

When motoring through South London to a luncheon appointment on 9th April, I saw the shocking announcement on the placards : " Germany invades Denmark and Norway ".

The following day I read all three main News bulletins, containing more details of the naval actions off Norway and Sweden. It looks as if we have lost a good many men, and three of our destroyers, but we have also bagged several of the enemy's, and so have the Norwegians.

We broadcast a most important message in Norwegian and Danish to the shipping of those two countries, saying, " Do not be deceived by the message broadcast telling you to proceed to Spanish or Italian ports; it was put out by Germany. Come to Allied ports, where you will be treated as friends." It would be interesting to know how many ships were saved from the clutches of the enemy by means of this message.

. . . . .

I read several News bulletins on 13th April, and at 7.45 p.m. I announced the Queen, who gave a perfect broadcast performance.

At 10.15 an announcement came in that an important official statement would be reaching us at any moment, to be broadcast in both the Home and Forces programmes. We carried on with records and apologies for the delay until at last, at 10.45, it came, and it was certainly worth waiting for. It contained the news that the Navy had forced Narvik and had sunk seven German destroyers —a superb achievement.

The next day (14th April) more details came in of this operation : three of our destroyers were damaged, but none was sunk.

This news was followed by an official Admiralty statement that the whole of the Baltic had been mined and the German coast sealed up. I read a detailed account of this complex operation in the nine o'clock News.

. . . . .

Four days later I was temporarily transferred to Bristol. On my arrival there I had tea in the board room at Broadcasting House in Whiteladies Road with Gerald Beadle, the West Regional Director, and his staff. Afterwards I met many old B.B.C. friends and was conducted round the studios, and over the various buildings scattered around Redland and Clifton which had been taken over by us for use as temporary studios.

. . . . .

On 28th April, a Sunday, I announced the afternoon concert given by the B.B.C. Symphony Orchestra in an improvised studio at the top of the C.W.S. Building in the Tramways Centre. This studio was eight floors up, and from its windows one could see the country for miles around. This concert was conducted by Gregor Fitelberg, who had been Chief Conductor of Polskie Radio, the Polish equivalent of the B.B.C. He was one of the few Polish musicians who managed to escape from Warsaw, after being nearly three months in the ruined city, where he carried on with his work during several days' intensive bombardment.

. . . . .

The following is the sequence of events from the news of the invasion of Holland and Belgium, to the evacuation of Dunkirk.

10*th May*. In the early morning I met "Sophie" Dixon, who told me that in the 7 a.m. bulletin it had been announced that the Germans had invaded Holland and Belgium, and were now bombing Brussels and towns in Northern France. They used the same evil formula as before—viz., "they were only doing it for their protection".

Both the Dutch and Belgian Ambassadors spoke before the six o'clock News. Baron Cartier de Marchienne of Belgium, a dear old man whom I have announced several times, and who has been in this country for years, spoke well, and was obviously very moved by the occasion. Mr. Chamberlain resigns and Mr. Churchill agrees to form a new Government. Serious news from Holland; Princess Juliana, Prince Bernhard and their family now in England.

.   .   .   .   .

On 15th May an account of the fierce battle raging on the Meuse was broadcast in the News. The Dutch Army has now laid down its arms, after fighting most gallantly against great odds, having lost about 100,000 men. The enemy are reported to have lost some 400 planes.

The following day a recorded version of President Roosevelt's speech to Congress was broadcast, in which he urged the speeding up of plane deliveries to the Allies. He also appealed for production to be increased for America up to 50,000 planes a year.

The news from Belgium is bad : there have been terrific losses on both sides, but we are confident. Germany has lost over 1,000 planes during the past week.

Here in England, with the countryside at its glorious best, it seems difficult to realise that in France and Belgium one of the bloodiest battles in history is now being fought out.

17*th May*. News very grave. Brussels and Antwerp have now fallen, but, in spite of this, one can detect a quiet air of confidence in those in authority.

The B.E.F. have had to fall back in conformity with the French retirement on the right from Namur and Sedan. How like 1914 it all sounds once more.

.   .   .   .   .

19th May. News of fighting no worse. The French are moving up reinforcements, and the R.A.F. are doing a wonderful job of work. Church at 11 a.m. Prayers for the King and country, and National Anthem sung at the beginning.

* * * * *

21st May. John Snagge came down from London to see us at work and tell me about the new emergency measures taken there, in view of the serious situation.

German claim of fall of Arras and Amiens announced in the News. Weygand has now taken over command : what has happened to Gamelin ?

* * * * *

23rd May. News still grave, but not catastrophic. Fighting now reported round Boulogne. Slept in office at Broadcasting House, to be in close touch with London.

* * * * *

25th May. It looks as if the Germans have taken Boulogne and are trying to cut our communications. Let us hope that Weygand will be able to prevent this. Day of prayer to-morrow (Sunday), as asked for by the King.

Again slept in Broadcasting House. Severe fighting in France continues, but no further details yet.

* * * * *

28th May. To London on duty. Arrived at Oxford Circus and saw the awful heading on a placard : " Belgium surrenders ! "

* * * * *

29th May. Saw John Snagge, who told me that Eric Dunstan is returning to help out. Just as I was coming away I met Sir Stephen Tallents, who said, " I think you ought to be in London; your voice is so well known ". In my carriage when travelling to Bristol were a number of race-goers, who got out at Bath; they were returning to London again by the 5.40. Nobody seemed in the least perturbed about the serious plight of our army before Dunkirk.

Directly I got back I had an interview with Gerald Beadle, West Regional Director, a fine administrator, most cultured and urbane, a man who inspires quiet confidence in all who work under him, who has a way of getting things done smoothly and quietly without any fuss—in short, an ideal man to be in command in a crisis. He

discussed the defence of our vital buildings with Philip Wade—
then Defence Officer—and myself. Later in the day I enrolled in
the B.B.C. Platoon of the L.D.V., then in the process of formation.

. . . .

30th May. First news of evacuation of B.E.F. from Dunkirk;
the men magnificent, the Navy and R.A.F. doing giant's work.
Fortunately the weather is perfect—a great blessing.

. . . .

On 1st and 2nd June the News bulletins were full of the details
of the wonderful progress being made with the evacuation of Dunkirk, and this in spite of furious enemy attacks on our ships. At
7.30 p.m. on 1st June I announced the concert given by the Symphony Orchestra and conducted by Sir Adrian Boult, which began
with the " Overture 1812 ". It was in the programme planned
weeks previously, and was not put in at the last moment.

. . . .

On 2nd June, before the News at 9 p.m., Mr. Eden spoke about
the situation :—

" Although the Germans stated three days ago that the
British Army in Flanders was surrounded and annihilated,
four-fifths of it and tens of thousands of French troops
have already been brought over, and the evacuation still
goes on."

. . . .

On 4th June Beadle and Philip Wade (an M.C. of the First
World War) decided that our more important buildings must be
guarded by L.D.V. personnel, and that night I did my first spell
of guard duty, and found it quite cold about 1 a.m., in spite of it
being the month of June.

The next night the Prime Minister made an inspiring broadcast
and told us of the magnificent defence of Calais by the Rifle Brigade
and the 60th Rifles. He said that 335,000 troops had been evacuated
from Dunkirk : " It was a miracle of deliverance, but not a victory,
nearly 1000 guns and all our transport had been lost." Later I
announced the Symphony Concert in the Colston Hall, which began
with the National Anthems of the Allies, followed by :—

" We have heard from the Prime Minister, and from the
French military communiqués that the withdrawal of the

Allied Armies in Flanders is complete. To mark the
occasion of this great deliverance, and by way of tribute to
the heroism of those who have fallen, and those who are
saved, we perform the Eroica Symphony by Beethoven."

.   .   .   .   .

Throughout the second week of June a terrific battle raged on
the Somme and Aisne fronts, the R.A.F. doing wonders in support.
At the end of the week came the grave news that the Germans
had crossed the Aisne in two places, but in spite of this, somehow
or other one was calmly confident of the result.

It was remarked that there were, too, many young men around
who had not been called up, and I found myself thinking of the 1914
days, and asking why they did not volunteer at once.   I suppose the
truth was that there was little or no equipment for them; the loss
of so many guns in Flanders was a great calamity, and later I heard
that would-be volunteers were being told to wait until they were
called up.

By now the L.D.V. of the B.B.C. had begun training in earnest on
the Bristol University O.T.C. ground, under Sergt.-Major Stacey,
Chief Instructor to the University, a most inspiring soldier from the
Somerset Light Infantry; we were fortunate in having him, and the
facilities the University so kindly provided.

.   .   .   .   .

On 14th June we had to make many changes in our programmes
following the very bad news that the Germans had that morning
entered Paris.   The French line was still intact; they had with-
drawn to avoid the destruction of the city.   M. Reynaud was sent
a message from our Government renewing the pledge we had
already made, to continue the struggle at all costs.

.   .   .   .   .

M. Reynaud again appealed to America to act before it was too
late.

Following the Queen's broadcast in French to the women of
France, which was magnificently done, I announced a special concert
at 10.10 p.m.

Three days later, while I was speaking to the Bristol Rotary Club,
the news came in that France had asked for an armistice.   There
were many more last-minute changes in our programmes because of

this shattering piece of news. I stayed at Broadcasting House all night, keeping in close touch with London.

The next day men from my platoon were to have fired on the range, but the parade was cancelled at the last minute by the Commanding Officer, without any reason being given. It looked as if the military authorities were conserving all ammunition for use in the event of invasion.

. . . . .

Sequence of Events from the Fall of France to the Battle of Britain

Sunday, 23rd June. German terms amounting to complete surrender accepted by France announced in the News; the army to be disarmed and demobilised, the fleet surrendered. Mr. Churchill put out a statement that " the British Government had heard of the acceptance of the terms with grief and amazement. No such conditions could have been submitted to by any French Government which possessed freedom, independence and constitutional authority ! "

. . . . .

That night General de Gaulle broadcast from London that a French National Committee was being formed in London to maintain the independence of France and help the war effort of the Allies. I can hear his voice now : " C'est moi, Générale de Gaulle qui parle."

Enemy increasing air activity; fire precautions and security measures tightened up; lectures on gas by an N.C.O., who kept referring to it as GAAS !

. . . . .

On 27th July, after a noisy and spectacular night, in which we had a raid and a thunderstorm going on at the same time, the lightning setting fire to no fewer than thirty-two balloons, we got down to tackling the all-important problem of man-power.

A message from the Prime Minister was broadcast in the News saying, " Do not relax because the enemy has not yet attempted invasion."

. . . . .

During the first week of August the enemy made many air attacks, in which we gave considerably more than we received.

On the 8th on my way home to Portishead by car I was stopped three times because of air activity, and found that crawling through the country lanes with only side-lights on was no picnic.

On the 15th the account of a heavy enemy air attack on the Thames area was broadcast in the News. The R.A.F. were magnificent: 180 enemy machines were shot down. We lost twenty machines, with fourteen of the pilots safe.

. . . . .

At the end of the month my wife and I returned to Bickley, Kent, for a few days' leave, and were enjoying the peaceful nights until, after a few day-time alerts, things suddenly boiled up on the 31st, when a terrific air battle began over the Thames Estuary in the early evening, forcing us to retire to the shelter, where we listened to it raging overhead. When it had ended eighty-five German planes had been destroyed, to thirty-seven of ours, with twenty-five pilots safe.

. . . . .

8th September (*Sunday*). As I came past New Cross in the evening when returning home from a " Follow the Drum " programme in London, I saw the warehouses in Dockland still smoking after yesterday's raid, and in the evening the glow still lit up the sky as the enemy returned to the attack, this time on the main railway lines entering London. Yesterday's reports said the Hun lost ninety-nine aircraft—about a quarter of his force was engaged.

. . . . .

9th September. I went to Chislehurst station early, and found that the Charing Cross line was out of action. At 11.15 I got a train from Bickley to Holborn en route for Paddington, but it took over four hours to get there. The passengers were wonderfully cheerful; some of them had been in the train for more than six hours.

Eventually I caught the 4.15 train from Paddington, which was very crowded, so was the station : the bombing was evidently driving people away from London.

. . . . .

10th September. At Bristol I took over operations command, and moved from Portishead into a flat on Durdham Downs, Clifton, to be near Broadcasting House.

. . . . .

11th September. The Prime Minister broadcasting to-night told us "that the bombings of London are part of Hitler's plans for the invasion of this country. Preparations for it are going forward on a great scale. Next week may be a very important week in our history!"

Buckingham Palace hit by a bomb; there were no casualties.

. . . . .

26th September. First daylight massed bomber raid right over Bristol to Filton, the works of the Bristol Aircraft Company. I saw thirty-five enemy bombers, in formation, flying low, with fighter escort buzzing around them. I thought at first they were our own planes, as there was no gunfire; then suddenly the A.A. guns opened up, and though many of the machines were destroyed, either by A.A. guns or by our fighters, some of them got through and did considerable damage, a large number of people being killed, as, unfortunately, one crowded shelter was hit.

. . . . .

29th September to 6th October. A period of intense activity, speeding up defence precautions, wiring, sandbagging Broadcasting House, Bristol, and the outside studios, also busy recording all the bigger shows—e.g., Scrapbook, plays—and in addition staff work, range, etc., with some overseas programmes thrown in at five o'clock in the morning.

RAIDS UPON LONDON AND BRISTOL, BROADCASTING HOUSE HIT

During a heavy raid on London on the 4th October, Broadcasting House was hit by a bomb, which did considerable damage to the upper floors and studios, and caused several casualties, some of them fatal. It exploded just after Bruce Belfrage had begun reading the nine o'clock News in the sub-basement. We heard the report of the explosion on the loud-speaker quite distinctly, and heard Bruce pause; then came a voice (it was Lord Lloyd's, who was in the same studio) saying, "It's all right" . . . and Bruce, as cool as a cucumber, carried on with the bulletin as though nothing had happened. It was a fine piece of work, because the blast came down the lift-shafts and ventilators and, scattering dust and soot over everything, blew open all the swing doors, including those of the sub-basement.

I was standing by at Bristol, keeping in close touch with London, and soon Godfrey Adams, who was Duty P.A. (i.e., Senior Executive Officer) in charge of the programmes, was speaking calmly to me, telling me to be ready to take over at any moment; but somehow London managed to continue without our aid. Adams had little information at the time, except that nobody was allowed above the second floor, presumably to allow the firemen and rescue parties to get on with their job.

.　　.　　.　　.　　.

1st October. I announced a programme of Elizabethan Madrigals by the B.B.C. Singers in the evening. Just as they began " Come, doleful Owl ", by Robert Jones, the sirens started to wail !

.　　.　　.　　.　　.

2nd October. Our company being part of the 3rd Battalion Bristol City Home Guard, the C.O. (Colonel Piper, D.S.O.) decided that we should have a battalion concert at the Colston Hall. Both the Symphony Orchestra and Henry Hall's band took part, the hit of the evening being Sir Adrian Boult's conducting of Henry Hall's band playing " Tiger Rag ". This is what the local paper said about it afterwards :—

> " He did physical jerks, performed weird and wonderful acrobatics—of which the high light was a leap high in the air—he strolled round the stage wagging a forefinger in the traditional style, leaned over the solo saxophonist's instrument, and listened anxiously, lest an unintended blue note emerge, and registered horror and alarm when a solo trumpeter gave a brilliant parody of Louis Armstrong."

It was grand, and the more amusing for being entirely unexpected. Then Henry Hall retaliated by most competently conducting the Symphony Orchestra playing the Overture to Mozart's " Figaro ".

.　　.　　.　　.　　.

3rd October. To lunch with Sir Walford Davies at his flat near Broadcasting House. I noticed that there was a music manuscript

194

on his table, and asked him about it.   He told me it was a string quartet he was writing, and that he had begun it while in Bristol —and this in the middle of the Blitz.

     .   .   .   .   .

5th October.   The Prime Minister's war review included references to 1,700,000 men in the Home Guard, and to the fact that the possibility of invasion was by no means ruled out—just what was wanted to supply a little ginger to some of the men.

     .   .   .   .   .

THE BLITZ

November 24th (Sunday).   I was rehearsing and recording " Star Time " with Yvonne Arnaud, Norman Shelley and other members of the Repertory Company at Redland Studio, recording beginning at 6.   At 6.20 the sirens sounded and we had to stop and go below into the shelters. After dropping parachute flares, the enemy released some high explosive bombs and incendiaries, and there was heavy and prolonged A.A. fire.   It soon became evident that this was no ordinary raid, but the " Blitz ".   Now and again I went up to look round, and saw many fires burning in the city below us, some houses on fire nearby, and some incendiaries burning on the road- way.   Just before 10 p.m. there was a lull, and I got back to Broad- casting House—the enemy planes were still dropping incendiaries. Fires burning everywhere, the whole sky lit up.   A water-main had been smashed, cutting off supplies.

Directly after breakfast the next day I went down Whiteladies Road, past the University, to the entrance of Park Street, to see the damage done by last night's raid.   One glance was sufficient to show that it was severe.   Many buildings had been gutted by fire caused by incendiaries : a furniture depository, a large store, two churches, many shops and almost the whole of Park Street had gone—a most depressing sight.   If only there had been fire-watchers available to cope with the incendiaries, dozens of buildings would have been saved.   Being a Sunday night, no doubt many employees were away for the week-end.   The streets were a network of fire- hoses, it being difficult for vehicular traffic to get by, and some of the walls were very dangerous.   In spite of this, hundreds of people were walking round to see the damage.   Police cars with loud-speakers were moving in and out, urging people to boil all water before drinking it.

Feeling most depressed, I returned to the studio to rehearse a duet with Betty Huntley-Wright and the orchestra under Ernest Longstaffe and tried to forget the scene outside; but just as we began the transmission the sirens sounded and London took over—enemy planes were coming over high up, to take photographs!

In the evening they again came over to raid Avonmouth, but our defences had been strengthened and, thanks to some " big stuff " put up by the A.A. batteries, little damage was done.

Gerald Daly, Engineer-in-Charge, Bristol, and " Tubby " Myers of the Engineering Division, an expert on the installation side, and a general favourite, have been very busy making emergency sanitary and water arrangements; now practically all the mains had gone. How near the war had come to us; so swiftly too! How many things one takes for granted in life, never appreciating them until they are suddenly snatched away. Fortunately, the Army had come to our aid, and sent us field water-carts, and we had relays of fatigue parties out fetching water for the canteen and for staff living nearby.

The following day I motored to the Colston Hall for the morning orchestral rehearsal, taking with me my wife's fur coat for Sidonie Goossens (principal harp), who lost all her belongings in the Blitz on Sunday night.

.   .   .   .   .

On 2nd December, after a busy afternoon rehearsing and recording, we had an alert early in the evening, and London took over from us. We soon realised that another full-scale Blitz was on the way; first came the showers of incendiaries, setting fire to the roof of Broadcasting House, but we quickly put them out.

It was most unpleasant at times, because the enemy planes began to drop high-explosive bombs, using the light from the fires as a target, and several times we had to lie flat on our stomachs as " whistlers " came down. Later, as things were a little quieter, I went back to Broadcasting House and helped to put out the Epilogue from the tiny security studio in the basement, Paul Beard playing the fiddle with scarcely enough room to use his bow, Dr. Welch reading the prayers.

About 10.30 p.m., when things were much quieter, but the " All clear" had not gone, Colonel Piper, my C.O., came in and said that a large bomb had fallen outside Cotham Fort, the T.A. Store, shattering the building and blowing rifles and greatcoats all over the place. Several people, including four Home Guard sentries, were missing. At 10.45 I set out with eighteen men, with picks and shovels, and we spent a grim night digging on the lip of a huge crater in the lurid light of many burning buildings.

Shortly after 3 a.m. Max Kester, one of the Variety Producers, came up to Philip Wade, the actor, who was with me, and whispered in his ear, " Philip, could you do with a pint ? "

" Could I blinking well not ! " said Philip.

" Well," said Max, " you see that torch moving about on the other side of the crater ?   That's Leon Goossens (the oboe player); he'll take you to it."

I did not see either of them again for more than half an hour; apparently there was a shattered pub on the other side of the crater, but the cellars were undamaged, and the landlord and his wife were at home to all helpers.

On returning to my flat on Durdham Downs, Clifton, next morning, I found that a bomb had fallen in the road just outside and smashed all our windows, killed our warden and two others, and deposited a 3-feet-square paving-stone on the roof; but fortunately nobody inside the house was hurt.

.   .   .   .

On the 9th December I had an early morning call from Peter Fettes. He had been on duty at Broadcasting House, Bristol, and had been up all night with Felix Felton, the Programme Director, making emergency plans for us to take over in the morning, because during the night a land-mine had exploded outside the Langham Hotel, causing severe damage to Broadcasting House, London, and other buildings in the district; serious flooding of the basement followed, endangering the apparatus there. There were several casualties, Broadcasting House was temporarily put out of action, and Maida Vale control room, which was incomplete at the time, had to take over; they all had a most difficult time. We had to take over nearly all the programmes scheduled from London. I was at Broadcasting House, Bristol, all day, and returned there at night to sleep in.

By the middle of December, Headquarters in London had started to tidy things up, and they began to take over some of the programmes we had been doing for them, in this way easing our burden and giving us a chance to take stock of the position.

On the 14th the Director-General came down from London to meet the heads of Departments, and told us about the chaos at Broadcasting House after the explosion of the land-mine; there were twenty-four casualties, including one policeman killed, B. E. Nicolls, the Controller of Programmes, badly concussed and cut by falling masonry, and Fred Bate (of the N.B.C.) injured in his office in Great Portland Street.

This Christmas was a quiet one, I am thankful to say; apart from presenting the Symphony Concert and reading the Epilogue, I did very little, and the Germans mercifully left us alone.

1941

THE new year was ushered in with a twelve-hour blitz at Bristol, in which some bombs were dropped unpleasantly close to us in Broadcasting House—close enough to rock the building and smash several windows. While the raid was in progress, I took the names of those sheltering in the basement, and found that they numbered just over seventy, far too many. The truth was that when the sirens sounded, many of the staff billeted nearby came along to Broadcasting House, for the companionship and the canteen facilities.

. . . . .

On 13th January part of Music's Headquarters in a house in Pembroke Road was destroyed by fire, including the important Music Library. The fire was not caused by enemy action, but by a fire-watcher of all people. He is reported to have said that he was bored with fire-watching, it was so dull, so he decided to set the place on fire to liven things up. Later, when inquiries were made, it was found that he had been sent to us by the Ministry of Labour, knowing that he had only come out of a mental institution in June, but they explained that because of the shortage of man-power they had no alternative. They might at least have warned us of his past history, so that we could have kept an eye on him. The tragedy was that most of the invaluable control-scores were destroyed, and these contained the timings of each work, the conductor's name and the date, written on the fly-leaf.

. . . . .

Two days after this I received a letter from a woman refugee who enclosed a most beautifully illuminated manuscript of some verses from St. John's Gospel which I had recently read in an Epilogue. It was in very small script, and looked like a mediæval missal,—an exquisite piece of work, and sent to me in gratitude for once (unknowingly) helping her with her English. " When I first came to this country," she said, "I did not know much English, and you were the first person I was able to understand."

. . . .

At the end of January, De Lotbinière, Outside Broadcast Director, came down from London to take Beadle's place as West Regional Director, and at once set about making preparations for the visit of H.R.H. the Duke of Kent.

. . . .

On 5th February De Lotbinière brought H.R.H. into the studio with Piggott, who had been his mathematics tutor at Dartmouth, and is now on our staff. They came in during the recording of an Orchestral Concert, which I was presenting. The Duke listened for a while, until the interval, then we were presented to him, and he asked us questions about the recording and the orchestra before going on to the Director's room for tea.

. . . .

The following Sunday, J. B. Priestley's postscript after the nine o'clock News having been cancelled, the Prime Minister spoke brilliantly for thirty-eight minutes at nine o'clock. He referred to the capture of Benghazi and the bombardment of Genoa. "From this port," he said, "a Nazi expedition might have sailed to attack General Weygand in Algeria or Tunis."

. . . .

Just as it was beginning to get dark on the 6th March I thought I heard cannon-fire, but it turned out to be machine-gun fire from a Nazi plane which had slipped in, low down between the balloons, and was spraying the streets with bullets. Kay Cavendish, who at that time was working for our Variety Department as a repertory artist, had a very narrow escape; bullets were spattering all round her as she bolted from the street to the shelter of a house. She told me later that she could see the man in the enemy plane quite distinctly.

We heard afterwards that our fighters swooped on the raider and shot it down as soon as it had left the city area and got out into the open country.

. . . .

On returning from the Norman Chapel of the Cathedral, where the Singers had been broadcasting a Palestrina Mass on the 11th, I

GERALD BEADLE, CONTROLLER, WEST REGION

SERGT.-MAJOR STACEY AND THE AUTHOR IN L.D.V. DAYS AT BRISTOL

met Piggott, who told me that Sir Walford Davies had died suddenly of heart failure. This was a great shock, as I had been talking to him in the canteen only three days before. Millions will miss his cheerful " Good evening, listeners all " and his brilliant talks on " Music and the Ordinary Listener ", " Music for Worship ", and his playing, for he had an exquisite touch. Music and the influence of music in the home were his life. Richard Capell said of him, " He was a man of overflowing humanity and zeal for the welfare of his fellow men ". Sir Adrian Boult said, " Millions have been encouraged by him to listen to the best music; his uncanny gift of illuminating the great masterpieces in homely non-technical language was the secret of his popularity ".

I went to Sir Walford's Memorial Service in Bristol Cathedral on the 14th. The B.B.C. Singers sang most beautifully, his own Introit, " The hour cometh and now is ", and his setting of the 121st Psalm and the Nunc Dimittis. Dr. Thatcher and Sir Adrian Boult acted as ushers and showed us to our seats. Two bishops were there, and Dr. Iremonger and Dr. Welch. Dr. Hunt, organist at Bristol Cathedral, was at the organ. I returned to work at Broadcasting House feeling very sad. What a gap the passing of Sir Walford has left in our lives! No one could fill it—he was unique.

. . . . .

On 23rd March I announced a fine recital by Astra Desmond. A superlative artist and the mother of grown-up sons, too. She looked quite majestic, standing erect, almost six feet in height, with her dark hair and her fine features, and wearing a dark green dress, with horn-rimmed glasses to match. She sings in Norwegian, Finnish and Greek, as well as in French, German and Italian, and always with that sense of ease that indicates the great artist. Only once in all the years I have known her did she ever cross swords with me, and that was when I referred to Conchita Supervia as " the world's only coloratura contralto ". I suppose I must have been especially impressed by the wonderful range of the Spanish singer's phenomenal voice.

. . . . .

On 25th March I prepared the presentation of a programme in honour of Greek Independence Day, given by the Orchestra, conducted by Clarence Raybould. I had only very short notice of this programme, but it seemed to go well. Raybould is such an excellent person to work with. He seldom criticises our work, but if he does, he is always constructive. In this case, when searching in my mind for a suitable approach, I had the good fortune to remember the opening words of the speech of Pericles on freedom and democracy (spoken as a Funeral Oration over the Athenians who fell in the first year of the Peloponnesian war), and I read a short extract from it at the end of the programme. Clarence Raybould kindly wrote me a note about it the next day, to the effect that it was " exactly right ". Actually it was a piece of good fortune that I happened to have come across it recently in my reading.

   .   .   .

 27th March. Mr. Churchill in optimistic vein : " Never have we been so strong or so hopeful as we are to-day."

 I was presenting a programme on the subject of spring at 9.30 p.m. with the Orchestra in the large studio. At 9.20 p.m., during a talk from London, we had an alert, but I told London that as there had been no gunfire, and we were in a so-called " security studio ", we would carry on at 9.30. As I began, " This is the B.B.C. Home Service, Oh to be in England now that April's there ", the guns roared out, mutilating the atmosphere of peace and spring which I had been so carefully trying to create, and making us all roar with laughter.

   .   .   .

 11th April (Good Friday). In the afternoon I announced the Parsifal Concert given by the Orchestra conducted by Sir Henry Wood. He seemed to be as full of life as ever, but told us that he had recently had " flu " and had not yet fully recovered. That night we had another horrid two-phase blitz. It began at ten o'clock with parachute flares and incendiaries; then came a lull and the " All Clear ", followed by a heavy H.E. attack, in which the enemy bombers used the fires as targets. The noise was terrific, as our barrage had been considerably increased—I had scarcely any sleep. The Coliseum, off Park Street, was completely destroyed. The next morning I went to see its ruins, and, on passing the University, saw Mr. Churchill and Mr. Winant surrounded by cheering crowds. They had come down from London to receive honorary degrees from the University, and were smiling and waving to the crowds, delighted at their reception. All this was going on as though times were normal and nothing unusual had happened the previous night, when in fact fire-engines were still busy putting out fires only a few yards away.

.   .   .   .   .   .

I understand that it is now settled that we shall go to Bedford. They are most friendly disposed to us there, and will welcome the Orchestra and the concerts. Also I hear that there is good accommodation, and several excellent halls which can be used as studios. The one drawback seems to be that the town is almost completely surrounded by either factories or aerodromes. Let us hope it will not be a case of " out of the frying-pan . . .".

.   .   .   .   .   .

On 6th April (Palm Sunday), after the performance of Bach's " St. Matthew Passion ", I read a short passage of prose by a Quaker writer, the music ending a few minutes early. The following week I read this letter in the *Manchester Guardian* :—

> SIR,
>   At the end of the glorious broadcast of the Matthew Passion on Sunday 6th April an equally glorious passage of prose was read. I wonder how many listeners recognised it as coming from the works of James Nayler, quoted in the Quaker Book of Discipline ?
>   The spirit which directed the inclusion of those words, which are one of the finest expressions of Quaker Doctrine, was a different one from that which recently moved the B.B.C. to forbid pacifists to broadcast. So many people wrote to you then criticising the B.B.C. that I feel one of us ought to express, through your column, our thanks to the B.B.C. for giving listeners this very beautiful passage from the literature of non-violent resistance.
>
> Yours etc.
BEN W. VINCENT.
>
> *Mount View, Queens Gate,*
>   *Bramhall.*

Surely it is one thing, as an act of policy, to refuse to allow a pacifist to broadcast, but quite another to broadcast a selected passage from the works of a pacifist writer ?

On 27th April came the serious news that the Germans had entered Athens, but in spite of this the Prime Minister in his broadcast review of the war position, said that ". . . in view of the aid now assured from America, the eventual and total defeat of Hitler and Mussolini is certain ". He then went on to tell us that of the 60,000 troops sent to Greece, 48,000 had been evacuated.

Early in May I found that more and more of our staff were going to Weston to sleep at the B.B.C. Hostel, making my task as operations officer Bristol most difficult in the event of an emergency, when swift action by men immediately available might be imperative.

The blitzes continued at irregular intervals, and on the 7th May Windmill and Lewis's garage in Clifton and a furniture store opposite to it were destroyed. Audrey Cameron, the producer, who lived close by, did a fine job of work, helping to push out cars from the burning building, saving many of them. What " guts " she has— as I have had occasion to remark before. Far more than many men.

About this time Eric Fawcett asked me to record a short piece to be included in the weekly series introduced by Maisie Gay, the vaudeville star. Owing to arthritis, Maisie could not come to the B.B.C., but each week Eric used to go out to her home at Box, near Bath, with the recording gear, and she recorded her introduction from her bedside, followed by her signature tune, " There's life in the old girl yet ". There certainly was, for in spite of her disability she wrote me several most cheerful (almost saucy) letters, and the show was very popular, and ran for several weeks.

Later on she founded an invalids' fellowship club, in which members undertook to write to one another periodically.

Henry Warren, the writer on country life, was then attached to our staff. He wrote the Empire Day programme, which was given by the Symphony Orchestra, conducted by Sir Henry Wood. It included Percy Grainger's "Colonial Song", a fine tune, and Sir Henry's own "Fantasia on British Sea Songs", which must have brought back many memories of the Queen's Hall and the Proms. At the end, as an Epilogue, I read "My own country", the little poem by Belloc, which includes this couplet :—

"In the month of May in my own country
All the woods are new."

. . . . .

The announcement of the sinking of the *Hood* by the *Bismarck* was given out in the News on 26th May. She was sunk by a chance hit in her magazine. Bernard Stubbs, formerly of our News Department, who was on board as a Naval Intelligence Officer, went down with her. The *Bismarck* was eventually sunk by the cruiser *Dorsetshire* 400 miles off Brest, after a long chase. The news from Crete was bad : the Germans were attacking with air-borne troops, and we lost several ships from their air attack.

. . . . .

Early in June we carried out a Home Guard exercise which brought home to us the dangers from within. Broadcasting House was expecting to be attacked by an enemy force coming from the direction of the Bristol Channel, at any time from 6 p.m. onwards. All reasonable defence precautions, such as manning strong points, look-outs, etc., sending out patrols to reconnoitre, were taken be-fore this hour. It so happened that in front of Broadcasting House there were some flower-beds, which were in process of being dug over by the gardeners, and at the side were two piles of bricks, where repairs to the garage were being made, by a local con-tractor's men. An hour before zero, the gardeners, labourers, masons, etc., changed places with the enemy, who had made it worth their while to do so. The enemy were all experienced actors, and their make-up was impeccable, and all were hard at work at 6 p.m., and no suspicions were aroused. Shortly after six o'clock, on a given signal, they entered the Home Guard Commander's office, and, seizing his rifle, attacked and overpowered the sentry from the rear, then rushed the guard and held up the operations room and took us all prisoners.

This was a clever and slick piece of work, proving the value of observation and make-up—in fact, it was just the sort of ruse that the enemy might have employed to gain access to the building and blow up the vital gear in the control room.

.   .   .   .   .

I had recently lost a handkerchief, which was found by Stephen Jack, the actor, who kindly returned it to me with this charming little verse :—

> " Unlike the jewels of King John
> This was not lost in Washington,
> But lying on a studio floor
> It missed its master all the more."

.   .   .   .   .

On 19th June I had an interview with B. E. Nicolls, the Controller of Programmes ; he is an old friend, on whose staff I served when he was London Station Director at Savoy Hill, succeeding Rex Palmer in that capacity. I began by congratulating him on his recent memorandum on announcing in general, and in particular on his advice to avoid introductions of the type, " Beethoven had the tooth-ache when he wrote this work ; it has not been performed for eighty years, and that is why we are playing it to-night ". Then I criticised the war-time standard of announcing, pointing out that new-comers since the war had had scarcely any training at all. He agreed, and told me of the steps being taken to rectify this situation.

I then attacked the Corporation's policy of allowing first-class microphone performers to drift away into other jobs because there appeared to be little or no future for them in microphone work, instead of encouraging them and recognising their talent and paying them according to their ability, in order to retain their services. It was a position best summed up in a parody of Gilbert's well-known lines :—

> " Stick close to your desks and steer clear of the mike !
> And you'll all become rulers of the B.B.C."

Nicolls laughed at this, and I went on to quote the case of Harman Grisewood, in support of my argument ; Harman being one of the finest broadcasters alive, who now seldom goes near a microphone, and had recently become an Assistant-Controller. Nicolls agreed on the general principle.

From this point our conversation ranged chiefly from fire-watching to Home Guard duties, and we parted good friends, as we always have been.

I had not seen him for some time, and I thought that he had aged a good deal since he was wounded in the explosion of the land-mine last year. A keen gardener who knows the British Flora and Geological Formations well, he seemed to be more nervous than he used to be—at least, that was my impression. He probably knows more about broadcasting than any other man in this country, having served in many branches of the programme division. He has a wonderful memory and, with his great ability, tact and disarming smile, coupled with a fine physique and a remarkable dome-shaped head, should surely have been a bishop. How majestically he could wear a cope, and how dignified that head would look beneath a mitre !

On Sunday, 22nd June, Mr. Churchill spoke before the News, telling us of Germany's attack on the U.S.S.R., and of our decision to help Russia in any way we can. Heavy fighting was going on in Russia, with severe losses on both sides.

Early in July I met Lady Violet Bonham-Carter, a B.B.C. Governor, then on a visit to Bristol, and had a long talk with her about News-reading and its difficulties, and also about music, with special reference to the B.B.C. Symphony Orchestra. This, I maintained, was a great national asset, and should be used as such, at any rate in war-time. I stressed the importance of its going out and about all the big cities, so that the players could become better known and the people given an opportunity of seeing what they looked like. I argued that it was an invaluable instrument for helping to maintain national morale, and asked, "Why not a tour of all the blitzed cities as a start ? "

She was a most sympathetic listener, and encouraged me to talk, and promised to look into some of the points I had raised. But, though the Orchestra did, later on, go to the main Service centres and to some large American depôts, a tour of the blitzed cities, as such, never materialised.

On 11th July I returned to London to read some News bulletins and announce the opening night of the Proms, a six-weeks season sponsored by Keith Douglas, under the auspices of the Royal Philharmonic Society, the Orchestra being the London Symphony Orchestra. At the rehearsal at the Albert Hall I saw Ivor Walsworth, the Programme Engineer, and Lady Wood, and prepared my plans. Later I saw Sir Henry and tried to persuade him to say a few words at the beginning of the concert, but he pleaded that " it would upset me so much musically ". However, he did promise to make a short speech on the last night of the season.

From 21st to 28th July there were various farewell parties in Bristol. I was extremely sorry to leave, as people were very kind to us during our stay, and I had made many friends. The Pembroke Road Home Guard gave a farewell party to Colonel Piper, the C.O., which he attended, in spite of the fact that he had heard only the day before that his son had been killed in action. On the 24th, at Dr. Welch's party at the Club, I met the Bishop and the Dean. The latter was very amused at a heading in the local paper, which announced " Religion leaving Bristol ".

We arrived at Bedford at the end of the month, and on 8th August I announced the evening concert given in the Corn Exchange there for the first time. It was a fair-sized hall, and the acoustics were good, but as a concert hall it could not compare with the Colston Hall in Bristol. As there was an invited audience, and the members of the Orchestra were in evening dress, I, too, changed.

I announced the programme from the platform, standing beside Sir Adrian, and as I took my place he whispered in my ear, " Fine ! back to the old tradition ".

The 10th August was a day long to be remembered, because, after a Symphony Concert in the afternoon, conducted by that fine musician, Julius Harrison, in the evening there were two outstanding broadcasts, one by the Queen—by far the most lovely piece of broadcasting by a woman I have ever heard; her voice, so cultured and so appealing, is rather sad in quality, and yet most attractive, her phrasing being well-nigh perfect.

Later Quentin Reynolds excelled himself, introducing a new form of Radio technique, and speaking directly to Hitler, addressing him by his former name, " Mr. Schickelgruber ".

Shortly after Reynolds had finished speaking, and while we were praising his effort as a brilliant piece of work, I received an S.O.S. to go to the Bunyan Studio (i.e., the Bunyan Chapel converted into a studio) and read the Epilogue for the Forces at 10 p.m., as Robert Speaight, who had been engaged to read it, had not arrived. I was rushed there in a Staff car, and arrived only just in time. As I finished reading, Speaight appeared, looking worn and worried and generally hot under the collar.

He told us that his train from London was very late, and so full that, in spite of a first-class ticket, he had had to stand all the way, and when he eventually reached Bedford station there was no Staff car to meet him, and he could get no taxi; he therefore had to walk to his hotel, carrying a heavy bag. He then rushed off to the Parish Church—the Epilogue had formerly been read in a side chapel in the church, but recently, because of the difficulty of blacking out the windows, it had been transferred to one of the studios—tried to get in, but found the door locked. Eventually, in despair, he was seen by a police sergeant hammering on the door and shouting dramatically, " I want the Epilogue ! . . . I want the Epilogue ! " The sergeant persuaded him to return in his car to the station, where they telephoned the B.B.C. headquarters at the Cavendish Hotel. The commissionaire did not know where the Epilogue was being broadcast, but rang control room, who told him, and off they rushed in the police car to the Bunyan Building, getting there just too late ! Poor Bobby ! I was sorry for him. But at least he had the consolation of being there in good time for the second reading—in the Home Service at 10.38.

.   .   .   .   .

On Saturday, 23rd August, I went up to London to announce the last night of the " Proms ", which in spite of bombing and the destruction of the Queen's Hall, with its old associations and convenient situation near Oxford Circus, had been patronised by the greatest crowds in their long history. " We are now realising ", said Thompson, the Concert Manager, " how much money we turned away at Queen's Hall." Sir Henry, true to his word, spoke to the audience before the concert began, reading a few sentences written out on a postcard, eulogising the support the audiences had given to the concerts in spite of Hitler and all his gang. It was a very wet night, but this did not damp people's enthusiasm, for the Albert Hall was packed. There was the usual cheerful care-free last-night atmosphere, all the principals of the orchestra being cheered as they took their places, and the audience enjoying them-selves immensely in the " Fantasia " based on British Sea-songs, by Sir Henry himself.

．　　　．　　　．　　　．　　　．

In the second week of September I took a party of men on to the range at Stewartby, some five miles out of Bedford, at the head-quarters of The London Brick Company, Ltd., the range being situated in one of the worked-out lodes or clay-pits.

In spite of the rifles being unfamiliar, some of the old soldiers shot remarkably well, but I was far from happy with mine. These rifles had been lent to us by the Bedford Police, and the constable who handed them over was shocked at the idea of using boiling water to clean them after firing (standing Army practice). " What," he said indignantly, " put water in my rifles ! Never." So we pulled them through and handed them back to him with many thanks.

．　　　．　　　．　　　．　　　．

On 23rd September I read six Epilogues, one after the other, in order to record them for Nairobi. We now have a Transcription Service which is making a large number of records in this manner, and sending them overseas in order to project the British way of life in various foreign countries, as well as in the Empire. Quite a lot of this work is carried out in the studios at Bedford.

．　　　．　　　．　　　．　　　．

13*th October.* Great excitement at Broadcasting House in London over the " enemy voice " which suddenly began cutting in yesterday, both during the News and after it, during the W.A.A.F.'s programme. Strict orders have been issued that all programmes must go on up to the last moment of their schedule, to give the interrupter no loophole. Shortly after this, when Alan Howland was on duty, he read the News practically up to the last second, with no pause whatever, and at such a speed that all the

Voice could do was to utter over the last sentence a despairing, " That's not fair ".

.   .   .   .   .

At the end of that week, in preparing my presentation material for a concert to Europe by the Symphony Orchestra, I was amused to find that the Overseas Presentation wished Paul Beard to be referred to as " concert master ", and not as leader, as we normally do in this country. When I arrived at the studio the joke was on me, because Paul was away ill, and Marie Wilson, his deputy, was leading, and I certainly could not call her " concert mistress ".

In the end I compromised by saying that the Orchestra was " led by " Marie Wilson.

.   .   .   .   .

PEARL HARBOUR AND ITS SEQUEL

I had to announce the Sunday afternoon Chamber concert at the Bedford Modern Girls School on the 6th in full operational kit, having come there straight from the Home Guard Exercise " Scorch ", there being no chance of changing beforehand. At 9 p.m. that night Alvar Lidell gave out the momentous news that Japan had attacked the United States at Pearl Harbour, without warning. Everyone is wondering if this will be the turning point of the war. Whatever the reaction, it is obviously of the greatest significance.

In the evening we listened to President Roosevelt's speech, which came through very clearly—a most dramatic and all-important moment in our history. The Prime Minister followed him at 9 p.m., but, perhaps because it was an anti-climax, I did not think he was quite up to his usual form. I then went to Bedford School to do the presentation of " *Alexander Nevsky* ", with Robert Donat in the name-part, Dallas Bower producing. Some of the music was thrilling. How strange that this play about a national hero and the way he freed people from the enemy in the Middle Ages should follow the wonderful news of the entry of the United States into the war.

.   .   .   .   .

13*th December.* At 7.30 I announced a programme, called " Salute to America ", in honour of America's entry into the war. It was almost a last-minute show, with very little rehearsal, because of the swift, sly way the Japs began hostilities—" sneaking up to America and kicking the back-door open ". Gilliam produced it, and, thanks to the many experienced men in the cast, we got through without any mishap. But it was an anxious business. Bobby Speaight, Laidman Browne and Ivan Samson all were in it.

.   .   .   .   .

17th December. A sad piece of news came to me in a letter to-day from Mrs. Lambert, who wrote from Norfolk to tell me of the death of her husband (A. J. Alan). This was a shock, as I did not know that he had been ill. She told me he had been in a Norwich nursing-home for some time, following an operation in the summer, from which he never fully recovered. So passes a most original mind and engaging personality—a great artist : the greatest radio story-teller yet. He was rightly regarded as one of the few great names in Radio.

.   .   .   .   .

Colonel Stafford, Bedford Director, sent for me the next day to tell me that before the concert on Sunday, the 21st, to be given in honour of Stalin's birthday, there was to be a party to entertain guests from the Russian Embassy. He asked me to help him entertain them, and also if I could furnish a guard of honour. Apparently London thought the Ambassador and his staff ought to be invited, but in view of the distance, and the fact that Mr. Maisky was in Moscow, it was considered unlikely that they would accept. But they had accepted, and the problem now was to arrange for the reception and luncheon to follow, at very short notice. As it was a Sunday, there were difficulties about getting a local caterer to undertake it. In the end, the Corporation's own Catering Department handled it from London, and made an excellent job of it, considering how short was the notice. To help Stafford to entertain his guests was one thing, to furnish a guard of honour quite another. However, I undertook to find some kind of a guard to be at the entrance when the cars arrived on Sunday, and proceeded to make the necessary plans. All but one of the guard were members of the Orchestra, and the final rehearsal was to be on the Sunday morning, immediately before the luncheon. I therefore saw Sir Henry Wood, who was conducting, at the Friday rehearsal, and he agreed to let the Orchestra off at 12.30 on the Sunday morning, to give me a chance of assembling and inspecting the guard before the convoy arrived at 12.50. Also, I wanted the men to get the " feel " of their rifles when presenting arms wearing gas-masks in the " ready " position—i.e. on their chests.

Imagine my anxiety when not one of the guard had even come in sight along the road from the Corn Exchange by 12.40, and I was almost frantic when at last I saw two of the men approaching at the double about two minutes later, the others following a short way behind.

I had just time to fall them in and call them to attention as the cars arrived—no time to inspect them, let alone give them any arms drill. As a Russian Admiral got out of the leading car they presented arms, doing it very smartly. The Admiral then carefully inspected the guard, followed by a General of the Red Army and an Air Force General, and they then walked inside the Bunyan Building to be received by Stafford and his staff. As I dismissed the guard, one of them—an ex-sergeant of the Royal Marines—came up, saluted and said, " May I confess sir, that in all my service I have never been nearer to dropping my rifle on parade than when presenting arms to-day—thanks to that damned gas-mask ? " That was a candid enough confession, and we had a good laugh about it. He then went on to explain why they had been unable to get away from the rehearsal before 12.40, instead of at 12.30, as Sir Henry had arranged. Almost at the last moment the Overseas Programme Division decided to record the symphony; therefore, instead of rehearsing only a few passages, as Sir Henry had told me he intended to do, the Orchestra had to play through the whole of the work. I was lucky to get a guard at all.

Later, nearly all my anxieties were dispelled, when Stafford whispered in my ear that the Russian General had asked him if the guard of honour was made up of Regular soldiers ! This remark I discreetly passed on to the men as soon as I had an opportunity.

.   .   .   .   .

At Christmas-time I was asked to take part in a programme which involved my reading, as though in a News bulletin, part of a typical script by my old friend " Stainless Stephen ". This was the sort of thing I had to try to " put over " : " ' Well, pets ', announced

Brainless, causing a thrill to run through his lady listeners (comma) by the warmth of his greeting (semi-final), ' some of you may be wondering what I'm doing here again (semi-conscious) spoiling a perfectly good programme. Speaking in confidence, the B.B.C. (capital letters) found itself on the horns of a dilemma (step-child to a buffalo) now the new list of pronunciations has come into effect.'

"Well, we've all got our troubles. For instance, my boy, who's been taking his examination, has just written to his mother, ' Have failed in all subjects, prepare the old man.' I've sent him a telegram : ' The old man's prepared; prepare yourself '. Old man indeed ! I'll mop up his strategic points, and it won't be a pincer movement either.'

1942

IN the second week in January, on returning from a few days' leave in Devon, in a train crowded with troops, I noticed that, in addition to the usual driver and fireman, there was an R.E. Corporal on the footplate. I suppose this is only a precaution in case of invasion, but, in view of enemy air activity, in the words of Sid Walker, " It makes you think, chum; it makes you think."

    .   .   .   .

On 22nd January, when the Japanese, thanks to their great air superiority, were making much too rapid progress in Malaya, Dr. Clifford, an Australian in charge of Overseas Music at the B.B.C., gave us a lecture about Overseas broadcasting, stressing its great influence in the Dominions and Empire. He told us what a demand there was for good music in the Pacific, and how widely our efforts were appreciated, adding that all the members of his department were hopelessly overworked as a result.

    .   .   .   .

On 29th January I announced a Symphony Concert of the works of Delius, given in the Bedford School Hall—an excellent hall for sound, owing to the height of the roof. This concert, which was conducted by Sir Adrian Boult, was introduced by Eric Fenby, who for many years, after the composer's sight had failed, has been his amanuensis. He gave us a graphic account of how they worked together, illustrated by the Orchestra, and in particular from " The Song of Summer ", a work dedicated to him.

    .   .   .   .

On 1st February, a Sunday, it was snowing hard in the morning, and at 11 a.m. Mr. Middleton telephoned to me from Northampton to say that he could not get to Bedford because of the snow. I told him not to worry, and said that I would read his manuscript for him. I had a perilous cycle ride into Bedford, for we were then living seven miles out on the Kimbolton Road, but arrived there in under an hour and a quarter. When I got into the town I found that snow-ploughs were being used. I rehearsed and read Middleton's script, which seemed to go fairly well, so far as I could judge. The following day I received a short note from John Green, the producer, thanking me for taking over in this emergency, and hinting that my love of gardening had stood me in good stead.

That week we had still more snow, it being as much as six feet deep in places, making the going very difficult, but the main roads were not too bad, because snow-ploughs had been used on them.

.   .   .

What a dreadful bogey timing is ! The curse of Radio Production. Would that we had a programme that had no fixed points in it, like the 6 p.m. and 9 p.m. News bulletins—one in which it really did not matter if we ran two or three minutes late by the end of the evening.

The Symphony Concert in the Corn Exchange, Bedford, at eight o'clock no 22nd April was conducted by Sir Henry Wood, and Sir Henry had persuaded Arthur Bliss, the Director of Music, that he could do both the Fidelio Overture by Beethoven and the Elgar Symphony in fifty-eight minutes; but I was against this plan, arguing that it was much too risky. However, Bliss said that he would take the responsibility, and I informed London of the decision, and of the risk, requesting them to give us right up to the last moment and to cut the closing announcement, if necessary.

In the end it became a neck-and-neck race with the clock, the last chord coinciding with Big Ben's first stroke of the hour at nine o'clock.

Bliss seemed very upset about it, saying that Sir Henry took the first movement of the symphony too slowly. The truth was that Sir Henry, now getting on in years, relied too much on timings he had noted fifteen or twenty years ago.

.   .   .

While the Orchestra was at Bedford there was a weekly series of half-hour programmes on Saturday evenings called " The Orchestra Entertains ". On 25th April Clarence Raybould was conducting and, in checking over the order of the music, was horrified to see that the Librarian had put out a French orchestral arrangement of Handel's Largo. He was so incensed at this that, to prevent the

216

B. E. NICOLLS
(DIRECTOR OF HOME BROADCASTING)

FLORENCE MILNES, B.B.C. LIBRARIAN

possibility of it ever happening again, he tore the music into shreds and threw it on the floor in utter disgust.

We had to send post haste for the Librarian and tell him to find something else. After a while he returned with a selection from "Carmen", the parts being handed round while the concert was in progress.

.   .   .   .   .

The following day was "Youth Sunday", and in the evening we broadcast a special service from the Chapel of St. Paul's Church, conducted by Cardinal Hinsley, Archbishop of Westminster.

He gave a stirring address to the young people of the country, and at the end pronounced the Blessing. Dr. Welch was there, also Monsignor Elwes and Alec Robertson, who were acting as liaison for us with the Cardinal—a necessary precaution because His Eminence had been ill with heart trouble, and there was some doubt whether he would be able to come up from London. He did, in fact, have a slight heart attack just before the service, which naturally made us all rather nervous. I wonder how often, if ever since the Reformation a Cardinal has spoken from a side chapel of a parish church of the Church of England?

.   .   .   .   .

May 6th. This morning I received a letter, sent on from the Head Office, from a Scottish woman, now home on leave from China, saying that seeing my photograph in the *Radio Times* reminded her that : " three years ago my husband and I were stationed in a lonely spot on the coast of North China. It was a very great treat to turn on the wireless and hear you give us the news. We felt that a dear friend had actually come into the room and was speaking to us personally. It was so amazingly clear—just as if you were in the room. We would like you to know that we have a warm place in our hearts for you."

.   .   .   .   .

On 19th May I went to London to see John Snagge about future plans. He told me that a system of full continuity was beginning in June, whereby every minute of the programme will be covered by a shadow studio, manned by a complement of announcers and engineers, ready to take over at a moment's notice. This would mean a bigger announcing staff in London, and in consequence, the

Director-General has ruled that the most experienced announcers must now be in London. In Snagge's view I was the only one whom the public had never forgotten, and I was therefore to read News bulletins, though there would be times when I could still present some of the musical programmes from Bedford.

It was agreed that I should report on 20th July, after taking some leave and making the necessary plans for handing over the Presentation Unit and my Home Guard Command in Bedford. Apparently there is a War Office ruling that no News-reader shall serve in the Home Guard.

·   ·   ·   ·   ·

On 17th June I went with the Symphony Orchestra for a week's tour in Wales, going first to Cardiff, where we were welcomed by the Welsh Director, Hopkin Morris, and his staff, who had kindly made all the necessary arrangements.

The Orchestra had a great reception wherever it went, and I have many happy memories of the kindness and hospitality of the University students at Aberdare Hall, who fed members like fighting cocks, and even gave up some of their well-earned vacation to wait on them at table. We seniors, in the hotels, did not do nearly as well, the food being poor, so much so that more than once several of us (including Sir Adrian Boult, who loves good food) went to Aberdare Hall as guests.

I recall the Civic Centre at Newport, a fine group of modern buildings on a hillside, and the glorious Brangwyn Hall at Swansea, one of the most magnificent Civic Halls I have ever seen, standing in the centre of an imposing group of modern buildings designed to form one symmetrical and most pleasing whole.

The hall, which must hold 1,500 or more, is the home of the famous Brangwyn panels, most of which were stored for safety during the war, but there was one remaining in the reception room, a large canvas, superb in colour and design, which suggested the Queen of Sheba's " apes and peacocks " theme, the central motif being a huge flowering palm. Would that we had such a hall in the centre of London.

On Sunday night 21st June a choral and orchestral concert was broadcast from one of the Cardiff theatres, Part 1 being choral and Part 2 consisting of a Beethoven Symphony. Many of the singers, who came from the mining valleys, stayed on to listen to Part 2, but, as they had trains to catch, they began to creep out towards the end of the Symphony. This naturally did not please Sir Adrian, and in his little speech of thanks at the end he included a protest about the exodus, saying that he was not used to conducting the Orchestra as an "outgoing voluntary".

.   .   .   .   .   .

Early in July I handed over my command to Eugene Cruft, the principal double bass of the Orchestra, and returned my uniform to the Quartermaster, retaining only my haversack as a memento, on payment of four and sixpence, and said good-bye to the officers and N.C.O.'s. So, for the second time in my life, I said farewell to His Majesty's uniform; last time it was in 1922, when I left the Indian Army (on the disbanding of my regiment) after eight years' service.

.   .   .   .   .   .

When I went back to Broadcasting House, London, on 20th July, I had to spend some time getting to know "the run of the ship". There had been so many changes since I went away in April 1940, especially in the three floors underground, which, for security reasons, became very overcrowded during the war.

I read the six o'clock News, and, not having done so for so long, was very nervous; but after the first few minutes I began to get into my stride again, and when I read the nine o'clock News I was much happier. To be an efficient News-reader requires constant practice, and practice helps to give self-assurance—a very important factor, because without it one cannot concentrate properly; and concentration is essential.

That evening Robert Robinson, a new announcer, invalided out of the service from Libya, came in and read the Parliamentary Debate in the middle of the nine o'clock News. He had style, a good clear voice, and shaped well.

On the 30th I met Christopher Stone, who came in to broadcast a programme of records. He appeared to be very fit, but I noticed that he looked a good deal older. He told me that he was busy making munitions, getting up early each morning and cycling six miles to the factory, wet or fine.

.   .   .   .   .   .

At 7.10 p.m. on Sunday, 9th August, I read the weekly News Letter, a summary of the weeks' events, which was always a difficult job, because one had to try to cover so much ground in a mere twenty minutes. On this occasion I spoke quickly, with scarcely any pauses between the sentences, but even so I ran ten seconds over the scheduled time. R. T. Clark, the Home News Editor, who wrote it, said that I was doing 153 words a minute. "R.T.", who scarcely ever left the building during the war years, could write brilliantly for the voice, and I seldom altered a word, though he always said, " Alter anything you like if you find it difficult to put over, as long as the sense remains the same."

Talking of reading News bulletins at speed, consistent with maximum intelligibility, the average number of words read by the Home Service announcers in the nine o'clock News—i.e. in fourteen and a quarter minutes—is 2,140.

Later I went to the Albert Hall to the orchestral rehearsal for the concert in the evening, and during the interval I discussed with Sir Adrian Boult the steps the authorities were taking to try to reduce the echo in the enormous hall. This has always been a major problem. They have now tried extending the canopy above the brass and drums, and this has definitely reduced the echo and improved the acoustics. Sir Adrian seemed very pleased about it, and, looking round at the horseshoe-shaped auditorium, pointed out that there would be room for many more people if it were reseated. "It dates from Victorian days, when ladies wore crinolines," he said. At present it holds about 7,000.

.   .   .   .   .

THE MALTA CONVOY AND RAID ON DIEPPE

Wednesday, 19th August, was the most exciting day in the news room since the Battle of Britain, because of the accounts coming in of the raid on Dieppe. Casualties had been heavy on both sides, but a six-gun battery, a radio-location station, an ammunition dump and a flak battery were destroyed, and our new tank landing-craft were used for the first time. I had a fine bulletin at 6 p.m., which went on for twenty-five minutes. Most of the nine o'clock News was a repetition of the six o'clock, but it also included an eye-witness account by Commander Anthony Kimmins of the air attack on the Malta Convoy—a most graphic piece of broadcasting.   This was an epic action by the Fleet Air Arm, and (towards the end) by fighters from Malta, who beat off the fierce attacks on the convoy by the enemy.   Our losses were severe, but at least sixty-six enemy aircraft were destroyed.

The following day I read the nine o'clock News, and this included Frank Gillard's eye-witness account of the Dieppe raid.   This also was a most vivid piece of radio reporting.

Saturday, 22nd August, was a day I shall long remember, for two reasons : it was the day on which I had to register with the forty-nine-year-olds, and it was also the day on which I announced the last night of the Proms, when Sir Henry made this little speech at the end :

" My dear friends, this brings our glorious season to a close.   It has been one of extremely happy co-operation with my colleagues, Mr. Basil Cameron and Sir Adrian Boult, the London Philharmonic Orchestra and the B.B.C. Symphony Orchestra.   Before bidding you adieu, I must thank you and tell you what a wonderful audience you are.   How you listen !   Your attention is so encouraging and exhilarating.   And now we look forward to meeting next year in this great old Hall, I hope in days of peace."

On the 25th August I read both the 9 p.m. and the midnight News, the latter containing the tragic news of the death of H.R.H. the Duke of Kent in a flying accident in Scotland.   There was scarcely any other news.   After a suitable pause, therefore, I put on a record of Sir Walford Davies's " Solemn Melody ", without making any announcement.

The next morning I was up early in order to go to the News room in good time to read through the News, which included an obituary notice of the Duke of Kent.   A sad business.   All but one of the Sunderland's crew were killed.   The Duke was going to Iceland on R.A.F. duty, and so died on active service.

On 29th August I read all three night News bulletins. There was a full account of the Duke of Kent's funeral in the six o'clock. John Snagge, who was present, gave a very clear description of it in the nine o'clock News. It was a difficult job well done.

.   .   .   .   .

The staff position had become so difficult, because of the call-up, that John Snagge told me he had no hope of any leave. Roy Rich has now been " de-reserved " (what an expression ! and an official one, too), and will have to go. This will mean more work for those of us who remain, but I am thankful I have only broadcasting and fire-watching now—no Home Guard worries. Some of the News-readers consider that they should be regarded as specialists and do this work and Continuity only, being bent on trying to separate the functions of News-reader and announcer. Personally, I disagree. I hold that one of the announcer's most important jobs is to read the News, but also most important is his task of presenting talks, plays, recitals, etc., and his contact with artists in the studio. I am quite certain, too, that if I went on doing nothing else but reading the News I should get very stale, and the public would at once recognise it. In fact, staleness creeps in all too easily as I am reminded by a letter which I have just received from my old friend, S. K. Ratcliffe, a most experienced broadcaster and commentator, with great knowledge of the American way of life in general, and American politics in particular. He says that he was glad to hear me on the air again after an absence from England of three years; and after saying encouraging things about my " unstrained clearness and modulation ", he goes on to argue that a twenty-minute bulletin is too long, as evinced by the fact that " You tend to lose animation towards the end ". How true this is ! One is giving the whole time, and this means both a mental and physical effort, and of course there is always a chance of some evidence of fatigue to the critical ear.

.   .   .   .   .

Early on 4th November there was good news from the 8th Army, but much better was to follow, and I arranged for a special Cairo communiqué to go out at 11 p.m.

Bruce Belfrage, as News-reader on duty, got back from a programme at the Monseigneur Studio, a news theatre which we had taken over temporarily, just in time to do it. It was a thrilling piece of news, the gist of it being : " Enemy in full retreat ".

Bruce told me the following day that he will never forget the 4th November, because of this and also because it was the day on which he sent in his resignation to the B.B.C.

. . . . .

American Troops Land in North Africa

On Saturday, 7th November, after a hectic afternoon and evening on duty, with bulletins brimful of excellent news from nearly all the Fronts, I got back to Broadcasting House from a recital in Oxford Street to find John Snagge waiting for me to tell me that news of really big things was expected in the morning. He said that he had been hauled out of the theatre at Windsor, and had only just arrived. After I had read the last News I had a conference with him about procedure in the morning. He said that this would be a great scoop for us, as it would only be in the late London editions of the morning papers, and the country as a whole would learn it from us.

. . . . .

The following morning, 8th November, I read the summary of the News giving the announcement of the landing of American troops at several North African ports, and John Snagge followed with the American and British communiqués. I then read the remainder of the News, all of which was excellent. We repeated it at nine o'clock.

. . . . .

Sunday, 15th November, was set aside as the day appointed to celebrate our victory in Egypt; there were services of thanksgiving, and church bells were allowed to be rung between nine and twelve noon.

. . . . .

One afternoon towards the end of November, Gordon McConnel, one of our most experienced and efficient producers, came to see me about the timing of programmes. He stayed for nearly two hours discussing this most important subject. His view is that no timing problem would arise if the discipline were stiffened up, if each producer were fined one pound every time he ran one minute over his schedule. He argued that in America, if there is even a three seconds over-run, an explanation has to be given by the producer to a committee appointed by the management to deal with such matters, and if they can do it, then we, the greatest purveyors of entertainment in the world, can do it too.

It sounded a most drastic remedy to me, but his words carried weight because, in all the many productions of his I have announced over the years, I have never known him to be more than half a minute out in his estimated timings. Before a show began he told you the rehearsal timing, and if there was any variation in speed during transmission he gave you an accurate estimate of the overall timing half-way through. If only all other producers had been so painstaking! But, then, Gordon was essentially a practical man—not one of the dreamy sort, lost in the beauties of his production.

. . . . .

In the nine o'clock News on 22nd November I read the announcement of the opening of the Stalingrad and Don offensive. It stated that 14,000 of the enemy had been killed, and 13,000 prisoners and much booty taken. This was the best news from that front for a long time.

On the 25th John Snagge and I gave a party in the Bolivar to the Department which was a great success, thanks largely to excellent staff work of Sheila Stewart, who not only helped me with the arrangements, but also acted as hostess. We said good-bye to Bruce Belfrage and Roy Rich, who were going into the Navy and R.A.F. respectively at the end of the month.

The guest of the evening was Florence Milnes, the Librarian, who behind the scenes, unnoticed by the hordes of people who come in and out of Broadcasting House, has done a wonderful job from the very early days. She began at Savoy Hill with nothing, built up a superb reference library at Broadcasting House, and then methodically proceeded to do the same thing in the provinces and in other London centres, such as Alexandra Palace, where special reference books dealing with visual art were required.

The conundrums she is daily asked by producers and script writers would drive me mad in a fortnight, but she calmly carries on, and somehow or other always manages to produce the goods.

After the bomb explosion, when the library was severely damaged, she worked like a galley-slave salvaging valuable books, deep in dust and debris. She has always been a good friend to the announcers, and to me in particular, and I was delighted that she was able to come as our guest. What the Corporation would do without her, I cannot imagine; but I often wonder if the senior members of the staff realise what she has achieved in such a comparatively short time, and the enormous goodwill value she must have on the credit side of any balance sheet of the Corporation.

. . . . .

During the last week of November I announced a recital given by the Blech String Quartet. This was an excellent combination, all the members of the Quartet being in R.A.F. uniform. I understand that they play in the String Section of the R.A.F. Orchestra, led by Frederick Grinke, now one of the finest string orchestras in the country.

. . . . .

On the 13th December I was in Continuity (the shadow control studio) from 6 p.m. until midnight, and was confronted with what might have been a difficult situation had I not looked ahead and taken the necessary precautions.

There was a Service from St. Martin-in-the-Fields, followed by the annual St. Martin's appeal, made from the church by the vicar. This, in turn, was followed by Robert Speaight's feature " God Save the King ", which concluded with a recording of the end of the Coronation Service from Westminster Abbey—the singing of the National Anthem by the choir, with organ accompaniment. Had the feature programme begun late or over-run, I should have been faced with the alternative of either fading out the National Anthem at the end of the programme, or of suppressing Big Ben, which was a " must ". It is one thing to have an appellant in the studio in charge of a responsible producer, quite another to have a vicar in his own pulpit, where he might easily forget that he had to work to a strict time schedule.

I therefore sent a message to the vicar that in no circumstances could he over-run when making his appeal, and if he did, I should fade him out, regardless of the consequences. The result was a most accurate series of timings throughout the evening.

. . . . .

On the Friday before Christmas I went down to the Merchant Navy Club just off Coventry Street, Piccadilly, to announce " Shipmates Ashore ", an excellent weekly transmission put out principally for the crews of Merchant Navy ships at sea, presided over by the indefatigable Doris Hare, with Debroy Somers and his band, produced by Howard Thomas. Many Merchant Navy men were there, and girls were invited from one or other of the Ministries in turn, to dance with them, the whole atmosphere being very homely and cheerful. It became a wonderful link with merchant-ships all over the world, and they had their own News bulletin, which we had to read, including a personal column. I well remember giving out the news that the wife of Seaman Blank had presented her astonished husband with TRIPLETS, and the cheers that followed.

So valuable was this human link, that members of the ships' crews came in hundreds to the club when on leave, to see Doris Hare, whom they all adored, and to take part in the broadcasts in one way or another, if only to join in choruses and afterwards tell their pals that they had done so. On this occasion Lord Leathers, the Minister of Transport, was the guest of honour, and made a fine speech, and the artists included Constance Cummings and Noel Gay.

.   .   .   .   .

On 21st December I went to Bangor, the home of the Variety Department during the last part of the war, to take part in the musical fantasy, " Pepi the Polar Bear ". I travelled up with Muir Matheson, who was conducting, and was met by Imlay Watts, who took me to the County Theatre, then used as a studio, where a rehearsal was in progress. From there we went on to another studio, where Ronnie Waldman was rehearsing " Monday Night at Eight ". As I entered, Ronnie came across to greet me and said, " Did you get my message ? " I had, of course, received no message; I doubt if there had ever been one. He then explained that he wanted me to act as the mystery voice in his show, and asked if I would think out something, and be quick about it. I agreed, and eventually decided to sing " You mustn't miss the last bus home "—a song which I found quite by chance on the piano. I set to work on it, and in the transmission it seemed to go well, Ronnie and the others laughing at my antics, dancing to the rhythm as I sang.

The next day we rehearsed " Pepi " all day and far into the night. There were many delays about cues and linking by the Orchestra, but eventually it was recorded and we retired to bed. Nova Pilbeam played the lead, and acted and sang most charmingly. Jack Melford was Pepi, I was the story-teller, and Henry Reed's music was a joy. The play was broadcast on Christmas Day directly after the main programme ending with the King's speech—a bad time, because so many people waited until the King had finished his speech and then switched off. This was a pity, as " Pepi " was a most enchanting fairy play with some very attractive features.

    .   .   .   .   .

On Christmas Day I was up with the lark to read the early News at 7 a.m. This contained a scoop for us. I remember the sequence well :—

> " This is the B.B.C. Home and Forces programme. Good morning, everybody, and a Very Happy Christmas to you all.
>
> " Here is the News, and this is Stuart Hibberd reading it. . . .
>
> " Admiral Darlan has been assassinated in Algiers " !

1943

EARLY in the New Year, John Snagge told me that a film about the life of King George V was about to be made at Denham, and that the producer, Havelock-Allen, had asked him for the details of the broadcasts of the final bulletin, so that he could be certain of historical accuracy. John then went on to say that he had been through all the Corporation's records, but could not account for the period from 9.25 p.m.—when the play ended—to 9.38 p.m., when I first read the penultimate bulletin : the one about His Majesty's life drawing to a close. I could not remember the details myself, but told him I would look them up in my diary. I found that I had made a complete schedule of our activities throughout that eventful evening, and this I was able to copy out and send to Havelock-Allen.

.   .   .   .   .

Sunday, 17th January, was a very busy day. Having broadcast all the morning, after a rest in the afternoon I had to return again in the evening for the production of " Scrapbook ", in which I had a part. As there had been a bad raid on Berlin by our bombers the previous night, I took the precaution of taking my tin hat with me in the evening. Everything went quite smoothly until 8 p.m., when we were busy broadcasting " Scrapbook " from the Maida Vale Studios. Then we had a " red ", and were ordered out of the studios and into the shelters, and there we had to remain while London's new A.A. defences got busy, the noise being terrific. The shelters were not exactly of the type to inspire confidence, being splinter-proof but nothing more; they looked so flimsy that some of the ladies refused to go inside them.

I stayed there until 9.45, when things quietened down, and my car came and took me back to Broadcasting House, and I was there at midnight, when Robinson read the News giving the Cairo communiqué telling us of a fifty-mile advance from Zem-Zem.

.   .   .   .   .

On 26th January, after reading the early morning News bulletins
I went to the Monseigneur Studio to rehearse, and while there I
had to arrange for a special Stalingrad communiqué about the
liquidation of the German Army. The next day we broadcast the

POCKET CARTOON

"*Well, if it isn't the
Widow Fatima, who is it?
Just tell me that!*"

news of the Churchill–Roosevelt meeting at Casablanca, a great
surprise, as the secret had been well kept. The *Daily Express* had
a most amusing cartoon by Lancaster depicting Winston, complete
with cigar, disguised as an Algerian woman, *yashmak* and all, carrying a water-pot on her head.

. . . . . .

On 2nd February Freddy Allen told me that the narrator of
" War and Peace "—a very famous actor—" nearly capsized the
boat and all the cast in it " when, by a slip of the tongue, he stated
that " the Prince approached it with an air of histolity " ! How
easy it is to make this kind of Spoonerism I know only too well.
It was a colleague of mine who once referred to " the Bathroom

Orchestra at Pump ", and I myself once said " heel and slate " for " hail and sleet ", so I found it comforting to reflect that it sometimes happens even to the greatest of actors.

.　　　.　　　.　　　.　　　.

On the evening of 17th February owing to the illness of Hubert Foss, I had to take his place at short notice, and read his manuscript about Bliss's " Music for Strings ".　Foss, listening from his sick bed, thought it went fairly well, and was kind enough to write a note saying, " I fear my script was of rather a personal type, but you gave it exactly the right touch of conviction . . .".

At any rate I enjoyed reading it, because it was splendidly written, and I am very fond of listening to works scored for a string orchestra; I think they broadcast better than any other combination of, say, more than twenty instruments.　In my opinion by far the best of all instrumental combinations for broadcasting is that used for the Schubert Octet.　Horn, plus wood-wind and strings; here one can hear each instrument with the utmost clarity throughout.

.　　　.　　　.　　　.　　　.

At Mr. Middleton's request, I travelled down to Kingston-on-Thames towards the end of February to speak for him at Bentall's, the big store there.　He is their gardening adviser, and a great favourite with all the staff.　He took me to a large hall full of people, where he introduced me as an old B.B.C. friend, and of course as a " voice ".　I spoke for half an hour.　After it was over there was the usual rush for autographs, and I found myself surrounded by a jostling mob, reminding me of a Rugger scrum, until rescued by Middleton himself with the help of some of the staff, and taken to one of the director's rooms, where we recovered our breath and cooled down a little.

What a craze this autograph-hunting is !　And it seems to be on the increase : there are always crowds of autograph-hunters outside Broadcasting House whenever any well-known personalities are due to appear in the programmes, particularly on Saturday nights for " In Town To-night ".

One Saturday night shortly before the war, a colleague of mine, who had been much pestered on going in and out of Broadcasting House in the course of his duty, could stand it no longer.　He seized the first book thrust into his face and scribbled in it, " Elsie and

Doris Waters ", slipping away before the astonished and disappointed youth could realise that he had been tricked.

This game of collecting autographs has its amusing side, however. Sheila Stewart has a son, who, on coming home for the holidays the other day, told his mother that she was " coming on ", because " it only takes three of your autographs to swop for one of Alvar Lidell's now ".

.   .   .   .   .

Group-Captain Keith, a fine type of R.A.F. officer, with a great experience of the Service, has joined us, and I have been trying to coach him.   He was very keen, plying me with all sorts of questions, some of them posers, as he had a most practical mind.   He was the inventor type, and was on the armaments side of the R.A.F. towards the end of his service.   During the evening Alvar Lidell rang up from Bedford.   He is at Cardington, near there, doing his recruit's course in the R.A.F.   When I asked him how he was getting on, he replied, " Oh, all right, but I am having some trouble with my boots ".   " Tell him to soap his socks," said Keith.

.   .   .   .   .

On 15th March I noticed that there was a paragraph in an evening paper which proved that the working of Continuity is making its mark on the listening public.   This is how it ran :

" Continuity Announcer Speaks : ' Before the nine o'clock News, in fifteen seconds from now, you may like to hear a movement from the Violin Concerto in E minor by Mendelssohn, played by Yehudi Menuhin and the London Philharmonic Orchestra conducted by Sir Thomas Beecham. . . . Ah, here is the nine o'clock News.' "

.   .   .   .   .

On 23rd March I went to Maida Vale to broadcast one of the series " Front-line Family ", a popular overseas transmission, which had been running for a long time.   There I met several old friends I had not seen for a considerable time : Harcourt Williams, the actor, who said some pleasant things about our work as announcers and News-readers ; Ralph de Rohan, who was broadcasting as the " Wicked Uncle " when I joined the B.B.C., and has not altered a bit since then ; and Carleton Hobbs—or " Hobbo ", as he is affectionately known—a superb radio actor and narrator, who was one of my staunchest supporters at Bristol in the B.B.C. Home Guard, a grand man. It was a joy to meet these three again, and talk about old times.

. . . . .

On 29th March I read the one o'clock News, and at the end of the bulletin a " flash " came through to say that a communiqué from Tunisia would shortly come in with good news. I arranged for this to be broadcast after the reading of the postscript at 1.27. It contained the announcement that we had now occupied the whole of the strongly defended Mareth line. Later it was also put out to the Forces.

. . . . .

Throughout almost all my early service, and until I left London for Bristol in April 1940 during the war, there was one person who influenced me more than any other in my determination to stick to broadcasting as a profession, and steer clear of the various attractive administrative opportunities arising from time to time in a greatly expanding public service. This was Arthur Lloyd James, Lecturer in Phonetics at the School of Oriental Studies in the University of London, and afterwards Professor.

It was his faith in English as the greatest language in the world, and his conviction of the vastness of the power of the spoken word through the medium of wireless, as a force for good or evil, together with his appreciation of the great responsibility and wonderful opportunity given to us in the B.B.C., that made its mark on me, plus my own innate love of music and my admiration for Sir John Reith as a leader and a man of vision.

Strangely enough, it was in trying to obtain better conditions for my fellow-announcers that in 1929 I had my only " row " with Sir John Reith, which nearly led to my resignation, and it was largely due to the intervention of Lloyd James, who kindly took me aside and said, " Do not persist in this policy of defying your seniors, even if with the best of motives ", that I climbed down and apologised to Sir John for my opposition to him, knowing that if I had not gained my point, I had at least drawn attention to an unsatisfactory state of affairs; and this, in due course, was rectified.

ALVAR LIDELL AS A RECRUIT AT CARDINGTON

"OH, SIR! ___ STUART HIBBERD SAYS HE'S GOING TO READ IT, AND IT ISN'T HIS TURN"

I met Lloyd James soon after the General Strike in 1926, when he came to broadcast to schools on the English language. Shortly afterwards he was called in to advise us about Announcers' English, which was having a great influence on the speech of the country. This led to the formation of the Committee on Broadcast English under Dr. Robert Bridges, of which Lloyd James became secretary. I met him several times at the meetings of this committee, which included Bernard Shaw, Forbes-Robertson, Logan Pearsall Smith and Lascelles Abercrombie. Lloyd James was the perfect technical expert; surrounded by a pile of dictionaries, he gave us historical data and sound advice, when difficult decisions had to be made, his preface to "Broadcast English, I", being a good example of his work—a masterpiece of writing on the spoken word.

He was a rather thick-set man of average height, with dark hair turning grey, which had begun to be a little thin on top. He had an excellent speaking voice and a keen ear, and could reproduce any sound in any language, and analyse sounds made by others, point out the faults, and explain how to correct them. He had a pleasant smile and a keen sense of fun, and a little habit, when thinking hard about a problem, of leaning back in his chair, half closing his eyes, and tucking his chin inside his collar, as he slowly brought out his solution. A hard worker, and one who delighted in his subject, he was a fine man in every sense of the word, and greatly liked by all those who came into contact with him. It was with the deepest sorrow, therefore, that I learnt of his tragedy and subsequent death on 24th March. Here was a war casualty just as much as if he had met his death in action, as it is quite clear that had there been no war, and consequently no frustrations, which crowded in upon him and preyed upon his mind, he would have gone from strength to strength in his profession and built up a world-wide reputation.

I can here only try to express my own sense of personal loss, and re-echo the sentence written by "The Broadcaster" in the *Radio Times* that "we would like to record our respect for the high services he rendered to the B.B.C. for many years in the matter of Spoken English, upon which he was so scholarly and resourceful an adviser".

.   .   .   .   .

On Sunday, 11th April, I announced H.M. the Queen, who was

speaking principally to the women of the Empire. I announced
her at nine o'clock, following the chimes of Big Ben, as follows :—

> " THIS IS LONDON.
> " In a few moments you will be hearing a message
> from Her Majesty the Queen to the women of the Em-
> pire.
> " Ladies and Gentlemen, Her Majesty the Queen."

Those words were the cue to the engineers to go over to Windsor
Castle, from which the Queen was speaking.   She spoke admirably,
as she always does, in a charming and very clear voice.   She spoke
easily, sincerely and most convincingly, without any suggestion of
hurry or anxiety about timing.   I mention this because the estimated
timing of her speech was seven minutes.   I said, on seeing the script,
" At least nine minutes ", and in fact, it took twelve minutes.

It was superbly done.   " You have earned the gratitude and
admiration of the world in these years of sorrow and achievement," she said, " and it is high time someone told you."

She went on to speak of the time coming when the boys returned
home again, and of the new homes they mean to make for the young
wives of the future.   Then, pointing out that our precious Christian
heritage is threatened by certain adverse influences, she continued,
" It is the creative and dynamic power of Christianity which helps
us to carry the moral responsibilities which history is placing upon
our shoulders."

.   .   .   .   .

During the first week of May I heard with great sorrow of the
death of Leslie Heward, at the early age of forty-five.   He was a
most competent conductor and a superb musician—facts recognised by all who had played under his baton.   At the time of his
death he was the conductor of the City of Birmingham Orchestra,
having succeeded Sir Adrian Boult in that capacity when Sir Adrian
left to take over our newly formed Symphony Orchestra in 1930.
I first met him in 1925, when he conducted a concert in the Savoy
Hill studios given by the Cape Town Orchestra, of which he was
then the conductor.   Later he played piano duets with Victor Hely-
Hutchinson, who also came from South Africa and had known him

out there, and subsequently he conducted our Orchestra on many occasions.

I shall always remember him for his fine interpretations of the Symphonies of Sibelius.

. . . . .

The late bulletin on 7th May contained excellent news of the capture of Tunis and Bizerta, but better still was soon to follow.

. . . . .

To celebrate the splendid news from Africa, broadcast on the night of 12th May, it was decided that we should broadcast a special concert by the Orchestra the next night, and I was detailed to go to Bedford and announce it. It was a fine concert, which included Elgar's Enigma Variations and Beethoven's Fifth Symphony. Its impact on listeners is best described by repeating the opening announcement, which was as follows :—

" This is the Forces Programme.

The War in North Africa is over—Von Arnim has been captured.

These were the brief but pregnant headlines of the News broadcast this morning.

In celebration of this great victory, we are substituting for the miscellaneous orchestral programme advertised a tribute to our forces in Africa and those of our Allies.

The concert is given by the B.B.C. Symphony Orchestra, Leader Paul Beard, Conductor Sir Adrian Boult.

It begins with the stirring march ' Stars and Stripes ', by John Philip Sousa."

. . . . .

Under the auspices of Ensa, the Symphony Orchestra paid visits to each of the three Services in turn, beginning with Aldershot on Sunday, 23rd May. We went down by train from Waterloo, and from Aldershot station onwards by buses to the Garrison Theatre.

We had excellent audiences throughout the week, and after the last concert on Friday, 28th May, the Orchestra had to play two encores, which brought the house down. Then the G.O.C. (General Evans), who had attended all the concerts, made a most charming and witty speech of thanks, to which Sir Adrian replied.

The next day we went to Portsmouth, to the Navy. There, too, we had a tremendous reception, Commander McGregor being a most wonderful host, thinking of everything, even to having a fatigue party, under a petty officer, standing by to help the engineers fix up their microphones in the roof. It was here that during a rehearsal a middle-aged seaman was seen standing up, swaying from side to side, enraptured by the music, and on being asked if he was enjoying it, replied, " It gets yer, don't it ? Worse than drink."

. . . . .

On Saturday, 19th June, I announced the opening night of the Proms, as I generally did, at the Royal Albert Hall. We now have a box of our own there, with a small control room directly behind it, fitted with a window through which we can give visual signals to the Programme engineers—a great improvement on the old plan, when the engineers were tucked away in a back room, several floors up. There was the usual packed first-night house. Sir Henry, now fully recovered from his recent illness, seemed in excellent form when I spoke to him in the artists' room before the concert began, though I thought he looked a little pale. Lady Wood was arranging the famous white carnation in his button-hole as I went in. According to Press reports there were 6,000 people present, and Sir Henry remarked afterwards, " This is the finest and most enthusiastic reception I have ever received, and from the largest audience ever to attend at my beloved Proms."

It was in this season of Proms that Dr. Vaughan Williams conducted his new Symphony in D (No. 5), a most impressive work, quiet and contemplative in mood, in great contrast to his 4th Symphony in F minor.

. . . . .

On Sunday, 25th July, we dropped 2,300 tons of bombs on Hamburg—the greatest raid ever made—and this was followed up by a daylight raid by the Americans. That night I had several good News bulletins, followed by a flash at 11.15 announcing that Mussolini had resigned. There were full details of the exciting story in the midnight News. R. T. Clark and Harrison, the News Editors, were up all night working on the story, with the result that Harrison wrote a splendid piece about it, which I put out at 7 and 8 a.m. the following morning. It stated that Badoglio had taken over for the King. What next, I wondered?

．　　　　．　　　　．　　　　．

Harry Anderson, a London taxi-driver, gave a fine postscript on 1st August. He told us how he had recently taken two assessors to a badly blitzed area, " where the devastation was something terrible ". As they got out of the cab they heard the sound of a woman quietly singing. Walking over piles of rubble, they saw two little houses left almost intact, and in front of one of them was a rather stout woman, washing the doorstep. When she saw them, she stopped singing and asked, " You ain't seen me b—— milkman around, 'ave yer? " In the very worst of the bombings, he said he had never seen any signs of panic.

．　　　．　　　．　　　．　　　．

On 20th August, after a strenuous time, beginning with the early News bulletins, I went to Rupert Street to announce " Shipmates Ashore " at the Merchant Navy Club. There I met Howard Thomas, the producer, Debroy Somers and his band, Maudie Edwards—the Welsh girl who does such clever imitations—Gerald Cooper and that great actress and fine musician, Yvonne Arnaud.

Miss Arnaud greeted me warmly, and asked, " How many years have we been friends? " I reflected for a few moments, and then said that I thought it must be about eighteen years since we first met at Savoy Hill, when I was with Rex Palmer. I had seen her, of course, more recently, the last occasion when she had just recovered from a serious operation. I remarked at the time, I remember, how sorry I was to hear about it; to which she smilingly replied, " My dear, I've been filleted ", and we both had a good laugh.

．　　　．　　　．　　　．　　　．

On 31st August we learnt, to our great sorrow, of the death of John Hilton—a fine man, and one of the best of broadcasters. He was so human and sympathetic, and always absolutely natural; there was never any make-believe about his broadcasting, and he did not hesitate to call a spade a spade if he thought the situation demanded it. That night John Snagge read three appreciations of his work, one by the Director-General, one by Dr. Mallon and one by Luker of the Talks Department, who had been closely associated with him in his work for several years.

It was said of John Hilton that he treasured as his greatest reward a sentence in a letter from a listener which ran: "You have the happy knack of making life seem extra good."

. . . . .

Wednesday, 8th September, was an historic day—the day on which it was announced that Italy had surrendered unconditionally. This was the sequence of events as it affected me. At 5.15 p.m. John Snagge told me the news and said that the Director-General had just rung through ordering me to read the six and nine o'clock bulletins. There was a stop on the news until 6 p.m., as General Eisenhower himself was putting out the official statement. At 6 p.m. I made the preliminary announcement, saying that the bulletin "contained some of the best news of the war so far". The Eisenhower communiqué and Badoglio's statement then followed, about one and a half pages long, read by John Snagge. I then read the rest of the News and repeated the Eisenhower communiqué at the end of the bulletin. At seven I did the "World Goes By", and was just about to go out to get some food when I received a message which read: "Don't go; there is a special programme at eight by the Orchestra from Bedford, and you are to do it". I went to Snagge's room, where I found all three 'phones ringing— the planners had cancelled the Mendelssohn programme and substituted a special Victory one, and had not told us about it. I got on to Bedford, and found that the first item was the Symphony in C by Beethoven, then went to the studio and wrote out what I was going to say at three minutes to eight.

The other announcements I had to think out in the continuity studio while the concert was going on in the Bedford School Hall. We ended on time. Then came the nine o'clock News, which included a recording by General Eisenhower, after which we were revived by much-needed sandwiches and coffee—there had been no chance of any food earlier.

. . . . .

Monday, 15th September, was the beginning of my trip to Cardiff with the Symphony Orchestra en route for St. Athan, the big R.A.F. station some 20 miles outside Cardiff, where the Orchestra gave several most successful concerts in the large station cinema, as they had earlier in the year to the Navy and the Army at Portsmouth and Aldershot.

When I returned to London I made an official report on the tour, and in it, while stressing the great success, I ventured to point out that it had been a mistake to include the Walton Symphony in the programmes—much too "strong meat" for an R.A.F. station audience.

At the reception after the programme at St. Athan, the C.-in-C. (Air Marshal Barratt), a very human person, said that he was quite sure that if it had been a Canadian audience there would have been " cat-calls and whistles " while the symphony was being played.

Sir Adrian was, I know, very upset at its inclusion in these concerts.

. . . . .

Sunday, 3rd October. I have often wondered if the general public have any conception of what a broadcaster's life is like, particularly in war-time. I was reminded of this thought when I met Freddy Grisewood in the canteen at 7.15 this morning. He told me he had got back from Cannock Chase at 2 a.m., where he had been taking part in the " Dig for Victory " campaign. He had had hardly any sleep, and was now having a snack in the canteen—what should we do without our canteen, I wonder?—and was then going straight on to Guildford to take part in the broadcast of the Harvest Festival Service from a little country church just in the lea of the Hog's Back. I saw him again a few hours later, as he returned to make his contribution to the " I Know What I Like " series.

On October 3rd Mr. Middleton also came back to broadcast again at his usual Sunday afternoon time, after an absence of four months. He has been ill, but is now fit again and very busy.

He is, of course, unrivalled in his own line as a broadcaster. His secret? I think the answer is simple. He is absolutely natural, he is himself—such a very human, lovable personality. No wonder the public adore him!

. . . . .

Early this month (October) I received the following criticism of

my pronunciation of an Indian name from a Mr. Hugh Merrick of
Gerrards Cross, cleverly put into verse :—

> No chief Announcer should be proud
> Of his pronouncing OUDH as OWD
> (Let it be clearly understood
> We're all aware that it is OOHD);
> For, since, in History at school
> The most unmitigated fool
> Cannot avoid the Begums, who'd
> Their normal residence at Oudh,
> Announcers should not be allowed
> To soil the air with things like OWD,
> For if they were not strangely dumb
> They'd know that it was OODH, Begum !

To which, after a consultation with Miss Miller, our phonetics
expert, I got her to draft out the following reply :

> If you asked, upon the road
> For this 'ere town, and called it ODE,
> You never would be understood;
> And if you chanced to call it OOD
> The chances are they'd laugh aloud
> And tell you that its name is OWD.
> Begums come and Begums go,
> But this for certain truth I know :
> That in the town itself out loud
> They always call their city OWD,
> And if you doubt me go and see
> And listen for yourself, like me !

(Strictly speaking, Oudh is a province; " city " and " town " are
poetic licence !)

·　　　·　　　·　　　·　　　·

On the morning of Sunday, 31st October, I announced a concert
given by the band of the Grenadier Guards which included an
overture by Suppé with a strange title : it was called " Paragraph
3 ". Whether this had any reference to Para. 3 of the Emperor's
Regulations of the Austrian Army or not I do not know, but it all
sounded very official.

Incidentally, Suppé, probably best known for his overture " Light
Cavalry ", rejoiced in the following six baptismal names : Fran-
cesco Ezechiale Ermenegildo Cavaliere Suppé Demelli.

·　　　·　　　·　　　·

1st November was the day on which the new Continuity Suite was brought into use, after many tests and rehearsals by the staff who were to use it. It is a small, compact studio in the sub-basement, with a main transmission volume control, a master control for all programmes originating outside that studio, fitted also with a speech microphone and control, gramophone units, and a rehearsal switch, which can be used to operate the gramophone unit while a transmission is in progress. I foresaw a possible danger here—the human element of forgetfulness creeping in—and sure enough before the first week was out a colleague had superimposed two bursts of the overture to the " Bartered Bride " on the morning service.

. . . . .

9th November. The staff position is getting quite serious, so many of our staff are ill. Freddy Grisewood came back to us to help out for a while, but he also is a sick man, and cannot do much, and now, on top of it all, Peter Fettes has been called up—not to soldier, but to play the clarinet in the R.A.F. Bomber Command Band.

. . . . .

14th November (the 21st birthday of the B.B.C.). I took part in the feature programme "Twenty-one Years of Broadcasting ", produced by Glyn-Jones and Lawrence Gilliam. It was thirteen minutes too long at rehearsal, but the producers cut it so severely that in the end we finished seven seconds before 10.30—our schedule time.

There was a message of congratulation from the King as follows :—

" In peace and war alike it has proved itself a great national institution, rendering high service to the State and to millions of listeners all over the world.

" I wish the Corporation all success in the future, when broadcasting will play a part of ever-increasing importance in the lives of us all."

. . . . .

On 17th November I read my paper on " The Coming of Age of the B.B.C." to the Royal Society of Arts, speaking in the library of the Society in its superb Adam House in John Adam Street, Adelphi.

A Fellow of the Society who was present at the Lecture afterwards wrote to me as follows :—

> " I write to tell you of my experience in both seeing and hearing you at the same time. . . . Your voice sounded exactly as it comes through the loud-speaker— a slight shock—it seemed uncanny, almost unnatural that the voice which we know so well from the B.B.C. should be coming from the mouth of a living person."

      •   •   •   •   •

Tuesday, 30th November. I heard the sad news to-day of the sudden death of Arthur Catterall; Jack Shinebourne, who was the 'cellist in his quartet, told me it was due to heart failure. He was a fine player and a great leader, and was appointed leader of the B.B.C. Symphony Orchestra on its formation in 1930, and it was largely due to him that the string tone of this orchestra was so magnificent. He will be greatly missed both here and in his native Manchester, where he had a large connection.

      •   •   •   •   •

It was on Sunday, 5th December, that Theodor Brok, the former Mayor of Narvik, gave his postscript following the nine o'clock News. It was a superb script, but Herr Brok was very tired after eight hours in the train; also his English was poor—so much so that the producer realised that it would be both difficult and wearisome for English listeners to follow. He therefore sent an S.O.S. to me asking if, after Herr Brok had begun, I would step in and take over at an agreed point, Brok coming in again for the last paragraph. This I agreed to do, but I could not rehearse until 8.50, because I was looking after Esmond Knight, who was making the appeal at 8.45. We had just time for one complete run through, and at 9.14 were on the air. I felt rather like a substitute called out to field in a cricket match for somebody who had been injured. It was all part of the day's work, and by listening carefully to Herr Brok I tried to capture the spirit of what he had said.

The producer thought our " duet " went well, and soon there were several 'phone calls to that effect, including one from the Director-General. Later I received many letters about it, one from the Norwegian Editor, speaking for himself and many Norwegian friends in this country, who were most impressed. Another came from a Wing Officer in the R.A.F., and included this sentence, " If ever you feel depressed or tired out with broadcasting . . . will you remember that in the one rendering last night of the speech of the Mayor of Narvik you did a great service to mankind ? "   Then, finally, some days later, came an official letter of thanks from the Norwegian Naval C.-in-C. (Such letters are among my greatest treasures.)

. . . . .

I read the one o'clock News on Thursday, 16th December, and it contained the first intimation of the Prime Minister's illness— a bulletin issued from No. 10 Downing Street.

He had had a cold, and now had a patch of pneumonia. It did not sound too good. However, I at once made up my mind to read it in an ordinary tone of voice, so as not to cause undue alarm.

While I was reading the item preceding it, Freddy Allen came in with a message from the Director-General saying, " Don't be too solemn about the P.M.'s bulletin."

. . . . .

The outstanding Christmas programmes this year were the play by Dorothy Sayers, " He That Should Come ", the main feature " We are Advancing " and the " Grand Good Night to the Forces " programme.

During the Christmas holidays, when no papers were published, we had three scoops :—

1. General Eisenhower's appointment as C.-in-C. of the Second Front.

2. The Russian victories at Kieff.

3. The sinking of the *Scharnhorst*.

. . . . .

THE MILITARY BAND

When I joined the British Broadcasting Company in 1924 there was a whole-time permanent Station Orchestra, called the " Wireless Orchestra ", led by Kneale Kelly and conducted by Dan Godfrey, Junr.

Dan Godfrey soon realised that there was also a demand for concerts of military band music from the studio, in addition to outside broadcasts of famous regimental military bands. At his suggestion a band of players was assembled from the wood-wind and brass of the Wireless and other London orchestras. Known as the " 2LO Military Band ", it used to play in the studio two or three times or more a month, usually on Saturday nights, but it was still a scratch band, and it was not until August 1927 that the Corporation decided to form its own Military Band on a permanent basis, similar to that of the Orchestra, and appointed Lieut. B. Walton O'Donnell of the Royal Marines as conductor.

O'Donnell was a jovial, good-looking Irishman—" Bandy " to his many friends—a man of many accomplishments and great personal charm. A fine musician, good sportsman and a strict disciplinarian—in short, a good all-rounder. He never spared himself, and expected those who served under him to be hard workers, too, and soon he had got together the nucleus of a band from the best players available up and down the country, and in due course moulded them into the finest military band this country has ever heard, or is ever likely to hear in the years to come—a band which was probably the most outstanding combination of its kind in the world. Apart from famous overtures, marches and selections from operas and musical plays, the repertoire was very restricted. Few composers had ever written anything for the Military Band, but now, under Walton O'Donnell's leadership, all this was changed. Not only were the more popular classics brilliantly scored for the Military Band by such gifted arrangers as Gerrard Williams and R. J. F. Howgill, but composers were encouraged to write original works for this combination. Holst, Vaughan Williams, John Ireland and O'Donnell himself all wrote works for it. Here is a typical B.B.C. Military Band programme of the middle nineteen thirties :—

 1. Overture " The Mastersingers " by Wagner.
 2. Persian Dance from " Khovantschina " by Mussorgsky.
 3. A group of tenor songs sung by Jan van der Gucht, accompanied by the Band.
 4. Three Spanish Dances by Granados, arranged by Gerrard Williams.

Before the war the B.B.C. Military Band had many admirers, both at home and overseas; it was said to have a vast audience in Nazi

Germany whenever it was on the air, and this is not surprising when one remembers that it included players of such eminence as Charles Leggett (cornet), Haydn Draper (clarinet) and Robert Murchie (flute), to mention only a few.

After ten years of broadcasting, Walton O'Donnell was made conductor of the B.B.C. Northern Ireland Orchestra, and handed over the conductorship of the Military Band to his brother, P. S. G. O'Donnell, also of the Royal Marines. "Bandy", however, was not destined to stay long in Northern Ireland, for, as I have recorded earlier, to our great sorrow, he died quite suddenly in August 1939.

P. S. G. O'Donnell carried on the tradition of the band, so finely established by his brother, and during the war, under the B.B.C. dispersal scheme, took the band to Glasgow, where it did excellent work until it returned to London in February 1943 for a few months before being disbanded.

P. S. G. O'Donnell then retired—heartbroken—and some two years after his retirement he, too, died.

I know, of course, that the Military Band was an expensive combination to maintain, but in view of the great part it played in our programmes—in more senses than one—and in our national life, the high standards it set and its world reputation, it is a tragedy that the decision was taken to abolish it. Moreover, this action was taken in war-time, when one would have thought that rousing martial music played by a military band of such prowess would have been at a premium.

So the B.B.C. Military Band passed on, and all that remains is a memory in the minds of those of us who were privileged to work with it; and often as I walk down the long corridor of the Maida Vale studios, past the big orchestral studio, towards that which was formerly used by the Military Band, I can sense the quick step of "Bandy" behind me, and hear his cheerful greeting as he overtakes me, and expect to hear the noise of the Military Band tuning up as someone opens the studio door to pass inside.

1944

 EARLY in the New Year I received this letter from my friend Andrew Stewart in Scotland:

"DEAR STUART,

"This may amuse you; it's an extract from a letter to Hugh McPhee from the Rev. Alexander Macdonald of St. Columba's, one of the Glasgow Gaelic churches. He had been visiting the Highlands recently, and one day, when preparing to listen to the one o'clock News with an old Highland woman, he heard her say: 's e in bodach fhein a tha 'u drugh ami.' ('It's the old man himself') . . . This was you!"

. . . . .

On 15th January, in the six o'clock News, I broadcast a warning message about some ephedrene hydrochlor tablets, which had been given in error to a Glasgow mother for her baby. The next day I was thankful to learn that these tablets had been returned, unopened, by the father of the child.

. . . . .

On 1st February I announced Mabel Constanduros, who, with Grandma, was appearing, in her own inimitable way, in the Kitchen Front. It is nearly twenty years since I first announced her at 2 L.O., yet she is just as nervous and excited before a broadcast as ever. She is really a great artist. She told me that she never sleeps a wink all night before a broadcast like this. Too excited. And after all these years!

. . . . .

In the ten o'clock News on 23rd February I read the first part of Mr. Churchill's speech as it came in. It was a good, strong, fighting speech—no letting up, and no specious promises about victory this year—in short a " nose-to-the-grindstone " speech.

. . . . .

Saturday, 26th February, was an historic date, because it marked the closing down of the Forces programme. This is the actual announcement I used on that occasion :—

" It is now eleven o'clock, and so we have come to the end of the Forces Programme. But in saying good night this time, we also say good-bye. At 11 a.m. on 18th February, 1940, the Forces programme came into being. Now, after four years and nine days, it closes down. To-morrow, in its place, there will be the General Forces Programme. Good night, everybody . . . and good-bye."

GOD SAVE THE KING

1st March. From " Punch ".

THE ANNOUNCER

Alered man was with us for the nonce
That by the morwe erly wolde annonce
The dayes news al hot as it bifel;
His voys as cler was as the chapel bel :
And wonder was it, as it semed me,
Men mighte here his wordes, thogh they be
Y-spoke a hundred myle awaye, and ferre.
Evere his tale was of the kinges werre
Ageyn the blake and mightye hostes of Pruce :
Of Italye he spak, and Fraunce, and Ruce
When-as he hadde coghed and tolde his name;
And certes ther nas no man coude him blame
Thogh that the soun was twisted on his tonge
Of straunge tounes, if they were crulle or longe.
In o voys spak he gode newes and ille,
For al was but as griste to his mille.
Al blithe at the springing of the daye
" God-morwe everichoon " he wolde saye;
When-as the squeeking pippes sounede eight.
And thogh that it was new and somdel streit
He kept the reule of his fraternitee
To speken alway faire and fetisly.
Certes he was of reeders alderbest;
In parfait accent was ful muche his lest.
A bettre entoned man was no-wher herd;
This worthy nouncer was y-clept HIBBERD.

On Saturday, 4th March, the Henry Wood Concert due to be given at the Albert Hall was cancelled, because of the large amount of broken glass, caused by the explosion of a bomb, which it had not been possible to remove in time. In its place a special studio concert given by our Orchestra, and conducted by Sir Henry, was broadcast from Bedford. During the interval in this concert I read a tribute to Sir Henry, specially written for this occasion by Sir Arnold Bax. It was a fine piece of writing, a vivid picture of Sir Henry at work and relaxing at home painting in his studio. It ended by pointing out what a national institution he had become and stating that he had purified and enriched the musical taste of at least two generations, and improved the quality of orchestral playing out of all knowledge.

.   .   .   .   .

On 11th March I went to Bristol with Sir Adrian Boult and the Symphony Orchestra for a week's tour, during which we gave concerts at Bristol, Cardiff, Newport and Ashchurch, an enormous American supply depot near Evesham. The Orchestra was everywhere given a great reception, especially by the American troops when it played Sousa's famous march, the " Stars and Stripes ".

The food at Ashchurch had to be seen to be believed. It was here that I first tasted " apple butter " with cheese, and very good it was, too; also butterscotch pudding—a kind of coffee cream. All the food came from America, packed in tins, and there seemed to be an unlimited variety, especially of canned fruits.

The American troops were all most friendly and hospitable, and in spite of the long journey from Bristol, and a rehearsal followed by the concert, we thoroughly enjoyed our day.

After lunch we watched the American Transport Corps at work, collecting crates containing jeeps, one at a time, from a dump about 100 feet high, by means of a specially adapted truck. This had two proboscis-like steel arms in front, which it pushed under the crate, lifted it a few inches, then backed, turned and scooted with it across the yard, like a forest ant seizing a grub and dashing off with it. The crate was dumped before a group of men, who quickly smashed it, pulled out the jeep components, and in a matter of a few minutes the jeep was assembled and driven off to a parking-place on a flank.

.   .   .   .   .

On Friday, 24th March, I attended the luncheon given by the

B. WALTON O'DONNELL
("BANDY")

The B.B.C. Military Band in the Concert Hall of Broadcasting House

Musicians' Benevolent Society to Sir Henry Wood, in honour of his seventy-fifth birthday and the fiftieth year of the Promenade Concerts. Frank Howes, Music Critic of *The Times*, was in the chair, and Sir Adrian Boult, B. E. Nicolls, Clarence Raybould and many other artists and composers were present. I sat next to C. B. Cochran, now very lame and leaning heavily on a stick when walking. We all signed a book, which was given to Sir Henry as a memento.

The fanfares, played by the Trumpets from the Royal Military School of Music, were most impressive, one by Arthur Bliss being written especially for the occasion. There were also some verses written for Sir Henry Wood by the Poet Laureate, John Masefield, which I spoke after the toast " Sir Henry J. Wood " had been proposed by the Chairman and drunk by the assembled company. They were headed : " To Sir Henry Wood on the occasion of his seventy-fifth anniversary and in commemoration of the fiftieth year of the Promenade Concerts ".

> " How many thousand times have you upheld
> A batonette between two multitudes,
> Each hushed to ready and receptive moods,
> Waiting your mind's impulsion that will bring
> Oneness to beat, to breath, to stroken string
> And beauty's presence, holding the house spelled ?
> Ah, many times to me, as to the race,
> You have compelled this ecstasy of law,
> Lifting the human pattern from its flaw,
> In the dry desert giving living dew.
> Lord of sweet music (and of Langham Place),
> To-day this Nation thanks and praises you."

On Wednesday, 29th March, the Radio Doctor spoke at 8.15 a.m. in the Kitchen Front on the subject of " Edginess ". I always find him most entertaining. He has the happy knack of imparting serious knowledge to his audience, put over in a care-free, jocular way. To-day he made a slip which was very funny.

Talking about food and " edginess ", what he *meant* to do was to suggest the adoption of a five-meal day as a means of overcoming this trouble. What he actually said—though he corrected himself at once—was, a five-*day* meal !

Friday, 31st March, was the day on which we broadcast a programme about the Church of St. Clement Danes in the Strand—now, alas! a ruin, after being bombed by the enemy. The theme of this outside broadcast, arranged by Michael Standing, was "Oranges and Lemons", in keeping with the old nursery rhyme, and, for the same reason, its title was "You owe me five farthings". Strangely enough, Peter Bax told me that he actually found five farthings among the ruins, on going there to sketch directly after the Blitz.

. . . . .

On 1st April I heard that the Director-General, Mr. Robert Foot, had resigned to take over the chairmanship of the Mining Association of Great Britain in succession to Sir Evan Williams. He had come to us from the Gas Light & Coke Co., Ltd., and had an extensive knowledge of the coal industry. Mr. W. J. Haley, formerly a Director of Reuter's, and now Editor-in-Chief of the B.B.C., has been appointed to take his place. He has been a successful journalist, and is, I believe, a voracious reader and a very live wire, as is indicated by the fact that he joined the Corporation only last September.

. . . . .

On 12th April we broadcast a fine performance of "The Messiah", Stanley Riley's singing of the bass solos being outstanding. For years he has been the principal bass of the B.B.C. Singers—formerly the Wireless Singers—and has given the best years of his voice to the B.B.C. Had he elected to sing as a free-lance artist his name would have been on everyone's lips. I only wish there were more opportunities of hearing him as a soloist. Unfortunately outside artists are nearly always engaged, and it is seldom that members of the B.B.C. Singers have a chance of doing any solo work. I am very glad to be able to pay tribute to a fine and sensitive artist, with a superb voice.

. . . . .

St. George's Day, 23rd April, was celebrated by broadcasting a special programme called "This Breed of Men" by Louis McNeice. It was a stimulating and original way of suggesting the thoughts passing through the minds of our men in the Services, now standing by for action.

. . . . .

Obvious invasion precautions now being taken by those reporters who have been detailed to go, when orders come through, bags being packed all ready to move, money in pockets, etc. John Snagge told me he had seen one bag packed and labelled " Florence Nightingale, Crimea ".

．　　　．　　　．　　　．　　　．

An amusing slip was made to-day, 26th April, by one of the junior announcers when announcing John McKenna. He said John McCormack, instead of John McKenna—not quite the same person, despite the same Christian name and surnames beginning with Mac. However, he realised his mistake, and did his best to put it right at the end of the first song. Then we heard this extraordinary statement : " I must apologise to listeners, and to John McKenna, for calling him John McCormack ". This made us roar with laughter. How John McCormack would have laughed, too !

．　　　．　　　．　　　．　　　．

On Saturday, 5th May, I listened to Cecil McGivern's superb programme on the work of Britain's railways, called " Junction X ". If ever an Oscar is awarded for an outstanding Radio production, " Junction X " should surely have first claim. It is undoubtedly the finest documentary piece of Radio ever conceived. Subsequently it was published in booklet form, and was on sale on all the station bookstalls.

．　　　．　　　．　　　．　　　．

On 15th May I broadcast a special, and most significant announcement for the Army Film Unit which ran as follows :—

" The Admiralty now want photographs of every inch of coastline, and more than that, every road, every railway bridge and every factory in the world. Look out all your snapshots and postcards from abroad.

" All three services use our files, and you who are listening to me now may have one photograph which will provide a vital missing part of the whole picture.

" Please send them to the following address :

Photographs,
Admiralty,
London."

We subsequently learnt that invaluable information, urgently required for the invasion, was obtained as the result of the response to this appeal.

Alvar Lidell, now with us again, having been invalided out of the R.A.F., told me about a most amusing misprint in the News the other day when describing a battle position. It said, “ The Germans had amassed an enormous concentration of lorries and YANKS ”!

The next day came the splendid news of the capture of Cassino and the tremendously strong monastery position. A general advance now in progress, the Gustav Line having been broken.

. . . . .

D DAY AND AFTERWARDS

On 31st May, John Snagge warned me that things were nearing the boiling-point, and that I must sleep in, and be prepared for any emergencies, and on 4th June there had been excellent news from Italy : Villetri and Valmonte captured; and so, on to Rome. That night I studied the official secret document marked “ Procedure for D Day ”. Snagge and Gilliam came in and worked on a feature about Rome until 2 a.m., the news of the fall of Rome having come in during the reading of the midnight News.

The following day the 8 a.m. News, read by Freddy Allen, included a “ News Reel ” about the capture of Rome, beginning with the tolling of the bells of St. Peter’s, followed by Godfrey Talbot’s commentary. There were difficult S.H.A.E.F. meetings during the morning between Snagge and Colonel Dupuy of Supreme Headquarters, who wished to make the first D-Day bulletin announcement himself. That night I had a conference with Snagge and Phillips, going carefully through the details of the secret operation order, to be prepared for action at any moment. At 11.50, just as I was preparing for bed, Phillips came into my changing-room to tell me that the preliminary warning had been received, and that I was to ring Hotine, the Senior Engineer in charge of operations and liaison with S.H.A.E.F. I changed back into my clothes, and found Snagge telephoning to Hotine in the duty room. Hotine seemed certain that the “ soft ” warning was coming that we must be prepared to act. Detailed instructions followed, and while Snagge (tired out) went to bed I copied out the proclamations to be made after the communiqué had been read, eventually getting to bed myself at 2 a.m.

I was awakened soon after 5.30 by the noise of hundreds of planes. I got up, and found that the " soft " warning had now been received, and that Bulletin No. 1 would be broadcast between 9 and 10 a.m. While I was shaving, Ryan, the News Controller, came in and asked for Snagge, but he had gone to S.H.A.E.F., and had left a note to that effect.

Freddy Allen read the 8 a.m. News, which included a statement from Allied Headquarters that people living in the western seaboard of France had been warned that a new phase of activity was about to begin, and that they must keep away from roads, bridges, etc. This was followed by an extract from a German source, saying that we had landed paratroops in France—in other words, they had stolen our thunder. B. E. Nicolls (Controller of Programmes) said it was a case of *reductio ad absurdum*. We were not allowed to trail the official communiqué which was bound to follow soon, and yet here it was, in substance, from an enemy source.

Freddy Allen was beside himself with delight. Prudence Neil, one of the announcers, said, "He looked like a cat that had swallowed a canary ".

The " hard " warning came at 9.20, and we acted according to our orders, Snagge reading it at 9.32 as follows :—

" This is LONDON. London calling in the Home, Overseas and European services of the B.B.C. and through United Nations Radio, Mediterranean, and this is John Snagge speaking :—

" Supreme Headquarters Allied Expeditionary Force has just issued Communiqué No. 1, and in a few seconds I will read it to you :—

" ' Under the command of General Eisenhower, Allied Naval Forces, supported by strong Air Forces, began landing Allied Armies this morning on the northern coast of France.' "

It was then repeated, and this followed :—

" That ends the reading of the Communiqué No. 1 issued from Supreme Headquarters Allied Expeditionary Force."

After this came the "alert" period, when, in accordance with orders previously issued, the peoples of France, Norway, Holland, Belgium and Denmark were told in English and their own languages about what was happening. Everything worked smoothly; Joseph McLeod in Continuity did his pre-arranged fill-up and a neat announcement, only "Music while you Work" being scrapped. A special News bulletin was put out by Snagge at 12 noon. He had been at S.H.A.E.F. Headquarters all the morning, I answering for him at Broadcasting House; after which we carried on as usual.

Following the 1 p.m. News the first War Report was broadcast, and again after the 9 p.m. News we had further War Reports by our correspondents on the spot.

At nine o'clock I announced the King, who was speaking "to his people at Home and Overseas", and was also heard throughout the United States of America.

After the King's speech I went with the Archbishop of Canterbury and Dr. Welch, Director of Religious Broadcasting, to Maida Vale to attend a special service of intercession for the Forces, in which the address was given and the prayers offered by the Archbishop. I kept them both waiting for me in a car outside Broadcasting House for nearly a quarter of an hour, until the end of the King's speech—the first time, I should imagine, an archbishop has been kept waiting by an announcer.

. . . . .

Saturday, 10th June, was the opening night of the Jubilee Season of Proms. I announced from the Albert Hall, and did a commentary on the scene at the end, when Basil Cameron, who had been conducting Part 2, brought on Sir Henry again and again, amid scenes of greatest enthusiasm.

It was an historic and momentous occasion. Earlier in the day, on the initiative of Joseph McLeod, the following telegram was sent to Sir Henry at the Albert Hall :—

"Homage and affectionate greetings from the B.B.C. Home announcers. We will be your assistant curators."

Early the following week I received a charming letter from Sir Henry in reply, saying :—

"Would you kindly convey to the B.B.C. Home announcers my gratitude and warmest thanks for their kind telegram of Saturday last ? I know I can look forward to their loyalty and support as assistant curators of my Promenade Concerts.

" Yours sincerely,

" HENRY J. WOOD."

.   .   .   .   .

On Tuesday, 13th June, while I was on night duty at Broadcasting House, there were two alerts from about 4 a.m. onwards, and once I saw a large red flash in the east, followed by a loud explosion. The next day the papers said : " An enemy plane was hit, and crashed with all its bombs in the Stepney district, killing several people and smashing up one hundred homes ". We now know that this was a most unfortunate report, because the " plane " referred to was actually the first flying bomb sent over, and this information told the Germans exactly what they wanted to know—that they had scored an inner with their sighting shot.

.   .   .   .   .

On the morning of the 29th I announced a schools talk about the Falkland Islands. They are windswept, but excellent for raising sheep, the local name for them being 365—in other words, one for every day of the year. Recently an advertisement appeared for a school teacher for these islands, to which one reply was received. When interviewed, the candidate said that she wanted to go to the Falkland Islands very much. " You know where they are ? " asked the Chairman. " Yes," she replied. " In the Hebrides " !

.   .   .   .   .

About this time we had many adventures with flying bombs, both at my home in Bickley and in London, one on the afternoon of 30th June coming unpleasantly near, and making us run for the shelter. I spent the rest of that afternoon helping to clear up piles of broken glass, and after tea went in to London to the Albert Hall for the broadcast of the Promenade Concert, only to find that it had been decided to call off the Proms altogether. It was, I am sure, a wise decision, but I wish someone had remembered to tell me about it. I rang Broadcasting House, and an armoured car was sent to fetch me. I felt an awful ass as I climbed into it outside the main entrance, watched by crowds of people who were wondering what on earth it was. Bush House was also hit that day, and there were a number of casualties, caused by flying glass. There is now an order that there must always be a stand-by News-reader on duty at Oxford Street during an alert, in case Broadcasting House is hit and put out of action.

.   .   .   .   .

On 1st July I went home after reading the one o'clock News, and while I was in Charing Cross station waiting for the arrival of my train, the sirens sounded. The train then came in and I got into it, as did hundreds of others; I counted nineteen people in my compartment. There, as we waited, reading our papers, we heard the noise of a buzz-bomb coming nearer and nearer, while taxis blew their horns and ships on the river sounded their sirens in warning; but there was nothing we could do about it. More and more were eyes glued to newspapers in a vain pretence that buzz-bombs were a mere bagatelle and we could not care less. How relieved we all were when the bomb exploded in the river near Blackfriars Bridge and we were able to breathe freely again !

.   .   .   .   .

On Monday, 3rd July, while I was reading the 8 a.m. News, which was due to be followed by the Radio Doctor's talk, the studio door opened and a Captain in Home Guard uniform entered, sat down opposite to me and looked at me as I read. I was very puzzled, and at first unpleasant thoughts of the possibility of an enemy agent having got into the building by putting on Home Guard uniform passed through my mind, and I thought how easily he could have disposed of me had he so wished; then I came to the conclusion that he was a speaker in the Overseas Service shown into the wrong studio, and I carried on. It was not until I switched off and spoke to him, just before the end of the News, that I realised that he was a doctor, who had come to speak in place of the Radio Doctor.

.   .   .   .   .

Quite apart from increasing numbers of buzz-bombs, we announcers had been having our share of struggles with Russian place-names, so that the arrival of the following poem from my old friend Tubby Myers, the engineer, who said it had been written by his secretary's father, a Mr. Harrison of Birmingham, produced just the right dose of comic relief required :—

The news is marvellous, I thinksk,
We've Poggibonsi, Minsk and Pinsk,
And, better still, we're pushing on, see?
Past Pinsk and Minsk *and* Poggibonsi.

The Nazi Warriors had to flee
From both the " insk-ses " M. and P.
While Alexander got them groggi
In Italy at bonsi-Poggi.

So Hitler's hopes at Minsk and Pinsk
Go Urgle-gurgle down the sinksk,
And as his front line further shrinksk
We'll soon get round to saying " Dvinsk ".

But as for Wop pronunciation,
We're puzzled by your Corporation.
When first we heard of Poggibonsi
Those g's were hard just as in " gone ", see?

Then Joe Macleod, the dirty dog, he
Refused to call our bonsi-Poggi.
Oh no! he tried another dodge : he
Began to call our bonsi-Poggi.

How cheerful sounded Bonsi-Poggi
Just like a gay tail-wagging doggi.
But Joe Macleod's dull version—Poggi
Is like a suet pudding—stodgi!

We'll put up with the awful luck
We had with Africa's Buk-Buk.
Announcers gave us *such* a look,
And said " Tut-tut, that there's Book-Book ".

And later on only a mug
Dared reference to the River Bug
(Which is very hard on a poet 'cos
There is no rhyme at all to Boog).

Believe me, I am very sore.
Please don't refine me any more,
And leave me, please, my bonny, sonsy,
Cheerful, sprightly, Poggibonsi!

. . . . .

In the 8 a.m. News on 21st July there was the sensational announcement of the attempt on Hitler's life, read by Freddy Allen.

Hitler's voice was recorded, explaining that the attempt had been made by a small, disgruntled clique of now unemployed officers. This was obviously a blind, and the attempt was probably part of a large-scale, well-planned revolt.

.   .   .   .   .

On 10th August I went to Bedford to announce a concert billed as "Fifty Years of Proms". It was a programme to celebrate the fiftieth anniversary of Sir Henry J. Wood's first Promenade Concert at the Queen's Hall on 10th August, 1895. The concert was to have been conducted by Sir Henry in the Corn Exchange, but unfortunately he was taken ill while in Bedford, and Sir Adrian Boult conducted for him. As soon as I arrived in Bedford I went with C. B. Rees of Music Department to the Bridge Hotel to inquire for him, and Lady Wood told us that he was definitely better, and that Lord Horder was pleased with his condition, but there was still a possibility that an operation might be necessary.

She then gave us a message from him, which I read out to the audience in the Corn Exchange during the concert :—

> " Give my love to all my dear musicians and my dear friends of music. I am disappointed I cannot be with them to-day, but tell them I shall soon be with them again, and then we'll finish the Jubilee season with a Victory season."

But this, alas, was not to be; in the News on 18th August Alvar Lidell announced his death. I was very sorry to hear this, as we had all hoped that he was well on the way to recovery; he just lived for the Jubilee season of Proms, and happily saw it through. He died in Hitchin Hospital after an acute attack of jaundice, at the age of seventy-five. How much he has done for English music, especially orchestral playing! And how we shall all miss him in the B.B.C.! As Sir Adrian said, " He will always be remembered for his selfless service to all music ".

.   .   .   .   .

I went to Bedford again on 25th August, this time to join the orchestral party en route for Luton for a concert given in the huge canteen of Vauxhall Motors, holding over 2,000 people. The canteen was heavily damped for sound, the roof being thickly padded to reduce the clinking noise of cups and saucers. I found it most difficult to make myself heard, and in the end was forced to use the public-address system, much against my will.

The news of the fall of Paris had come in the 1 p.m. News (read for me by Richard Wessel). I therefore opened the concert by saying, " We begin most appropriately, with a triumphal march, ' The Triumphal March from " Aida " by Verdi '." It was very hot in the packed canteen, Sir Adrian was boiling—there seemed to be no air at all—but we had a marvellous audience, and this was very rewarding.

On 23rd August I went from Bedford to Hitchin to Sir Henry Wood's funeral, the service being held in the fine old parish church there. It was sung by the B.B.C. Singers, with Dr. Thalben Ball at the organ; there was also an orchestra, made up of players drawn from famous London orchestras, the music including " How lovely is Thy dwelling-place ", by Brahms, and a movement from Bach's Brandenburg Concerto No. 6, in addition to Chopin's " Funeral March ". The singing of the 23rd Psalm was most moving.

6th September. A short while ago I was announcing " Shipmates Ashore ", the Merchant Navy programme from their club in Rupert Street, and read the special News for them, when a number of African toys, made of raffia-like material and representing some kind of small jungle animal, were given to the children of sailors who had been lost in action. They were the gift of some kind Nigerian chiefs from Ikot Ekpene, and were greatly appreciated by the children. In the News I read out a message of thanks from the children, knowing that the Chiefs would be listening, and doing my best to pronounce the African name correctly. To-day I received a note from Alfred Dunning, the producer, enclosing this extract from a letter of the District Officer of Ikot Ekpene, Nigeria :—

> " Your announcer is to be congratulated on his Ikot Ekpene. To have said it so feelingly, without having felt it and scratched its bites, was the envy of us all."

9th September. At the moment things both here and on the Continent are very quiet, thanks to the magnificent work of our troops in capturing the launching-sites of Hitler's secret weapons.

We went down to the lovely Eynsford–Shoreham valley in Kent, and everywhere one looked one saw large, fat, barrage balloons tethered, as it were, every few hundred yards or so. It was as though a convoy of prehistoric baggage-animals of gigantic size had halted to be fed and watered for the night.

.   .   .   .

B. E. Nicolls appointed Senior Controller—an excellent choice. John Snagge, who has been hopelessly overworked for months, was at last persuaded to take some leave, and went down to Wadhurst, to stay with the Nicolls. Most unfortunately, while there, picking apples in the orchard, he fell off a ladder and badly injured his ribs and back.

Poor John! it was rotten luck, but a gift to the comedians— jokes galore about falling out of apple-trees!

.   .   .   .

On 9th October we received a letter from a Belgian lady which speaks for itself :—

Liberated Brussels, 7th October, 1944.

To the Announcers of the British
Broadcasting Corporation,
London.

" DEAR FRIENDS,

" May I begin this letter by saying that you became, during the grim German occupation, good and dear friends indeed to those English speaking Belgians, to whom you have constantly reminded the existence of a fighting Britain, one day coming to free us of the nightmare of the threatening Gestapo spectre.

" We had of course broadcasts from the B.B.C. for Belgian listeners, but I am one of those who also risked much by listening regularly to the ' Home and Forces programme ', broadcasts of foreign services being often difficult to catch, due to those exasperating German interferences.

" In those days of black distress, of anxiety, great

worry, persecution and yet desperate determination, a note of cheerfulness and cordiality was brought along by you, proving so great a help and assisting us frequently from desperation. You were the only English people of whom the 'verboten' and 'hated' language could be heard, and it sometimes proved a very great satisfaction.

"Many is the time when thirty to forty people a day anxiously enquired about the war to one they knew was listening in English. If you could realise the comfort you were bringing to people of occupied territories, who here and there, listen in great secrecy to your promising voices of better times ahead, welcoming voices quite apart from those of the enemies, the latter directed full of harsh menaces against us. Can you also imagine the awaitening, day after day, for the contact with the last thread of hope in our existence, the voice of Great Britain.

"When German propaganda was endeavouring to pour its poison into souls, probing into our inner thoughts without end, and the weak were inclined to become doubtful and sceptical as to ultimate results, I at least was one that could reassure those around, that matters somewhat differed from the enemy's arguments.

"Now liberation has come, and may I thank you for the brief moments of quiet happiness in between terrible devastating periods of German Nazism. Your help was most valuable in giving us courage.

"Think sometimes of the peoples still fervently expecting news from your lips, yours is a great mission!

"I repeat what the Belgians learnt to say when the British troops arrived : thank you, thank you, merci, merci.

Yours sincerely,

Note.—See Appendix A for two other letters, one from Norway and one from Holland.

. . . . . .

14*th October.* In the evening I saw many bombers returning from raids on Cologne and Duisberg. Buzz-bombs still coming over now and again. We had an alert at 2 a.m. Snagge is making good progress, and seems more cheerful, in spite of two broken ribs and severe headaches caused by concussion. He is strapped up now, and tells me that he is bored with doing nothing. It must have been a very bad fall. He fell backwards as the ladder went forwards, and was unable to put out his hands to break his fall. He will be away another two or three weeks, at least.

· · · · ·

On 15th October in the nine o'clock News I announced the death of Rommel. He was apparently killed in a motor smash caused by a raid by our fighter planes. R. T. Clark, Home News Editor, wrote an excellent obituary notice about him, which he read himself, sitting opposite to me in the News studio. But he read it much too fast. This was such a pity, as it was so well put together.

· · · · ·

On 25th October I went to Bedford to speak the Narrator's part in Honneger's "King David", which I had been rehearsing with Clarence Raybould, who conducted. The broadcast was from the Corn Exchange, an excellent hall for broadcasting an Orchestra and Chorus, the acoustics being very good indeed. I found it difficult to speak lines over music when the words were not allotted true musical values by the composer; yet he expects one to make certain climaxes in unison with the Orchestra as though it were, at these points, an accompaniment. I enjoyed the dramatic quality of the work and the stimulating barbaric music, for example " The March of the Philistines ", also " The Lament of David " : " How are the mighty fallen ? "—a fine piece of Oriental music.

· · · · ·

I came across a report from a paper which said :—

"Ersatz Alvar Lidells, John Snagges and Stuart Hibberds were to have been dropped into England by parachute in the first phase of the German invasion. These men, trained as News broadcasters and parachutists, were to land with the paratroops, who were to seize our broadcasting stations. Details of a plan to use our radio stations in such a way that faked instructions and news could be broadcast have come to light in liberated Belgium. When the invasion was feared and the B.B.C.

News-readers started to announce their names, the German Secret Service organisation opened a special school
in Belgium, to train and imitate them. Recordings of
Alvar Lidell, John Snagge and other broadcasters were
made. Germans (and Quislings) who could speak perfect
English and had the same tonal qualities as the B.B.C.
men were selected. B.B.C. methods were studied, and
everything was prepared to make the Ersatz programme
sound 100 per cent genuine."

. . . . . .

On 5th November I left London overnight for Swansea, en
route for St. Davids via Carmarthen, for the enthronement ceremony of Dr. Prosser, the new Archbishop of Wales. I thought
Carmarthen a most attractive spot, situated high up above the
lovely Towy Valley, in splendid dairying country. There I learnt
the meaning of the name Caer-Marthen, the stronghold of Merlin.
So I was in the Merlin country, the country of romance and legend.
From Carmarthen I went by car, with the Welsh Programme
Director, Watkin Jones, to Solva, near St. Davids, where he had
kindly arranged rooms for me, St. Davids, which is a very small
place, being full up.

We had tea in Solva, a beautiful fishing village in a deep ravine,
very Scandinavian in appearance, as the name suggests; then we
went on to St. Davids for the rehearsal of the ceremony in the
wonderful old cathedral, with its glorious tower, high Irish bog-
oak roof, and pillars many inches out of the true, due to the sinking
of the foundations. The cathedral is not visible until one is well
into the city; then the ground seems to drop away from beneath
your feet, and quite suddenly there it is below, a gem of Norman
architecture, with the ruins of the glorious mediæval Bishop's Palace
adjoining.

Having laid all our plans for the broadcast of the ceremony the
next day, and discussed details with the Archdeacon and the Archbishop himself, we returned to Solva, where I had plenty to think
about, the chief problem being how to recognise the bishops as
they appeared in the procession.

I shared a platform above the West Door with Talfan Davies, the

Welsh-speaking announcer, and from here we looked down on the congregation, and took it in turn to describe the ceremony and the colourful procession below us.

Unfortunately something went wrong with the red light which indicated when our microphone was live, and the only thing we could do was to listen on head-phones while watching the ceremony, and try as far as we could to avoid speaking while the officiating bishops were speaking or praying. This was sometimes most difficult to judge. The main criticism afterwards was that there were times when our commentary went on when it should have been silent, because it was spoken over the words of the Bishop.

.   .   .   .   .

On 22nd November, St. Cecilia's Day, I went to Bedford to announce a performance of " Alexander's Feast, or the Power of Music ", by Handel. There was some fine choral singing conducted by Leslie Woodgate, with Elsie Suddaby and Norman Walker both singing well; and some of the solos were difficult to sing.

I received a charming letter from Lady Wood, referring to the Jubilee Concert and the message I broadcast about Sir Henry, and adding :—

> " The broadcast in connection with St. Cecilia to-night brought it home again with renewed emphasis. How delighted he would have been to have heard your reading of his letter, fraught with so much interest for the future of music and musicians. He did so hope to see 22nd November, a day in the Calendar of Music on a par with that of Art, and such broadcasts as that of last night must help to bring his wish to fruition."

.   .   .   .   .

On Friday, 24th November, after reading the nine o'clock News I went to Studio 8A to announce a programme with a queer title : " Fifty Thousand Times ". It turned out to be a feature programme in honour of *The Times* newspaper, the 50,000th issue of which comes out to-morrow. There were several senior members of the staff of *The Times* present, and after the programme we had a small party in one of the conference rooms near the studio. There I met Messrs. Morrison and Kent of *The Times* staff and obtained their autographs on a copy of the 50,000th issue of *The Times*, as a memento.

Ralph Truman and Norman Shelley were wondering how I was going to pronounce " the 50,000th issue of *The Times* ", and I told them it was quite easy if in saying " thousandth " you left out the " d " and only pronounced the " th " at the end of the word.

. . . . .

THE GERMAN OFFENSIVE IN BELGIUM

On 18th December came the sudden and unexpected news of a German offensive on the Western Front. It looked as if the Americans had been caught napping, conditions had been foggy, our air superiority could not be made use of, and the Germans seized on a Heaven-sent opportunity. According to reports at that time received, there had been heavy casualties on both sides. Later we heard that the Germans had broken through the American Army front in two places, and advanced thirty miles into Belgium.

. . . . .

On Christmas Day I announced the Christmas Bells programme at 9.20, including the bells of Bethlehem, which came through most beautifully. Later I was in the feature called " Journey Home ", and I also broadcast the National Anthems of the Allies, which followed on directly after the King's speech. There was an awkward passage in the News that night—one referring to the " wide wedge west of Budapest ".

. . . . .

The New Year's Eve programme was called " As a Great Year Ends ". Lawrence Gilliam and Louis McNeice were the producers, and Robert Donat and I shared the narration. It was divided into several parts, which entailed a lot of preparatory work, with a final run through from 6.15 p.m. onwards that evening. In the transmission I led off at 10.45. First came the Regional sequence, which I did, then the review of the year, which Robert Donat did, and the European sequence, after which I again joined him for the finale.

1945

A JOURNALIST friend and critic, himself a first-rate broadcaster, wrote to me about the New Year's Eve programme and approved of my efforts, ending with :—

"Pitch and pace, animation, interest (as *you* know, a cardinal matter) was entirely right.

"Donat's beautiful voice, tones, vowels, were a joy. But too often he slowed down, dropped his voice, and gave it for a few moments the sentimental sound that listeners, all of them I believe, dislike.

"I think he forgot the essential point, now and again, that in radio exposition and recitative, *animation* must be kept up. The listener must know that the speaker is first of all delivering with *interest* in every sentence."

Here are words of wisdom indeed for all who are interested in the art of broadcasting !

.   .   .   .   .

On the afternoon of 29th January I went into the announcers' room and found both Freddy Grisewood and Freddy Allen there. I asked Allen about the Russian bulletin, and he confessed that he had said, "Marshall Cherniakowski's Force-ki's" in the News a few nights ago, much to everyone's delight.

It was the old story of the Russian communiqué arriving at five minutes to nine, just as one was about to go to the studio. There was no time to look it through beforehand, and it generally included place or proper names difficult to pronounce. The best plan was to get the Editor to underline the names with a red pencil, which at least gave one a chance of glancing at them. The main thing to do was to decide what you were going to say, and to say it with conviction.

Things in radio, as in life in general, by no means always work

out according to plan. On 19th January at 9.15 p.m. I listened to
Peter Creswell as Charles I in the " King's Tryall ". This was
most impressively done, and I was enjoying it, when, at a very
dramatic point in the play, where Charles makes an impassioned
appeal to the Commons to be tried by the Lords and Commons,
we were suddenly given fifty or sixty bars of " Boogie Woogie ".
Someone had slipped up in the control room, plugging in a wrong
circuit on top of the transmission. There seemed to be almost
half a minute of it, in fact it was only nine seconds, but it quite
ruined the atmosphere. I was so busy investigating the facts and
arranging for the apology that I missed the rest of the play.

.   .   .   .   .

In the News last week I only just escaped having to read
a paragraph containing this dreadfully long German name:
RÄMUNGSFAMILIENUNTERHALTSBEITRÄGE. Luckily there was
enough News without it, but apparently it is a portmanteau word,
made up of Rämungs-familien-unterhalts-beiträge, meaning contributions for the entertainment of evacuated families. When
divided up in this way it loses all of its terrors.

.   .   .   .   .

On 5th March, thanks to the genius of Cecil McGivern, we were
able to broadcast another fine piece of documentary radio, on the
subject of Mulberry Harbour. What a master of this type of Radio
he is. McGivern is to Radio what Grierson is to Films.

.   .   .   .   .

On Saturday, 10th March, I was reading the nine o'clock News,
which included a message from Mr. Churchill to General Eisenhower about the recent victory, in which he referred to " your far-
reaching and triumphant combinations ". It was with great difficulty that I marshalled all my powers of self-control to continue
reading without any trace of hilarity in the voice !

.   .   .   .   .

On 24th March I returned from Bristol, where I had been sent
to meet the Regional Programme Board and try to clear up some
outstanding problems of presentation, and found that things on the
Western Front were moving fast. MacGregor, Assistant Controller News, came in and told me that the balloon had gone up,
and together we made arrangements about breaking into pro-

grammes with up-to-the-moment news. However, this was not necessary, because the communiqué came in just before the end of the 1 p.m. News, and was read by Frank Phillips.

There was an excellent bulletin at 9 p.m. that night, which I read, and it was followed by a brilliant piece of reporting by Wynford Vaughan Thomas in War Report.

In the six o'clock News the next day there was an account of the splendid progress being made all along the Rhine front, but we were obviously beginning to come up against much stiffer opposition. In the nine o'clock bulletin there was good news from the Eastern Front, too.

At 10.30 p.m., after the play "The Man Born to be King", I went up to my office on the fifth floor, which I shared with Joseph McLeod, and which is above the main entrance—a room with French windows opening on to the balcony outside. As I entered there was a heavy explosion, and the French windows moved suddenly in and out with the blast as a V2 fell quite near. We both rushed out on to the balcony, and from there we could see a huge mushroom of smoke and sparks rising up half a mile high, a little to the east of us. Then came the inevitable clanging of bells as the fire-engines and ambulances dashed to the spot, which turned out to be Whitefields Tabernacle in the Tottenham Court Road, used during the war as an hostel. I walked round there the following week and saw the severe damage that had been done to the surrounding buildings; there was a pile of rubble some thirty feet high, and through it stuck out six iron pillars—all that remained standing of the original Tabernacle.

·   ·   ·   ·   ·

I was reading the midnight News on Good Friday, 30th March, when a most unusual thing happened. In the bulletin was an account of the fall of Danzig, and the Editor had decided to lead off with this, instead of with the news from the Western Front; but after I had read the first page of the Danzig news I was confronted not with page 2 of that story, but with the second page of the Western Front story. I paused, re-arranged the Western Front pages, and carried on, then the Editor came into the studio and sorted out the pages, and I re-read page 1 of Danzig after the

Western Front story, following on with pages 2 and 3, and so restored the continuity.

I wonder how many people noticed the repetition?

. . . . .

On Easter Monday, Carleton Hobbs was to read "Lift up your Hearts" before the 8 a.m. News, and almost missed his broadcast. There were hardly any buses about at this hour and no taxis. Eventually he got as far as Piccadilly Circus from High Street, Kensington, on an L.C.C. dust-cart, and then had to run for it.

. . . . .

On Friday, 13th April (note the day and date), a glorious spring day, with the apple-blossom now fully out, we heard the sad news of the sudden death of President Roosevelt. It was a dreadful shock to us all, as we felt that he was our friend, and quite suddenly he had gone, and we knew that he could not be replaced. A message from Broadcasting House came through soon afterwards to say that I was to go to Bedford in the afternoon for a special memorial programme.

I saw Laurence Gilliam and John Snagge, and found out as much as I could about their intentions, and then left by the 4.40 train from St. Pancras, travelling up with Sir Adrian Boult. He had been caught only just in time at Waterloo as he was about to enter a train for Salisbury on a visit to his old father. Arrived in Bedford, we had a meal and then went to the rehearsal. Gilliam and Robert Speaight were in the studio, having come up by car, bringing the script with them.

This programme, entitled "In Memory, Franklin Delano Roosevelt", was one of the most moving Radio experiences I have had. The reading by Robert Speaight of "Let us now praise famous men" and the music were magnificent. It included part of the Eroica Symphony, one of the Enigma Variations, and the most beautiful "Adagio for strings" by the American, Samuel Barber.

There were my words which followed Speaight's reading:—

"We in Britain, who now pay this act of homage to Franklin Delano Roosevelt, are remembering his achievement. We honour the President of the United States who, by his courage and vision, guided his country through

economic chaos and catastrophe; Roosevelt the demo-
cratic statesman who saw, and proclaimed from the beginning, the nature and menace of Fascism : Roosevelt
the friend of Britain, who brought the resources of his
country to our aid when we stood almost alone against
the Axis Powers. Roosevelt the war leader, who has
played his determining part in the grand victorious strategy
of the United Nations, Roosevelt the man whose voice
heartened and sustained the hopes of his fellow men in
every continent of the world."

Then, at the end :—

"We take our leave of Franklin Delano Roosevelt,
four times President of the United States, in the words of
that other President who died, as he has died, in the
moment of triumph, for the cause in which he spent
himself."

Then Speaight followed with Lincoln's famous words :—

"With malice towards none; with charity for all;
with firmness in the right, as God gives us to see the right,
let us strive on to finish the work we are in; to bind up
the Nation's wounds; to care for him who shall have
borne the battle, and for his widow and orphan; to do all
things which may achieve and cherish a just and lasting
peace among ourselves, and with all nations."

Then followed Bach's " Sleepers Wake ", played by the orchestra.

.   .   .   .

On St. George's Day, 23rd April, the reports coming through
from the Russian Front indicated that they were right through the
main Berlin defences and well within the suburbs, so that exciting
news about the German capital might reach us at any time.

I began our St. George's Day programme with a concert of
music for this day, which included a tribute to the heroes of England,
with special reference to the Battle of Britain, taken from " The
Island ", by Francis Brett Young :—

> " Who were these paladins
> Anonymous and immortal ?   Whence this breed
> Of heroes born to fend the direst pass
> Our Island ever knew ?   They were the seed
> Of the mild, unadventurous Middle Class :
> The sons of parsons, lawyers, doctors, bankers,
> Shopkeepers, merchants, chemists, engineers,
> Who in this desperate day
> Won for our wings dominion of the skies."

After this I had to go and rehearse my "mystery voice" in "Monday Night at Eight", to which torture I had weakly agreed when approached by Ronnie Waldman.   On this occasion Dickie Murdoch was the acting-chief-torturer, but he let me down lightly, by asking me to read, as though in the News, a dreadful piece, all written in Cockney.   It must have sounded very funny, for I had to translate it as I went along.

For my mystery voice I became a very old man, speaking on the subject of "The Cuckoo in Spring", and I think it foxed most listeners.   This is how it ran :—

> " The Cuckoo is a merry bird,
> She sings as she flies.
> She brings us good tidings
> And tells us no lies.
> She sucks little bird's eggs
> To keep her voice clear,
> That she may sing cuckoo
> Three months of the year."

On 25th April, after announcing the Radio Doctor following the 8 a.m. News, I was surprised to hear him refer to a man who had been seriously ill and then " took a turn for the nurse ".

.   .   .   .   .

DEATH OF MUSSOLINI.   FALL OF BERLIN

Rumours of a link-up between the Allied Armies of the East and West in Berlin had not been officially confirmed.

The news came through two days later, while I was standing by for it, ready to break into programmes, when, to my surprise, I heard Freddy Grisewood give it out in the six o'clock bulletin. The Controller had made a last-minute decision that it should go out at the beginning of the six o'clock News, and not afterwards, as previously arranged.

.   .   .   .   .

On 29th April I read all the gruesome details of Mussolini's death in the nine o'clock News. He had been shot like a dog, together with members of his Cabinet and others, at a village on Lake Como, and his body afterwards publicly displayed in Milan, hung up like a turkey in the Christmas market. That night we heard, too, that both Venice and Munich had been captured.

. . . . . .

On Tuesday, 1st May, I received orders to report at 9 a.m. the following Thursday. Things are certainly moving very fast. When I arrived at the office at 5 p.m., John Snagge had just gone out to see the atrocities film about the German concentration camps. As I worked on, a message came through from R. T. Clark, the Home News Editor, asking, " Can you arrange to break into programmes ? The German Army in Italy has surrendered unconditionally." The time then was 6.45 p.m. I made the necessary arrangements for a break at 7 p.m., and gave it to Freddy Allen to do before the Talk scheduled for that time. He was delighted. This was a great historical event, *nearly one million prisoners being taken.*

At 10.15 p.m., after a busy evening, very much on the *qui vive*, another call came from R. T. Clark : " Berlin has fallen. Will you please arrange to broadcast this news ? " I did this myself. Here are the actual words I used :—

> " We are breaking into our programmes for a second time to-night, this time with some splendid news from Moscow : Berlin has fallen. Marshal Stalin has just announced the capture of the capital of Germany, the centre of German imperialism, and the cradle of German aggression. The Berlin garrison laid down their arms this afternoon. More than 70,000 prisoners have been rounded up so far to-day."

. . . . . .

On 4th May I was attending conferences all the morning, busy working out details of procedure. Everything hinges on the time fixed for zero hour, which will begin with a statement by the Prime Minister.

That evening I read the six o'clock News, which was of historic interest, because it was the last bulletin broadcast preceded by the name of the News-reader. John Snagge read the nine o'clock News, announcing, at the end of it, the cessation of the custom of naming the News-readers, the original reason for it—security identification—having lapsed. In this News the announcement was made of the surrender of Denmark, North Holland and North Germany.

. . . . .

On Saturday, 5th May, I read the early News bulletins, which included an interesting statement from a German official source on " Why we lost ". . . . " Air Power the answer."

The Schedules for V.E. Day were now filling up fast; many of us waiting on at Broadcasting House for zero hour. Nothing much happened until Monday afternoon, except that at mid-day on Sunday the News contained the story of the patriots' rising in Prague and an account of their radio call for help. At 4.30 p.m. on Monday afternoon, Godfrey Adams (Programme Planner) came in and told me that General Eisenhower had put out a communiqué about the signing of the surrender terms, and we found that General de Gaulle had alerted the people of France in the early afternoon. All this time that we were waiting for something to happen, flags were flying and planes were zooming above us overhead. Later we discovered that we had been waiting for a wire from Stalin, which did not come.

At 7.45 p.m. that evening, on the authority of the Ministry of Information, we broadcast a statement that to-morrow would be V.E. Day. The Prime Minister would be speaking at 3 p.m., and His Majesty the King at 9 p.m. This announcement was repeated later on, and I began the nine o'clock News with it, going on to describe the German surrender, giving an account of how it was carried out at Rheims, and a list of the signatories. I was on duty until midnight, and saw many bonfires with their reflections in the sky; a few rockets went up now and again.

At 1.30 a.m. I was awakened by a fearful thunderstorm, which continued for more than two hours. It was as though Mars was having a final fling at us in his death-throes.

The next day, 8th May (V.E. Day), was a very long one. I was up betimes and broadcasting before breakfast, and later came a busy period in the office of conferences, checking cues and schedules, inserting this and leaving out that, and all the time I was answering for John Snagge while he rehearsed " Tribute to the King " and Victory Report.

Snagge announced the Prime Minister at three o'clock, I read the six o'clock News—twenty-five minutes of it—with the Prime Minister's recorded speech. The " Tribute to the King " went excellently. His Majesty spoke very well indeed, but took thirteen and a half minutes, so that, with the National Anthem, played by the Symphony Orchester in Bedford, it was almost 9.15 p.m. before I began the News.

After it was dark, we went out to see the flags and the flood-lighting. There were hundreds of flags, but only a few flood-lit buildings. It was a most impressive scene, with crowds everywhere in the streets and on the pavements. I returned to read the midnight News, which included the King's speech, the first sentence of which I can never forget :—

> " As these words are being spoken, the official end of
> the war in Europe is taking place . . ."

And with a feeling of great relief and deep thankfulness for having lived to see the end of a Second World War, I went to bed, and to sleep at once.

.   .   .   .   .

We had been promised a new broadcasting lay-out in this country as soon as reasonably possible after the war, and plans were well advanced when V.E. Day came on 8th May.

The framework of the new scheme, as outlined by the Director-General, was that the broadcasting service should consist of three programmes, two being contrasting programmes, one on medium wave, and the other on medium and long wave; the third was to follow later and to be quite distinct from, but complementary to, the others. This latter programme would be broadcast only from 6 p.m. onwards.

The transition from a war to a peace footing was swiftly carried out, and at the end of July the General Forces Programme was replaced by the Light Programme. It was not possible to start the Third Programme until sometime later. Meanwhile the Director-General rightly insisted that criticism of the scheme should be withheld until the Third Programme had become established, because it was an integral part of the scheme as a whole.

During the war there had been some criticism of our war-time method of working, on the ground that too much was concentrated in London, and too little shared out among the Regions, but the advantages of centralisation as a war-time expedient were realised, and as soon as the war ended it was decided to give the Regions autonomy in practically everything except the News. This granting of Regional autonomy meant that we, in London, had to allow for Regions to come in and go out, at choice, at the end of each section of the programme, and, to allow for this, a ten-second interval for switching was agreed to, coming at the end of each section.

Before and during the war a good deal had been heard about the healthy stimulus of competition, and in discussing post-war broadcasting the Director-General welcomed this idea, and suggested that there should be an element of keen friendly rivalry between the Home and the Light programmes; but in practice this did not materialise, the character of the two programmes being entirely different, one slick, non-stop, specialised, often sensational and hearty, the other non-specialised, leisurely in tempo, and thought-provoking, with the avowed object of " reflecting and illuminating the world in which we live ". So marked was this contrast that within a month of the scheme beginning I had no idea what was being broadcast in the Light Programme when I was on the air, nor did I know who was the announcer on duty, in theory my immediate competitor.

Just before the new pattern began to take shape I announced a superb book-talk by Compton Mackenzie. What an admirable broadcaster he is, with his clear, well-modulated voice, his original and critical mind, and his vast store of knowledge, based on travel, observation and wide reading. On this occasion the only criticism I had to make was that he tried to crowd too much into his allotted fifteen minutes, and towards the end had to hurry; and this kind of talk demands a leisurely, contemplative approach. His numerous anecdotes and his fund of stories were always at hand to illustrate any experience, and his memory was staggering. He assured me afterwards that he could clearly remember a nurse of his, who left when he was eight months old. In his youth he went to a Kensit meeting at the Queen's Hall, concealing a cauliflower under his coat, which, at an opportune moment, he lobbed gently from above, scoring a bull's-eye on the unfortunate Kensit, and knocking him out.

. . . . .

Early in June there was Vaughan Thomas' description of King Haakon's return to Norway. How effectively nostalgia can be broadcast! Never before had I heard such full-throated cheering sustained for so long, by what was obviously a vast concourse of people.

. . . . .

Following on the election of a Labour Government at the end of July came the news that the atomic bomb had been perfected, and the first one was dropped on Japan on 5th August, its effect being two thousand times that of the R.A.F.'s ten-ton bomb. Three days later Russia declared war on Japan. I put out this piece of News at the end of the Promenade Concert on 8th August, and the next day the news that Japan had surrendered was given out in the one o'clock News. As I came through Oxford Circus after this, I thought everyone had gone mad. A.T.S. and W.R.E.N.S were standing on the top of Peter Robinson's building showering down paper on people's heads below, and holding long paper streamers, which billowed out in the wind. There was no official confirmation from the Government of this wonderful news, and it did not come through until, after a long period of waiting, it was announced by the Prime Minister at midnight on 14th August.

. . . . .

On 24th August I read the 6 p.m. News giving us our first post-war shock—the announcement that our financial position had now become grave, as the result of the sudden cessation of Lend-Lease.

At the end of that week I announced the " Last Night of the Proms ", notable for the superb singing of a young English contralto named Kathleen Ferrier, who is clearly in the international class. It has been a record season, more than 300,000 people going to the Proms this summer.

The following week saw the beginning of the new ITMA, with Tommy Handley in his most devastatingly frivolous form : " This is the Battersea Dogs Home Calling. . . . Here is the News. . . .

Sir Adrian Boult has just taken all the Poms (Proms ?) to the bottom of the garden." This week ended, however, on a sad note, for C. H. Middleton, most beloved broadcaster since Sir Walford Davies, suddenly dropped dead in his garden. In my opinion he was a war casualty, having worked himself to death. I wonder how many millions made a date with him each Sunday at 2.15 ?

· · · · ·

On 25th October I used the Continuity suite and its facilities to announce the King's speech from the Royal Albert Hall on the occasion of the centenary celebrations of the College of Science and Technology, South Kensington. Lord Rayleigh, the President, was to speak immediately before the King, and my task was to announce the King and go over to the hall on the applause following Lord Rayleigh's speech, being careful to avoid radiating any of his speech. I closed down the 9.15 talk by Mr. Glenvil Hall in the Continuity studio, began a programme of records of Paul Robeson to fill up the time until the King's speech was due at 9.40 p.m., and listened to Lord Rayleigh's speech on pre-fade. Having timed my announcement, and armed with a copy of Lord Rayleigh's speech, I knew exactly where to end the records and say my piece, in order to go over to the hall on the applause. It all worked out according to plan, but it needed careful timing and liaison with the hall and the engineers beforehand. Even so, it was not without its anxieties, because Lord Rayleigh began three and a half minutes early and ended just before 9.40 p.m.

· · · · ·

On Sunday, 28th October, I announced Godfrey Winn's talk on Holland in the late afternoon, after a chat with him and the producer about broadcasting in general. In spite of the detailed arrangements the producer made to regulate his speed, he ran over his allotted time, and was cut by Continuity just before the end of the last paragraph of a dozen lines or so in the script. Winn was most upset about it, as it had apparently happened once before, and this talk was planned to rise to a climax at the end, which was not broadcast, and he therefore argued that the whole point of the talk was lost. Aided by the producer, I did my best to pour oil on the troubled waters, pointing out that the cut was clearly and neatly made at the end of the penultimate paragraph, and that, in any case, the whole talk would be published in the *Listener*; but he was adamant, saying " What can one do ? . . . why did I ever consent to broadcast ? . . . there is no redress, not even an Editor to have it out with ", etc., etc.

.   .   .   .   .

On the last day of October I announced the Symphony Concert given by our Orchestra and conducted by Sir Thomas Beecham, which was a staggering exhibition of genius in action. The *Daily Telegraph* next day headed its notice " Beecham Reaches New Heights ", and with justification, for the Orchestra under his magical influence was superb. It is said that Toscanini once stated that there are two works in the repertoire, which are impossible to conduct, Wolf's " Italian Serenade ", and " Iberia " by Debussy. In this concert Sir Thomas conducted " Iberia " without a score.

.   .   .   .   .

At an Albert Hall concert on 14th November, this time conducted by Sir Adrian Boult, the soloist was Marjorie Lawrence, the Australian dramatic soprano, who was singing for the first time in this country. She is a victim of infantile paralysis, and has to sing sitting in a wheeled chair, being wheeled on and off the platform by her husband. A large woman, with a powerful voice, she needed all that she could produce to be heard above an orchestra of 110 or so in the hall, when singing the excerpt from the heavily scored Strauss Opera. She is very fair, and was dressed in apple-green and silver, with a green plume surmounting a coronet head-dress, which gave her a regal, oriental appearance.

That week I went to Film House, in Wardour Street, the Headquarters of Schools Broadcasting, to announce one of their discussion series, " To Start You Talking ". When I got there I was horrified to find that the subject was " Why should sex be a problem ? "

I may be old-fashioned, but I regretted that this had been included in the schedule, because I felt that the modern idea of " frankness " is being overdone. Sex is such a personal, intimate matter, and surely what is wanted is guidance, not discussion; and this can be obtained, if needed, from a priest, doctor or parent.

Luckily I did not have much to say, but the fact that I was there meant, in some listeners' minds, that I had given it my blessing, and directly I returned to Broadcasting House the Duty Officer told me that he had had several calls about my appearance in a broadcast of this type.

.   .   .   .   .

At the end of October we learnt, with great sorrow, of the death of Alan Howland, after a long illness. A colleague wrote in *The Times* on 1st November : —

> " He was a clear and accurate reader, one of the quickest readers in the Corporation, and was also well known for his many character parts and for his readings in the series, the Wednesday Story."

He was a born broadcaster and narrator, and his untimely death in the mid-forties leaves a gap which will be hard to fill.

1946

THERE were two memorable programmes early in the year. The first of these was the 200th performance of ITMA, on 21st February, which was a brilliant show, a fine example of the team work of the Kavanagh–Handley–Worsley triumvirate. The audience was mostly made up of senior B.B.C. staff and their wives, and I met many old friends there I had not seen for a long time, including Fred Yule, Hugh Morton and Tommy himself. I thought the show went very well. However, Francis Worsley was far from happy about it. He said we were not an ideal audience; the cast was nervous because it was a special occasion—as he put it, " Too many damned professionals, like yourself, in the audience, Stuart."

The second memorable programme was a musical event in March —the visit of the Huddersfield Choral Society, a magnificent body of 300 voices, to sing Beethoven's Solemn Mass with the B.B.C. Symphony Orchestra under Dr. Malcolm Sargent, on the occasion of the Henry Wood Birthday Concert.

.   .   .   .   .

It was after the nine o'clock News on 12th April that many listeners were surprised to hear me say rather testily, " What the Hell ! " on which reporters, scarcely believing their ears, at once rang up the B.B.C. to make sure that it really was I, myself, who had said this, and inquire the reason for it. The Press officer told me afterwards that there were hundreds of telephone calls. What happened was this. I had been supplied with an official cue sheet, which stated : " At 9.15. 'That is the end of the News ' . . . Pause . . . five seconds . . . then make the announcement of the talk."

I said my piece at 9.15, switched off my microphone while I coughed—there is a hand-switch on the table for this purpose— switched it on again, and began to announce McDonald's talk, as per the cue-sheet. Having spoken five or six words of this an-

THE ITMA TRIUMVIRATE

FRANCIS WORSLEY, TOMMY HANDLEY AND TED KAVANAGH

THE AUTHOR SIGNING AUTOGRAPHS AT THE B.B.C. EXHIBITION AT NORWICH

nouncement, I suddenly saw the red light flicking violently over
the studio window in front of me, and, thinking that this meant
that my words had not gone out, I muttered, "What the Hell is
happening now?", paused; then on came the red light, and I
repeated the interrupted announcement, only to discover later, when
the 'phones began to ring in the studio, that the first three words of
my ejaculation had gone out before the Programme Engineer cut
me off. By an oversight, the Programme Engineer had not been
given a copy of the cue-sheet, and she had, entirely without authority, buzzed out—i.e., signalled to the control room to take the studio
out—on hearing my words, "That is the end of the News". Control room, suspecting a mistake, but acting on the signal, took the
studio out, but at once flicked the red light violently. The Programme Engineer then buzzed in again, up came the studio, and of
course my remarks were broadcast. The next day one paper had
a photograph of me with a semi-banner headline, "Oh, Mr. Hibberd!" A French paper went one better, and used the headline,
"Révolution à la B.B.C."

The 26th April was the day on which we broadcast the service
from St. Sepulchre's Church, Holborn, on the occasion of the unveiling, by the Lord Mayor, of the stained-glass window in memory
of Sir Henry Wood; it was in this church that, as a boy, he learnt
to play the organ under Dr. Lott. In addition to the Lord Mayor
and his staff, there was an orchestra drawn from the B.B.C. Symphony Orchestra and the London Symphony Orchestra, conducted
by Basil Cameron, and the singers were the B.B.C. Chorus and the
combined choirs of St. Paul's and the Abbey, Lord Jowitt giving
the address. The window, which was designed by Gerald E. R.
Smith in collaboration with Frank O. Salisbury, depicts St. Cecilia,
the patron saint of music, seated with attendant angels at the organ,
and in the left-hand panel below we see Sir Henry Wood as a youth
playing the organ, and on the right the familiar figure of Sir Henry
conducting a Promenade Concert. The church was packed;
every musical figure of note in the country seemed to be there.
The following day I went with Sir Adrian Boult and the Orchestra to Norwich, where we were entertained to luncheon by the
Lord Mayor. We gave two very successful concerts there, and as

T

the B.B.C. Exhibition was then in that city, I was asked to go and say a " few words ", being introduced by the B.B.C.'s Director of Publicity, Kenneth Adam, as " What the Hell Stuart ". It was while we were there I heard that Frederick Thurston, the principal clarinet of the Orchestra, had decided to resign. A pupil of Charles Draper, he had been with us since the early Savoy Hill days. He was in the Wireless Orchestra when I joined in 1924. A magnificent player, we shall be hard put to it to find a successor.

Victory Day, 8th June, I spent at Broadcasting House, reading News bulletins and making announcements, as nearly all the work was done by the commentators on the route of the procession; but I did see some of the television, which was excellent, and made me realise what an attractive medium this is for actuality material.

At the end of July I took part in an amusing Arthur Askey show at the Paris theatre. He and Kenneth Horne were supposed to have a lighthouse to let for the summer months, and I was one of the prospective tenants who came along to have a look at it. They did their best to palm it off on me, but all their plans went wrong; I smelt a rat, and eventually they had to admit that I was very hard to please.

I was reading the nine o'clock News one night in early December when the announcement of the end of the American Coal Strike came in. This was a scoop for us, as it only happened at 8.30 p.m., and consequently was too late for the last editions of the evening papers. The Editor just managed to get it into the headlines as I entered the studio, and at the end of the bulletin we went straight over to Leonard Miall in Washington, who gave us the details. How Radio can score with up-to-the-minute news, if it comes in after-office hours and there is a man on the spot to report it, as in this case!

The outstanding performance in the Christmas Day programme was given by Ralph Wightman, who introduced a man named Cross from Dorchester. He was so homely and sincere in his approach, and forthright too, that I felt very proud of my native county.

1947

THE year opened with reminders to all householders that, mainly because of the aftermath of war, we were living in hard times. Electricity cuts were being imposed more and more frequently, as the severe winter weather continued, until, early in February, it looked as if, to save fuel consumption, we might be forced to put out only one programme instead of two—a kind of Light–Home hybrid. Fortunately this was avoided, though the hours of transmission were shortened.

Gales continued to rage for weeks around our coasts, so much so that Edward Ward and his Engineer, Charles Coombs, who had gone to the Bishop Rock Lighthouse, off the Isles of Scilly on 20th December, for the Christmas Broadcast, were marooned there until they were taken off by the St. Mary's lifeboat on 17th January.

An unkind cartoonist depicted them with long, flowing beards looking out from the gallery around the lighthouse, sighing for the day when the relief ship would be able to land some razor-blades.

. . . . .

It was early in February that an old broadcasting friend, Daventry 5.XX, having performed most noble service, closed down, and my mind went back to that July day in 1925 when, at the opening ceremony, a poem by Alfred Noyes was broadcast, in honour of the occasion :—

" Daventry calling . . . Daventry calling . . . Daventry calling . . . Dark
    and still
The tree of memory stands like a sentry . . . over the graves, on the
    silent hill."

. . . . .

It was in the middle of February that His Excellency the Governor of Tomtopia, having lost all his belongings in that inhospitable land, returned home, and promptly proceeded to lose his voice; then we realised that we were indeed up against it. However, after

24th February, when in one Leicestershire village the thermometer registered forty-one degrees of frost, Tommy recovered his voice; we had got over the worst, and things began to improve.

Meanwhile the Royal tour of South Africa was a tremendous success, and in rejoicing about this we were able to forget many of our troubles at home, but not on the night of 17th February, when we were to broadcast the King's speech at the City Hall State Banquet, Cape Town, in reply to an address of welcome by General Smuts, the Prime Minister. His Majesty's speech was timed for approximately 8 p.m., and we had been warned that it might begin earlier, and had therefore cut out the 7.30 talk and substituted a flexible programme of records instead, but the Cape Town time schedule went wrong, and it was 8.50 before the King began to speak, and I spent an anxious evening apologising for the delay and trying to find out what the situation there was. The liaison between the City Hall and the Broadcasting Headquarters was almost non-existent, and nearly all the information I was given was incorrect.

. . . . .

How easy it is to make spoonerisms when broadcasting, if for a fraction of a second your concentration is not 100 per cent on what you are saying. Only a few weeks ago a colleague of mine referred to the *Windering Monstrel*, and on 18th April, at the end of a long Weather Forecast before the 6 p.m. News, the Editor brought in the bulletin as I was reading. I looked up from my script for a moment to take it from him, and promptly said, " Temmer, Hums and Tyne " instead of " Thames, Humber and Tyne "; another colleague in similar circumstances said, " East Doggy and Forters ".

At the beginning of May the warship H.M.S. *Sluys* had been in the News, and the name had evidently been mispronounced by one of us, because the Commanding Officer sent us his visiting-card bearing the name of the ship. On the other side of the card was written :—

" When you announce
Something so choice
Don't mispronounce
H.M.S. *Sluys*."

—in other words, it is " Sloyce ".

. . . . .

On 25th May I met Mr. Clement Davies, the leader of the Liberal Party in the House of Commons, who was making the appeal for the Welsh Region, speaking from London. He comes from Montgomeryshire, and told me that the losses of the hill farmers during the severe winter were terrible. One old farmer said to him, " I had three hundred ewes, and now I have just buried the last one." . . . " I felt like crying," said Clement Davies.

. . . . .

At the end of May we broadcast a special concert of works of her own choice in honour of Queen Mary's eightieth birthday, given by the B.B.C. Theatre Orchestra, conductor Stanford Robinson. It was during the same week that a Dutch gentleman, a Mr. Van Hoffen, came over from Holland and presented me with a bound copy of the Dutch underground newspaper, as compiled by him after listening to one of our News bulletins read by me during the war. It was handsomely bound, and inscribed with my name on the fly-leaf. He told me that it was taken down at great personal risk, because at the time he was being carefully watched by the Gestapo, who were most suspicious of him—so much so that he did not even tell his wife that he was engaged in this important work. This proved to be a blessing, because the Gestapo later arrested her, and cross-examined her for hours on end, without any result, because she knew nothing.

I was very proud indeed to receive such a thrilling memento of the war.

. . . . .

In July, after listening to Molotov repeatedly saying " No ", our attention was diverted from the world scene to the exciting piece of home news of the Royal Betrothal—H.R.H. Princess Elizabeth becoming engaged to Prince Philip of Greece, a Lieutenant in the Royal Navy.

. . . . .

The next day we broadcast the unveiling, by His Majesty the King, of the memorial chapel in Westminster Abbey, dedicated " to the men of the Flying Forces who gave their lives in the defence of Freedom ".

It was the seventh anniversary of the beginning of the Battle of
Britain.

.   .   .   .   .

Early in July I broadcast a most unusual S.O.S. about some
poisoned pigeons, which ran as follows :—

" Three dead pigeons were picked up in Barnet this
morning, and it was found, on examination, that they had
been poisoned by cyanide. It is known that a fourth
pigeon was picked up by a man who said he was going to
eat it for his dinner.

" Scotland Yard warns this man *not* to eat the pigeon
and wants him to telephone Whitehall 1212."

I never heard whether he got the message in time or not.

.   .   .   .   .

An orchestral concert from the Orangery, Hampton Court Palace,
on 20th July, given by the New London Orchestra, under Alec
Sherman, was the cause of an unexpected crisis at Broadcasting
House. The concert had begun in the normal way, and the second
item, consisting of the Bach concerto in D minor for two violins,
had just begun, when it became obvious that something was wrong.
After a few bars of groping by the players, the conductor stopped
the Orchestra, there was some consultation, and then a new start
was made. At first we could not find out what had happened,
but soon the engineers at the Palace told us that it was very windy
in the Orangery, and just after the concerto had begun, the music
was blown off the soloists' stands, and they were unable to go on.
I cannot remember anything like this ever having happened at an
outside broadcast before. After the concert I made an announcement explaining what had occurred.

.   .   .   .   .

During the first week of August I read the report of the Debate
on the Emergency Powers Bill, which included some complex legal
points from Sir Stafford Cripps's speech, difficult to grasp at first
reading, also some hard hitting by the Opposition big guns, and an
amusing metaphor used by Mr. Eden, who, in referring to the ship
of State, said that all the Government had done was to move the
furniture from the first-class to the third-class saloon.

.   .   .   .   .

The last night of the Proms was broadcast in the Light Programme on 13th September, Peter Fettes being the announcer on duty in the Albert Hall. He told me that the audience had come prepared to rag everything possible, and was not content to wait for the horn-pipe in Sir Henry Wood's arrangement of British sea-songs at the end. Even the long and difficult cadenza for the clarinet was ragged. I was sorry for Ralph Clark, who was the soloist, as I remember Frederick Thurston telling me that this was one of the most difficult passages ever written for that instrument.

.   .   .   .   .

On 19th September I announced General Slim, who was giving a talk on "The Old Indian Army and its Traditions". He himself was a former Gurkha officer, and we talked about this fine race and the wonderful way they have of always supporting us. We also spoke of Pathans, Sikhs and Dogras, Jats and Punjabis, and he made the important point that the Indian Army was a British institution, a fine British achievement, a most effective instrument in keeping the peace in that vast Continent of many races and creeds, though he was still anxious about the communal disturbances, more than 100,000 deaths having resulted from them since the handing over of control.

.   .   .   .   .

On Saturday, 4th October, I had my first experience of going to the Radio Exhibition at Olympia on a Saturday and appearing in public there. When I arrived at 3 p.m. there were long queues of people all round the building trying to get in, and I had to fight my way upstairs to the Radio Council offices, where I was due to report. The great draw was television, and undoubtedly there were some fine exhibits of sets in action. I remember while waiting for Mr. Dyer, a member of the Council, being highly amused by an excellent television picture of a Punch-and-Judy show. I was taken to the control room, where I soon found myself " on the air " in the hall, while hundreds of people, filing by the glass walls of the control room, watched me in action. After broadcasting for half an hour or so, not only programmes, but also S.O.S. messages for lost children, I handed over to Joan Griffiths and left to return to the Council office. I did not get far, however; for I was at once pounced upon by autograph hunters, and could hardly write my name for the crush, until mercifully rescued by Mr. Dyer.

As I left, the police had their hands full trying to control the crowds, and the Council had got them to telephone to the Underground Authorities, asking them to stop passengers coming to Olympia, by erecting " House Full " notices.

. . . . .

On the last Monday of the Promenade season there were several complications, owing to an announcement which was to be made to the audience in the hall, and because the rehearsal timing had shown that the concert would end early. I therefore went to Continuity in order to take charge of things from there myself, and was just checking up with the hall, when the Senior Control Room Engineer strolled in to say " Sorry, no lines ". This was at 7.22, and the concert was due to begin at 7.30. In the eight minutes that remained I had to do some quick thinking, as, though in theory I should have been ready for any emergency, and was indeed ready for a few minutes' delay, I was not ready to put over a substitute programme at eight minutes' notice.

I held a consultation with Sam Bonner, the Senior Control Room Engineer, who told me that our Lines Department and the Post Office were working on the line trouble, and I therefore hoped that the delay would be only a short one. But my luck was out. At 7.30 I explained that owing to line trouble we could not get through to the hall, and that until we could I would put on a programme of records. This I did, being careful to work out a programme which more or less corresponded in type with the published one. I sent for Denys Drower to help set up the records and rehearse the joins, while I did the actual presentation and tried to deal with the line situation, hoping that every minute I should get the O.K. to go over to the hall. I was at a loss to understand the delay, as not for years had we had any line trouble of this duration with the Albert Hall. In the end I had to broadcast a complete concert, including " Till Eulenspiegel " and a Haydn Symphony, the last part of which I had to hand over to Drower while I went off to read the News. Only after the News, and having dealt with the Press Officer and the Duty Officer, both inundated with calls asking why there had been no Prom, did I learn what had happened. As it

was the last week of the Proms, it had been decided to televise the
final night on the following Saturday, and after the usual sound
rehearsal in the morning, the vision rehearsal began. This did not
end until well into the afternoon. When it, too, ended, the Television engineers told the Post Office engineers that they had finished
" and would not be wanting the lines until Saturday ", whereupon
the P.O. engineers whipped out not only the Alexandra Palace lines,
but the Broadcasting House ones as well. That was why we were
sunk when the time came to broadcast the Prom. In their efforts
to re-establish contact with the hall, they got as far as the Kensington
Exchange, but were unable to get on from there to the hall in time
for the concert.

    .   .   .   .

Included in the nine o'clock News was an item about a chess test
match. Luckily I saw this when looking through the bulletin beforehand. I knew I should almost certainly say " chest match ",
so I got the Editor to re-write the sentence to read : " England has
beaten Australia in a test match at chess ". This is just the kind of
thing that, read at sight, inevitably ties one up in knots.

    .   .   .   .

Stewart McPherson's birthday was on 27th October, and he
had been asked by Ronnie Waldman to express a wish in " Monday
Night at Eight ". This was to hear me give a running commentary
on an ice-hockey match, between Harringay Racers and Greyhounds.
I do not believe for one moment that he thought I should accept
the challenge; but when Ronnie asked me about it, I felt that I was
being put on my mettle. I therefore told Ronnie that though I
had never seen an ice-hockey match, I would accept, and hope for
the best on the day. Ronnie was delighted, and at once put me
in touch with Tom Stenner, the Publicity Manager at Harringay,
who gave me all the help and information he could, and asked me
to come and see the match between Harringay Racers and Wembley
the following Wednesday.
Meanwhile I buried myself in the library, trying to find out all
I could about the game, and proceeded to learn the names of the
teams by heart, because there was no chance of getting to know the
men individually and recognising them when playing. I did not
tell Stewart I was going to the Wembley match, but at half time I

discovered that he was there, and went along to have a chat with him. While he was giving me some tips as to the best method of giving an ice-hockey commentary, one of the staff photographers snapped us.

When the great day arrived I was anxious, but determined to put up a reasonably good show. Stenner and Brian Johnston met me, and the first shock was the news that there were three changes in the teams and some cuts in the script, leading up to my cue, to be given to me by Kenneth Horne from the studio. This meant, of course, ignoring the game and following the script, until I had got my cue.

We sat perched up above the penalty box looking down on to the ice, with fifty or more screaming boys and girls directly behind us— fans of the Greyhounds, who, when in full cry, made it almost impossible for me to hear my own voice.

The game began, and I had to switch my attention from it to my head-phones, in order to pick up my cue from Kenneth Horne and be ready to say my piece in the script; then, having said it, I had to begin the commentary on the game. It was not easy to pick up the thread quickly. Sometimes I found that I could not see the numbers on the players' backs, and the game moved so rapidly (there is no touch in ice-hockey) that by the time I had described a move by one player several others had come up and joined in the tussle, and I could not get out their names quickly enough. I did manage to put over the excitement and describe runs made by either side, using such phrases as " The Greyhounds' right wing is attacking like blazes ", " He's been robbed ", etc., etc., and soon the excitement rose to fever pitch as a rough-and-tumble developed in the Racers' goal. I was just beginning to stage a gigantic build-up, at last remembering some names accurately, when Horne yelled through the 'phones, " Stop, Stuart ! Stop, will you ? Stop. . . ."

In my excitement and desire to make a good show of it, I committed the unforgivable sin of an O.B. commentator. I forgot to give the score; also I was much too honest about the names of the players, instead of making them up, when I could not remember them. But it was all very good fun. I hardly slept a wink that night. I was doing the commentary all over again, and so much better than in the broadcast.

·   ·   ·   ·

THE B.B.C.'s JUBILEE

Jubilee Week began on the 9th November, and throughout that
week there were special commemorative programmes, beginning
with Bridson's Feature, " The Mirror of our Times ", on the Sunday
night. This was a good start, but most people afterwards thought
that it included too much about the war and too little about our
achievements in imparting information and encouraging discussion
in peace-time. Robert Donat was the narrator, an excellent choice,
but unfortunately he had an atrocious cold.

The following day I did the announcement of " The Programme
was Recorded ", presented by John Snagge—a programme " re-
viving memories of great occasions and personalities in broadcasting ". This was a splendid piece of work, which included a fine
description of the Derby by Woodroofe, Snagge's commentary on
the Boat Race in 1937 and 1939, and Harold Abrahams's exciting
description of Lovelock's famous race, when he won at the Olympic
Games in Berlin.

There were other excellent programmes throughout this week,
which culminated with the birthday one on the 14th, devised and
produced by Messrs. Barsley and Worsley, which included Harold
Nicolson, Ted Kavanagh, a specimen News bulletin of the old 2 L.O.
days, read by me, and, most entertaining, Mabel Constanduros on
the Buggins family's visit to the Zoo.

It was during this week also that I broadcast a short sketch about
A. J. Alan. I also took part, with John Snagge and some others,
in the Savoy Hill Scrapbook Television programme produced by
Robert Barr, in which my job was to turn the pages of the Scrapbook. All went well until I began to name the Co-Optimists and,
coming to Stanley Holloway, I could not remember his name. I got
away with it by a quick reference to " Sam, Sam, pick up thee
musket ", but had my leg well pulled about it afterwards.

.   .   .   .   .

The two great events at the end of this year were the Royal
Wedding on 20th November, and the Royal visit to Broadcasting
House on 4th December. I had little to do with the Royal Wedding,
which was a triumph for the Outside Broadcasts and Television,
except that I made the initial announcement and read some of the
News bulletins, and also announced a programme of " Music for

Princess Elizabeth " by Bax and Elgar—music which had been
dedicated to her—but I saw nearly everything on the television
screen, which was excellent.

In the case of the Royal visit, I was warned that the Royal Party
would come and watch me reading the nine o'clock News in Studio
3D (the normal News-reading studio in Broadcasting House until
a new News suite was completed in Egton House, adjoining Broadcasting House, in June of the following year) just after 9 p.m.   For
the first time since the war I was wearing a short coat with a stiff
collar when reading this bulletin, and I felt like a trussed turkey
and was very nervous.   But my luck was in, because the Royal
party were late, and it was 9.10 before I was conscious of the fact
that they were looking at me, in turn, through the studio window.
By that time I had recovered my nerve and more or less settled
down.   But I was thankful when it was over.

Later in the Council Chamber I was presented to their Majesties,
and the Queen asked me several questions about News-reading,
particularly about the bulletins we read during the war.   I was able
to tell her how people listened, at great risk to themselves, in the
occupied countries, taking down the News and issuing it secretly
in the form of news-sheets.

. . . . .

Of Christmas 1947 I remember the broadcast of the Christmas
bells in the morning, ringing in the spirit of Christmas from North
to South, culminating in the superb chimes of the bells of Bethlehem.

I remember, too, Sir William Jones' exquisite stanza from the
Persian :—

> " On parent knees, a naked new-born child,
> Weeping thou sat'st while all around thee smiled.
> So live that, sinking to thy life's last sleep,
> Calm thou may'st smile while all around thee weep."

Then, in lighter vein, there was Dickie Murdoch's virtuosity in
the Christmas " Much Binding in the Marsh ", singing comic words
to Luigini's " Ballet Egyptien " music, and the Boxing Day broadcast
of the Harringay Circus, when Stewart McPherson kept the commentary going brilliantly after four unsuccessful attempts to hand
over to John Snagge, who was with the elephants in another ring.
Stewart told us that he was fast coming to the conclusion that the

elephants must have devoured Snagge for their supper, but at length John came through, explaining that Sally—one of the elephants—had seized the microphone so effectively in her trunk, in order to speak into it, that she had torn out the leads, and it was no easy matter for the engineers to restore them in time.

1948

THERE was a buzz of excitement at Broadcasting House shortly after 7 a.m. on 8th January. While the charladies were busy scrubbing the floor of the entrance hall, an Indian, dressed in sandals, pyjamas and a *puggaree*, rushed into the building and tore up the stairs, chased by commissionaires and brown-coats (studio attendants).

The door of the council chamber on the first floor happened to be open, in he dashed and, sitting down in the largest chair, shouted, "I want to broadcast".

The council chamber is used for large committee meetings and receptions; but, as it is situated outside the central broadcasting tower, it is not equipped with microphones, but evidently he mistook it for a studio. Sergt.-Major Stacey—one of the senior commissionaires—always very much on the alert, at once took charge of the situation, and questioned him tactfully to find out what he wanted. He demanded to be allowed to broadcast, and criticised the B.B.C.'s attitude towards world affairs. He refused to go when requested, and became obstreperous. Stacey therefore dialled 999, and the police came and took him away in a car.

Although of no particular significance, the incident showed how easily a man intent on sabotage could rush into the building if he wanted to. Once before, in Savoy Hill days, a similar thing had happened. In that case it was a madman, who knocked the commissionaire down (he was an old soldier with a wooden leg) and ran up the stairs, causing considerable anxiety to T. C. L. Farrar, the announcer on duty, and the engineers. It took several policemen some time to corner and overpower him before he could be removed in an ambulance.

. . . . .

When I arrived at the B.B.C. on the afternoon of 30th January, I found everyone talking about the tragic death of Mahatma Gandhi, the announcement of which was given out in the News at one o'clock. Apparently he was shot by a Hindu at close range as he was on his way to his daily prayer meeting at five o'clock. He was seventy-eight.

That evening I read the nine o'clock News, which began with the headlines and was immediately followed by a recorded account of the murder by our correspondent, Robert Stimson, who had been an eye-witness of the crime. After this I had two or three pages about Gandhi's life and work before we broadcast part of a recording by Pandit Nehru speaking to the people of India, beginning, "The Light has gone out. . . ." The Prime Minister broadcast a personal tribute from Downing Street directly after the News at 9.15 p.m.

While I was speaking, unknown to me at the time, another voice became superimposed on my words (rather like the ghost voice of the enemy during the war, only louder and more leisurely in tempo), becoming so loud at times that I was scarcely audible.

It was most unfortunate that this should have happened on such an occasion as this, and the Continuity announcer made a suitable apology at the end of Mr. Attlee's talk.

The reason for the intrusion was not cleared up until the recording had been carefully analysed by the engineers, who discovered that the " Voice " was none other than that of the Outside Broadcast Engineer testing the Downing Street line prior to the Prime Minister's broadcast at 9.15. Owing to an operational error, this test, which had been in progress before nine, was not cut out after the reading of the News had begun.

.   .   .   .   .   .

12th April was the date of the unveiling of the Roosevelt Memorial in Grosvenor Square by Mrs. Roosevelt. I made the opening announcement, stating that the ceremony would take place in the presence of the King and Queen, that the Memorial Service would be conducted by the Archbishop of Canterbury, and that there would be an address by His Majesty, to which the American Ambassador would reply.

Richard Dimbleby was in Grosvenor Square to describe the scene, and it was obvious from his description, and from our own ears, that the two Guards of Honour of the Royal Marines and the United States Marine Corps were magnificent.

I read the 6 p.m. News, which included a recorded description of the ceremony by Godfrey Talbot. I could not help smiling at his reference to the "American Voice" of the opening speaker who announced the Archbishop, because he was not an American, but a Canadian who has lived for many years in this country—Lord Greenwood.

Earlier in the News, when leading up to Talbot's recording, I almost said, "The Star-bangled Spanner", only checking myself just in time. What a dreadful spoonerism that would have been, and how unfortunate on such an important occasion!

.   .   .   .   .

In June the long-promised reorganisation of the News Department became an accomplished fact, and the Home and Overseas News (but not the Foreign News, which remains at Bush House) moved into Egton House, which adjoins Broadcasting House and is connected to it by an underground passage. Undoubtedly there are certain advantages in having all the News in one building, just like a Fleet Street newspaper office, but from the operational point of view there are also certain disadvantages, which we found rather trying. Prior to this move we had dealt with only Home News editors, and we worked admirably as a team. Now we met Overseas editors as well, who wished to introduce overseas methods of presentation. Some of these editors were put over the Home Service men. This caused a good deal of uneasiness, which one sensed at once. In Broadcasting House all the preparatory work was carried out in one room, containing about a dozen people. In Egton House, however, we found ourselves in one corner of a very large room with thirty or more people dictating, copy-tasting and typing, and with messengers constantly coming and going. This is not an ideal atmosphere in which to prepare to read complicated details about the dollar deficit and the sterling area, such as Sir Stafford Cripps often refers to in his speeches. Also, in Broadcasting House the News studio was properly air-conditioned, with an even temperature all the year round. In Egton House there is no air-conditioning, only a fan system of ventilation drawing in

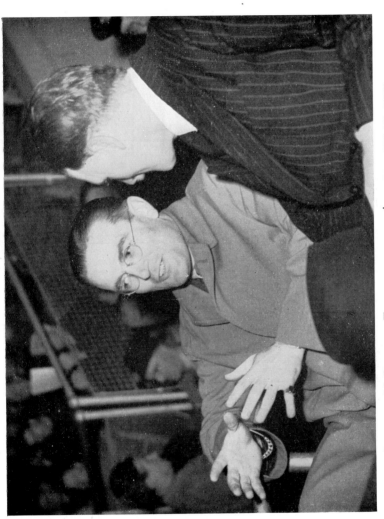

STEWART MCPHERSON EXPLAINS TO THE AUTHOR HOW TO GIVE A COMMENTARY ON AN ICE-HOCKEY MATCH

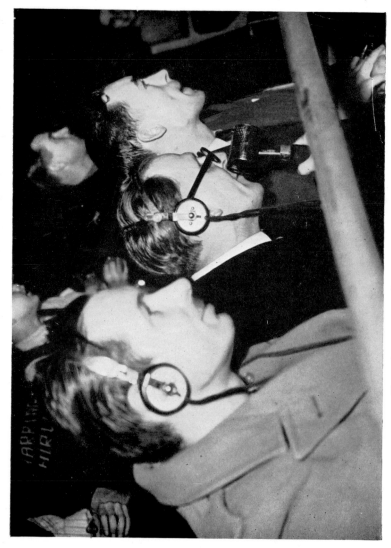

The Author in Action at Harringay

the outside air, with the result that one is often baked in summer and frozen in winter.

.   .   .   .   .

One night in August, a fly, stimulated by the warmth of the studio, and attracted by the beads of sweat on my brow, buzzed round me most persistently while I was reading the News; it even had the audacity to alight on my manuscript, and generally did its best to put me off. Meanwhile I retaliated by waving my hand at it, trying to swat it; but it got away, as I had to concentrate on what I was reading. The Programme Engineer, watching me through the listening-room window, roared with laughter at my efforts. He said afterwards that several bumps were broadcast, superimposed on the News.

In contrast with this, on 25th October when reading the six o'clock News I was so cold that I read the nine o'clock in a great-coat, with a muffler round my neck. Since then the ventilation engineers have improved matters, though the conditions can never be as good as those in Broadcasting House.

.   .   .   .   .

I announced the "Week's Good Cause" on Sunday, 13th June, which was given by Arthur Sculthorne on behalf of the National Deaf—Blind Helpers' League, and an excellent appeal he made, in spite of being himself both deaf and blind.

He brought a friend with him to help him with the rehearsal, and they used a simple method of communication which impressed me very much. All that was necessary was to hold his right hand, and write in block capitals with your finger on the palm of his hand any message you wished, and he read it at once. For example, his friend asked me to write my name on his hand. As soon as I had done so, he rose from his chair in front of the microphone, shook me by the hand and smiled at me, and said "Good evening".

He made his appeal earnestly and clearly, and, watching him as he spoke, I was struck by his fine features and pleasant smile. He had certainly triumphed over his disabilities in a most wonderful way.

Miss Leslie, the Appeals Secretary, afterwards told me that he had been blinded in a car smash, and had become completely deaf twelve years ago, as the result of bad catarrh.

.   .   .   .   .

The Olympic Games were opened by His Majesty the King at 3 p.m. on 29th July in the Empire Stadium at Wembley. A sentence from my opening announcement gives the key to the importance of the occasion :—

> " Before nearly 100,000 spectators, athletes of fifty-nine nations will march past the Royal Box. The Olympic Flame will be carried into the arena, and the Captain of the British Team, on behalf of over 6,000 competitors, takes the oath."

It was a hot day, ideal for the occasion, except perhaps for the massed bands of the Brigade of Guards, who, playing in scarlet and bearskins, must have found it very trying. However, they played for almost an hour non-stop—a fine feat of endurance.

The broadcasting of these games was a gigantic undertaking and, after some teething troubles, proved to be a triumph for the Engineering Division and the Outside Broadcast Department. Not only had they to arrange for transmissions in the B.B.C.'s Home, European and Overseas Services, but they had to provide facilities for all the fifty-nine nations taking part, and this involved the construction at Wembley of a spacious control room, with reproduction channels for playing disc recordings, and a large general-purpose room used for script-writing, equipped with a telephone exchange with specially designed call-boxes, from where one could speak to all parts of the world.

These were the closing words of my announcement :—

> " Back in the studio at Broadcasting House we recover our breath a little after that feast of colour, excitement and music from the Empire Stadium at Wembley, on the occasion of the opening of the Olympic Games by His Majesty the King, so ably portrayed by Wynford Vaughan Thomas."

.   .   .   .   .

All through the week-end 13th–14th November we were expecting the news of the birth of a Prince or Princess to H.R.H. Princess

Elizabeth, Duchess of Edinburgh. I was on duty, scarcely daring to leave the building, being ready to broadcast the news at the first opportunity. It had not come by 5.30 p.m. on Sunday, when I was relieved by John Snagge. I was not sorry to get home and enjoy some fresh air and a short walk. There was no news at 9 p.m., and I did not listen again until the News Summary at 11 p.m., when Snagge announced the birth of a Prince at 9.14 p.m. I was delighted to hear that it was a boy; and born on the B.B.C.'s birthday, too. How strangely archaic the wording of the official bulletin sounded: ". . . delivered of a Prince".

The next day John Snagge told me about the sequence of events. He was "alerted" at 9.50 from his home by Godfrey Talbot, who told him that he was then leaving for Buckingham Palace. This was the agreed signal to be prepared for the official bulletin within a few minutes. But before Talbot got there the Home News Editor 'phoned through to say, "It's come in, and it's a boy". The Light Programme just managed to get the announcement in at the end of their 10 p.m. News. John put it out in the Home Service at 10.20 p.m., fading "Rhine Journey" to do so, and going back to it again directly afterwards.

But in spite of our preparations, and the fact that we put out the announcement as soon as we could on both wavelengths, America beat us at the post, as one of our engineers listening direct to America heard it put out just before it was given at the end of the News in the Light Programme.

The next day, in honour of the event, I broadcast a programme of recorded music of works by British composers, which included a piece written specially for this happy occasion, called "Music for a Prince", by Herbert Howells. The programme also included some music called "Maytime in Sussex", composed by Sir Arnold Bax, the Master of the King's Music, which had been written for the Princess' twenty-first birthday, and part of Elgar's Nursery Suite, written for the two Princesses when they were children.

.   .   .   .   .

I was sleeping in, on duty at Broadcasting House, on 23rd November, when the telephone rang at 4 a.m. and the Duty Editor told me of the King's illness. A bulletin had been issued from Buckingham Palace at 1.45 a.m., and he had already told John Snagge about it at his home, and the latter wished me to read the early morning News, which would begin with the official bulletin. This stated that the cause of the illness was " arterial obstruction ", and added that " some anxiety exists about the right foot ".

The statement went on to say that the Australian Tour had been cancelled and that " His Majesty will be unable to attend any public engagements for at least six months ".

This was serious news, and a great shock to the country, because it was totally unexpected.

．　　　．　　　．　　　．　　　．

Christmas time found the Radio Doctor in his most devastating form, and in a talk about the sensory organs, just before he tackled the topical subject of what to do if you keep Christmas too well, he said that " tickling is only a tantalising trick of titillating the touch spots ".

A few weeks later Colonel Walter Elliot ran him very close when, in opposing the new Rent Restriction Extension Bill in the House of Commons, he called it " an intricate involution of ingenuity to cover the inadequacy of the housing problem ".

Both these efforts were outclassed in the report of the Parliamentary Debate on 22nd February, 1949, by Hugh Fraser, who, in describing a Government clause of the Steel Bill, dealing with licences, used a phrase worthy of the great Duke of Plaza-Toro himself; he called it " restrictive, ossifying, petrifying, atrophying, lapidifying, corrupting, stiff-necked, inflexible and cretinous ".

1949

BROADCASTING AND THE SPOKEN WORD

THE problem of writing for the voice and thinking in terms of the spoken word, as distinct from the printed page, has been with us almost since broadcasting began in this country. It was soon realised that a special technique would have to be developed, as what was required was shorter sentences than when writing for the eye and the use of as much colloquial English as possible.

This was made clear when some well-known scenes from Dickens were broadcast, and especially so later when, shortly after the B.B.C. had moved from Marconi House to Savoy Hill in 1924, Bernard Shaw was persuaded to read some extracts from his play, " O'Flaherty, V.C.", which had, of course, been written for the spoken word in the first place. But it was not until 1929–30 that, under the leadership of Mr. A. Lloyd James, our adviser in phonetics (afterwards Professor at London University), any serious attempt was made to persuade editors and producers to think in terms of the spoken word only, and to try to get authors and script-writers to write for the voice rather than for the eye.

We experienced broadcasters knew that, to be effective, it was necessary, when preparing scripts or News bulletins, to keep in mind three things : (1) To avoid the use of long sentences; (2) to limit the number of parentheses to two or three, at the most, and (3) to try to write sentences which slide easily off the tongue. For example, it was imperative to avoid such phrases as " The ruthless use of force ", or " The extraordinary orderliness of the room ", or expressions like " The Soviet-Finnish State ", because they are not vocal.

As to parentheses, if you are an experienced broadcaster it is not difficult to deal with two, and possibly three in a sentence, by varying the intonation each time, throwing each one away at different levels, as it were; but if more than three are included, it is very doubtful if you will succeed in making the meaning clear. For the same reason, long sentences are undesirable, and it is always better to use short ones, if possible. There are times when this is not possible—when, for example, one has to read a War Office communiqué or an Admiralty bulletin, written for the printed page, and not for the voice.

This also applies to reports of Parliamentary debates, and I once had to read this sentence verbatim—part of a speech by Lord Halifax delivered in the Lords on the subject of the gathering storm on the Continent in 1938. I have nothing whatever against the sentence as such, except that, because it is so long, it becomes a veritable verbal Hampton Court Maze, when read out loud. Here it is :—

> " If an issue were ever to be joined, I have no doubt at all about the ultimate outcome, whatever might be the varying fortunes of war or the duration of the struggle, but I find it very difficult to believe that with a certain prospect of resistance, with an awareness of the fearful consequences that must follow, and with the knowledge of the desire of all peoples for peace, and the readiness of all peoples to see matters settled by negotiation that those who might feel tempted to risk the arbitrament of war would not feel, if they might once convince themselves of the good faith of those with whom they had to deal, that it was wiser and more profitable to remove by negotiation the difficulties which inevitably arise in adjusting the claims and satisfying the needs of a constantly changing world."

I am glad to say that to-day producers do their best to get all broadcasters in their charge to introduce colloquialisms wherever possible, such as can't for cannot, isn't for is not, he'll for he will, etc., and News Editors are much more speech conscious than they were, though I believe there is still room for improvement.

On 6th January I introduced a new series of talks in the Light Programme given at 4.15 p.m. each Thursday, and designed to help the sick, the aged and invalids. The title of the series was " The

Silver Lining" and the first six talks were given by Canon Hutchinson of St. Bartholomew's, Brighton. He was followed by the Rev. Frederick Greaves of Bristol, and a number of excellent speakers, including two doctors, the Rev. Leslie Weatherhead, and Miss Emily Macmanus, formerly Matron of Guy's Hospital. Each week I did the introductions and the linking, and some interrogations to bring out important points, but all the spade-work was done by the Rev. John Williams of the Religious Broadcasting Department, ably assisted by Miss Bratt, who dealt with the correspondence—almost a full-time job on its own.

By the middle of the summer we had received reports from the Listener Research Department that our average weekly audience was about 2,400,000, and this figure was roughly maintained until the end of the year—a most satisfying reward for our efforts.

.   .   .   .

9th January (Sunday). Mr. Streeter, who bids fair to become a second Mr. Middleton, came to see me before his broadcast at 2.15 p.m. What a fine old man he is and how he exudes enthusiasm for his profession !

I enjoyed, but was most sceptical about, his suggestion of " wheeling the contents of the compost heap out on to the land in these moonlight frosty nights ", because, he argued, " the wheels make no marks, and you get a wonderful glow going in your body, and then you can go inside and enjoy your supper as never before ".

.   .   .   .

I was on day duty at Broadcasting House when, shortly after 5 p.m., a telephone message came through from Francis Worsley in the country to say that Tommy Handley had died suddenly that afternoon, following a seizure.

This tragic news was a great shock to us all, as no one had heard that he had been ill.

I had to get down to business at once and communicate with the Press Officer, the Duty Officer and the News Officer, who rang Worsley to confirm the message. There was then a hue and cry to find Ted Kavanagh to get him to write a short appreciation for the News.

Frank Phillips came in at 5.30 and carried on with the planning, while I went to the News Room to look at the bulletin. This con-

tained only a brief notice of Tommy's death, the appreciation by
Ted Kavanagh following in the 9 p.m. News.

It was all most upsetting, as Tommy was about my own age, and
we had known one another since 1924, when he appeared in the first
B.B.C. Revue at Savoy Hill and sang the patter song, "What I
want is a proper pot of coffee ".

I stayed on to read the three-minute appreciation in the 9 p.m.
News, which Ted Kavanagh had written. In it he paid tribute to
Tommy as " our greatest Radio comedian ", referring to him as
" one of the world's greatest laughter-makers ", and so, indeed,
he was.

Everyone I met in the next few days seemed to be staggered at
the news of his passing, and all agreed that they felt a sense of
personal loss.

I went to the funeral at Golder's Green with John Snagge and
other members of the staff on the 13th. Thousands of people were
present to pay their last tribute to him. There was a special choir
drawn from old musical friends, under Parry Jones, Charles Smart
playing the organ. The service was simple and short, and the
flowers were the most wonderful I have ever seen. There were
thousands of wreaths laid out on the turf surrounding the chapel.

On 27th January a Memorial Service, conducted by the Dean,
was held in St. Paul's Cathedral, which was attended by 4,000 people,
and there were also thousands of others outside in the street.

The Bishop of London (Dr. Wand) gave the address, and spoke
of Tommy Handley as " one whose achievement it was to bring,
week by week, to millions of our people an overflowing measure of
irresistible laughter, whose genius transmuted the copper of our
common experience into the gold of exquisite foolery ".

Earlier, in speaking of the triumphs of ITMA, I mentioned the
wonderful team-work of what I called the " Handley–Worsley–
Kavanagh Triumvirate ". The tragedy of the loss of Tommy
Handley, with the consequent disappearance of ITMA, was height-
ened only a few months later, when Francis Worsley, who had been
ITMA'S producer since its inception, died after a short illness on
14th September, at the early age of forty-seven.

.   .   .   .   .

I suppose we all have our little mannerisms and peculiarities when speaking, some colouring vowels more than others, some distorting them out of all recognition, as exemplified in the musical comedy song of fifteen years ago " How now, brown cow ? " when sung by Cockneys, Midlanders, North-countrymen and Scots.

I frequently do not colour my vowels enough—I make them too " white ", as they say; e.g. I frequently say "jest" for "just ", especially when using the phrase "just a moment ", so useful in Radio. I was not surprised, therefore, to receive a criticism about it from a listener in the form of a charming little rhyme on a postcard, as follows :—

> " I write only in jest,
> And I'm sure you know best;
> But with fury I bust
> When you say ' jest ' for ' just '."

Then he goes on :—

> " Would you dare to aver
> That a lady wears her
> Vust to cover her best ? "

．　　　．　　　．　　　．　　　．

On Saturday, 5th March, I went down to Plymouth to speak for Colonel Stafford, who is our representative there, and who at that time was looking after the B.B.C.'s exhibition of photographs in the City Museum. The Lord Mayor introduced me, and I had a splendid audience. Afterwards the Lord Mayor showed me a plan of the new city, which was most impressive, and I congratulated him on the progress already made. Even now one can see the outline of the new city beginning to take shape among the ruins.

I spent almost the whole of the next day in the train en route for Cardiff, where I had agreed to conduct the Sunday Half-hour, to be broadcast in the Light Programme at 8 p.m. from the Chapel Tabernacle, under the direction of Terry Richards. My train was late, and there was only time for a cup of tea and a sandwich before the rehearsal, which was followed at once by the transmission.

The chapel was crowded out—there must have been some 700 people there. It was very hot and stuffy, and, of course, all of them sang, as only a Welsh congregation can.

I was in the pulpit with the minister, with Terry Richards and the choir in the organ gallery immediately above me. The pulpit was very high, rather like that in St. Martin-in-the-Fields, and the microphone in front of us was not on the desk of the pulpit, but at the extremity of a telescopic stand on the floor in front.

Quite suddenly, in the middle of one of the hymns, the microphone slowly began to descend, until it had sunk below the level of the pulpit, and there was nothing that I could do to stop it.

Consequently I left the pulpit and went into the vestry to find the O.B. Engineer, and asked him to come and hold on to the microphone and put it up into its proper place while I said my next piece, afterwards going on to give my short address.

Whether it was caused by the exuberance of the singing, the heat, or the weakness of the stand I do not know, but it was my first experience of being faced with a slowly disappearing microphone, and I was lucky not to be speaking when it started its descent.

After the broadcast I spoke to the congregation for a few minutes on " Singing and the spoken word as expressions of worship in sacred music ", the choir, at my request, singing " God be in my head ", by Sir Walford Davies.

.   .   .   .   .

At the request of the Controller of the Light Programme and Music Programme Organiser, I undertook to present a series of twelve recitals at 4.15 p.m. on Fridays, beginning in the middle of February.

The name of the series was to be " May I Introduce " ?, the artists being either new to Radio or those who, for one reason or another, had been out of the country for two or more years, or whose professional career had been interrupted by the war.

Excluding the peak evening recitals by established artists, it was felt that there was little time allotted to recitals in our programmes, apart from one or two half-hours each week in the early mornings in the Home Service, and there were many young artists on our books who had had little or no opportunity of broadcasting, and it was thought that this series would fill that need.

I had the pleasure of introducing a number of brilliant young artists, and the series soon became established, and was regarded as being most successful.

I abolished the traditional way of announcing a recital, and, having

first presented the artists, with a few words about their achievements, I concentrated on the music, grouping songs and instrumental pieces by the same composer together, or Spanish, French
or Italian songs and pieces together, even if three consecutive works
were performed by three different artists. I also paid a great deal
of attention to the personal side, joining the artists in the studio
after the rehearsal and before the broadcast, getting to know them
and explaining my intentions in presenting the programme, making
certain that they all knew the order, and their cues. In this way I
gained their confidence—a most important point in ensuring a good
performance.

. . . . .

Writing in the autumn, and looking back over the year, three
things stand out in my memory : the wonderful summer (the best
I can remember since 1921, which was a " scorcher "), the most
exciting Boat Race of my lifetime, and the tour of the West Country
by the B.B.C. Symphony Orchestra, culminating in a concert given
in Truro Cathedral on 14th May.

The Boat Race was rowed on 26th March, and Oxford, who won
the toss, went ahead about half a length in the first minute, and were
leading by one and a half lengths at Hammersmith Bridge; but just
afterwards Cambridge spurted and pulled up, and as the two crews
shot Barnes Bridge they were almost level. Finally, Cambridge,
in a great finish, just pulled it off, by a matter of a few feet at the
winning-post.

John Snagge gave an admirable commentary on the race, and one
was kept in suspense up to the last second. The race was also
televised from a launch just behind the two boats, and with the help
of seven cameras at points along the course, the launch being
insulated against vibration, and the power for the camera coming
from a special petrol-electric generator.

Thanks to the fact that after Hammersmith Bridge the two boats
were seldom more than a few feet apart throughout the race, viewers
were able to keep them in sight most of the time. This fact and
the splendid weather meant that it was a triumph for the television
engineers.

. . . . .

I have always got on well with the Orchestra, and have many

friends among them, as I have also among most of the London orchestras, due to the contacts I have made in the course of my work over the years. In the difficult war-time days, when I was Defence Officer in Bristol and in command of the B.B.C. Home Guard in Bedford, it was the Symphony Orchestra who supported me so splendidly.

I was therefore especially pleased when the B.B.C. Symphony Orchestra did me the honour of asking me as one of the guests—there were only about half a dozen outsiders—to the dinner they were giving at the Savoy Hotel on 8th April, in honour of Sir Adrian Boult's sixtieth birthday. My old friend Ernest Hall, who has been principal trumpet of the Orchestra since its inception, and of the Wireless Orchestra before that, was in the chair, and an excellent Chairman he made. He has such a charming and lovable personality that he spreads a feeling of good humour wherever he goes. The Orchestra adore him, and so do his many friends in Beckenham, where he lives and is affectionately known as " Uncle Ernest ".

The dinner was held at the Lincoln Restaurant in the Savoy—a pleasant, large, air-conditioned room, which was never too hot or stuffy, as is generally the case on such occasions. There was a kind of family atmosphere about this gathering because nearly everybody knew everyone else. As we arrived we went up to the entrance and congratulated Sir Adrian and Lady Boult, who were standing there to greet us. I think all the members of the Orchestra and their wives were there (except Paul Beard, the leader, who was ill); Sidonie Goossens, principal harp, who sat next to Sir Charles Carpendale, was much admired, and later made a charming little speech in proposing the health of " Our Guests ".

Bill Fussell, the chief orchestral porter, and his wife were there, quite close to the top table. Bill is a great character, a Londoner, with the Cockney's irrepressible sense of fun, a man who is the living personification of the old soldier who, come what may, is never downhearted. He never seems to know defeat, and is one of the grandest men I have ever met. Long may he reign as king of the Orchestra's instrumental train, and in the hearts of all the members of the Orchestra.

Although it was a family, and not an official affair, that did not mean it was no ordeal for Sir Adrian, who made a most happily phrased and witty speech in reply to Ernest Hall's eulogy of him from early Liverpool days onwards, through Birmingham to the B.B.C., and one could sense the pride and affection that all members of the Orchestra felt for their conductor.

Later, in replying to the toast of " Our Guests ", Dr. Vaughan Williams, who was the principal guest of the evening, after expressing the greatest possible confidence in Sir Adrian, said he hoped that there would be no further talk of any other conductor, and that Sir Adrian would go from strength to strength in the future " as conductor of this great Orchestra ". Then we had a conjuror, and last but not least Gillie Potter, who, having heard earlier in the evening about the dinner, asked, as a great admirer both of Sir Adrian and the Orchestra, if he could come and make his contribution to the success of the evening by " addressing a few remarks to the assembled company ".

Arrayed in the famous straw hat and old Borstolian blazer, and carrying an enormous " Mother Gamp " umbrella, he came in smiling at us and raising his hat. Recognising me as he walked towards the platform, he began at once to rag me, bringing my name into almost every other sentence, and always following it with the raising of his hat and some such remark as " that is if the Chief Announcer, Mr. Stuart Hibberd, will permit me to say so," much to the joy of the audience, and to my discomfiture. It was all excellent fun, and it was most kind of him to come and entertain us on the spur of the moment.

. . . . .

The climax of the visit of the B.B.C. Symphony Orchestra to the West Country came on Saturday, 14th May, when a concert was given in Truro Cathedral—the first cathedral to be completed in England since the Reformation.

The Orchestra was placed in the transept, and in the half-light, and against a background of grey pointed arches and stained-glass windows, the music seemed to take on a deeper beauty and an added dignity.

The Gabrielli Sonata for two " choirs " of brass instruments, with which the concert began, and the Vaughan Williams Fantasia on a theme by Thomas Tallis, which followed, were both utterly right for this setting. Both belong to the realms of the spirit, though of course of very different ages, there being nothing of "the earth earthy" about either of them.

The Press reports, speaking of the Vaughan Williams work, afterwards said, "The strings of the B.B.C. Symphony Orchestra under Sir Adrian Boult gave a deeply moving interpretation of this noble work". This was true, and I am sure that those of us who were fortunate enough to be present will always look back on it as an unforgettable musical experience.

.   .   .   .   .

I cannot help feeling—and here I am expressing only my own personal views—that our present-day programmes are likely to produce a vast number of passive listeners, who take for granted everything that comes out of the loud-speakers, with little or no reaction to it. What is needed is a dose of shock tactics now and again, to disturb them from their lethargy and stimulate them into action—something on the lines of the Mais v. Maschwitz debate on living dangerously in the early thirties, and especially is this true in the case of musical programmes. It is not enough to listen, however intelligently, to the best music, and remain content to simulate a pad of blotting-paper and try to absorb it all, and then go away and do nothing about it.

We all of us have something of the creative urge in us, and there comes a time when it is necessary for us to be up and doing, and to begin making music for ourselves, whether by playing an instrument or joining a choral society, writing music or perhaps starting to learn a new instrument. We can all of us try our hand either at playing or singing, however imperfectly, or trying to write melodies, however simple, to our own great satisfaction.

It was to the credit of Sir Walford Davies that towards the end of his life he used the medium of wireless to persuade hundreds of listeners to sit down and write tunes for themselves—men and women who, had there been no wireless, would not have dreamt of attempting such a task, and this applied to people of all ages, including the very old.

Since his death the B.B.C. have gone on pouring out music of all kinds, but, with the exception of Alec Robertson in Music Magazine, there has been no appeal to listeners to be dissatisfied with this, and to turn to and get busy, making music for themselves. This, I feel, is a pity, because the Corporation is losing a great opportunity, and who could give the lead in the Walford Davies tradition better than Sir Adrian himself, or, if a younger man is preferred, Boyd Neel? Both are most gifted and experienced broadcasters.

. . . .

Looking back over twenty-five years of broadcasting, I realise how thankful I ought to be that I was privileged to serve under Lord Reith in the pioneering days of Savoy Hill.

I have tried in these pages to give the reader a glimpse of my life's work as a practical broadcaster, and I hope I may also have succeeded in suggesting something of the historical significance of broadcasting, and its impact upon the people.

The saying "*Autre temps autre moeurs*" applies equally to broadcasting as to most other things in life, and to-day we have to realise that Television is here, and that it has become a very real competitor.

Other things being equal, it can only be a matter of time before the majority of homes in this country are equipped with Television sets, as they are already with wireless. Not that I think that Television will entirely oust Sound Broadcasting, because Television demands all one's attention the whole of the time, whereas Sound Broadcasting makes demands on only part of one's faculties, and not necessarily all the time. One can knit and listen to good music, or prepare a meal while Sandy MacPherson plays the organ; also there are many programmes, such as Talks, News, Chamber Music, Eye-witness accounts, etc., where it would be boring to look at the originator the whole of the time. There are some types of programme—for example, Features and programmes like Vaughan Thomas' "Round the World in Eight Days"—which I think are better done by Sound Broadcasting than by Television, but generally speaking Television will score heavily in all actuality programmes, sporting events, State processions and national occasions, and will have a great advantage in plays, and in the transmission of films, enabling thousands to see first-class productions of ballet, opera and plays, such as those of the Stratford-on-Avon season, which formerly could only have been seen by those living in the great cities and large towns.

The sooner we broadcasters realise this, and face the situation, the better.

. . / . . .

It is a far cry from the "three-minute interval, please" of 1924, when programmes began each day at 3.15 p.m. (apart from an hour's lunch-time music) and the first general News bulletin was at 7 p.m., to the slick non-stop 9 a.m. to 12 midnight Light Programme of today, or the Home Service from 6.30 a.m. to 11 p.m., with ten News Bulletins a day between 7 a.m. and midnight.

Throughout the whole of this period there has been an increasing demand for sets, as shown by the licence figures, which rose from 990,000 when I joined in 1924 to well over twelve millions at the end of 1949. Taking a conservative estimate of two listeners per set, the potential listening audience must be something in the neighbourhood of twenty-five millions, and on National or International occasions this figure may be doubled or even trebled, when overseas listeners are added. Such figures are too frightening to contemplate, and if I once began to think in terms of them when about to broadcast I should probably be almost inarticulate—I prefer to stick to my original mind-picture, of speaking to one family or one individual only, and leave the numbers to the statisticians, and the social results of the impact of wireless on the people to the historians of the future.

APPENDIX "A"

COPY

Letter to Newsreaders—from V. Halsim of Larwik, Norway.

29th May, 1945.

DEAR SIRS AND GENTLEMEN,

I can't help writing and letting you all know what a tremendous comfort and help your voices has been to me, during these five long and dark years of oppression.

I have listened to you on an average of 6 hours a day, ever since the day of occupation, besides the sendings in my own language, so you will understand that I have had an all day job, just listening and getting the News, and I heard, out safely. It has been a game of wits with the Gestapo, with many falling into their hands, which you know was sometimes worse than death.

Now I want to finish this note by wishing you all lots of success and happiness in the future, and believe me when I sign myself as a very grateful listener.

Most respectfully,

GEORGE SOLVIG
VESTRE HALSIM.

Larwik,
Norway.

COPY

3rd May, 1945.

To Home Service Newsreaders of the B.B.C.

GENTLEMEN,

Perhaps you will receive a great lot of letters like this one, if so, please add it to your collection. It is meant as a recognition of your work as readers of the news

It is now about five years ago that I began to listen to the Home Service News and that this news began to form a welcome incident every day.

Indeed it was a welcome quarter of an hour at nine o'oclock in the evening, when your well-known voices told us the news of the day apart from its being good or bad.

My wife said we were with you when during the Battle of Britain we heard via the microphone of the bombardments on your cities. But afterwards, our hearts were beating faster when you told us in the morning news at seven o'clock—" Our bombers were out over Germany *again* last night ! "

I further remember the announcement of the startling beginning of the war with Japan at Pearl Harbour, and the heavy blow of your fleet in the Malayan waters, and of ours in the Java Sea.

Your voices we remember in the radio barrage at the beginning of the landings in North Africa.

The optimistic sound in your voices was undeniable when the news was good. That was the case when the Germans began to retreat in Russia, when the general capitulation of the invasion took place at Dieppe and the successful development since D-Day.

In general we listened with great pleasure to the B.B.C., but the news was always the epic of the day.

It did not last long before we were forbidden to listen to your stations by our " protectors " as we called the Germans, but this prohibition with all the threatenings, did not keep us from listening. It was only a little dangerous in connection with a possible treason.

This danger grew graver when we were obliged to deliver our radio-sets to the Germans. From that moment we had to listen *secretly*. But in spite of all Germans and their prohibitions and the betrayers they made use of, we have been able to listen to your news regularly.

The affair became very difficult however, when at the beginning of last winter, there was no longer electricity. From that moment, listening was limited to once a day, on an accumulator.

And then in the beginning of December we got in Delft, also the Germans called all men between seventeen and forty years and I too was obliged to " dive ", as we called such a movement. But . . . a radio-set came along with my friends and me into the " dive-place ", and we were able to follow the developments of the war.

So, under all circumstances, and notwithstanding all difficulties, we heard the news read by you, and our relation, although we are unknown to each other, became ever closer. For, the greater our difficulties, the more favourable the news was.

And now, at the bottom of our misery and hunger, we are hearing your voices telling us of rumours about peace and also of the manner in which VE-Day will be celebrated. Your communications about the bringing of food by air are daily confirmed by the noise of your Lancasters, and the Flying Fortresses of the Americans, when they are roaring over us at a height of 50 yards or less.

Now we are waiting for the announcement of peace, for I believe that at this moment all is all right behind the scenes. Whom of you will be the happy man to tell this news? Within the next few days I hope to know it, and then I'll post this letter immediately.

I write you this epistle, gentlemen, as a proof of my thankfulness for your telling us the news every day so accurately and clearly.

Finally, there is one thing I must write to you and that is my admiration of your pronunciation of all those difficult geographical names from all over the world, as there were Russian, Chinese, Italian, etc., and at last also Dutch names.

Gentlemen, once more many thanks for the support your voices gave us during the past years.* *As soon as " our Germans " are also in their cages I'll bring this letter to the post-office.*

Best wishes and many happy readings of good news!

Yours faithfully,

(*Signed*) H. BLOEMRAAD.

* The date of the postmark was some three months later.—S. H.

INDEX